Gertie

The Fabulous Life of
Gertrude Sanford Legendre,
Heiress, Explorer, Socialite, Spy

Kathryn Smith

Published by
Evening Post Books
Charleston, South Carolina

Editor: John M. Burbage
Designer: Gill Guerry

First printing 2019
Printed in the United States of America

A CIP catalog record for this book has been applied
for from the Library of Congress.

ISBN: 978-1-929647-44-6

Also by Kathryn Smith

*The Gatekeeper: Missy LeHand, FDR and the Untold
Story of the Partnership that Defined a Presidency*

Missy LeHand Mystery Series (with Kelly Durham)

Shirley Temple Is Missing

The President's Birthday Ball Affair

Eleanor Roosevelt Goes to Prison

To Linda and Leo

———— • ————

"I certainly have seen many things in my life, but I've always thought of my life as a natural progression of interests that led to events that led to more interests and events and so on and so on. Each sequence was an unconscious preparation for the next. The trick was to allow for chance. If I hadn't grown up around horses and the outdoors, I might never have known my love for them. If I hadn't seen those flickering African scenes of Paul Rainey during my childhood, I might never have believed such a trip was possible. And if I hadn't gone on the first trip to the Tetons, I might never have known the thrill of life in the wilderness. If I hadn't begun to travel, I might never have known how much there was to see and to learn. Half the battle is opportunity. The other half is the willingness to say 'yes.' For me, 'yes' was always easy."

———— • ————

— **Gertrude Sanford Legendre,** *The Time of My Life*

Contents

Prologue

— • —

It was early afternoon on September 26, 1944 when Gertrude Sanford Legendre stumbled out of a bomb-damaged building in rural Germany, sank onto a pile of rubble and cursed her own stupidity. She was in Nazi custody in Wallendorf, a village just over the Belgian border, that had been in Allied hands not long before. But the lines were changing so rapidly that Gertrude and three American companions had unwittingly crossed over to the enemy side that morning and were captured by German soldiers. What began a few days before in the bar of the Paris Ritz Hotel as a light-hearted road trip to get a look at Patton's Third Army in action had turned into a nightmare. Two of the men were seriously wounded. Their jeep driver, a young army private, was bleeding profusely and appeared to be going into shock.

All four of them faced uncertain futures as prisoners of war.

Gertrude — forty-two years of age, athletic and trim, a socialite from a prominent New York family — had worked for the American government's covert Office of Strategic Services in Washington and London for two years, fighting what she called the "paperwork war." Presiding over the cable desk at the organization sometimes jokingly called "Oh So Secret," she was privy to reams of classified information.

"I knew, from my work, of the activities of our OSS men in the field," she later wrote, "how they so courageously risked their lives day after day infiltrating enemy lines. I knew how they had passed as French peasants, as salesmen, as vineyard workers, with faked papers, *cartes d'identitie* and ration permits, to gather much needed information to be relayed to our listening posts over portable radio sets."

In short, she knew a tremendous amount about covert activities and would be a great prize for the Germans — and an intelligence disaster for the Allies. One of her companions was an army major in the OSS, the other an OSS lieutenant commander and naval pilot. Although Gertrude was a civilian, she wore the uniform of the Women's Army Auxiliary Corps and had an assimilated rank of first lieutenant. Keeping their work secret from the Nazi captors was paramount; they had managed to burn their identification cards before the Germans reached them, but none of them had the poison pills that were standard issue for OSS spies. They faced torture — and worse.

As a few scrawny chickens pecked the ground around Gertrude's sturdy army-issue oxfords, she raised her dark brown eyes overhead where planes circled lazily "like silver vultures." Suddenly realizing they were Allied planes, she considered using a pocket mirror to signal them, then rejected the idea as ridiculous. "Reason crowded in: Don't you realize you've blundered into trouble, and lots of it?" She thought briefly of Col. David L.K. Bruce, her boss at the OSS, and worried that he would be blamed for her capture. Then her thoughts turned to her husband, Sidney, stationed in Honolulu with the navy, and their daughters, eleven-year-old Landine and four-year-old Bokara, who were staying with relatives while she and Sidney served their country. She had left their framed photographs in her hotel room in Luxembourg, believing she would be returning in a few hours; how she wished she had brought the photos with her.

"Yes, I felt a dreadful sense of guilt," she confessed. "Why had I been so keen to plunge into such an adventure, which common sense would have forbidden? But adventure, that was it! The urge of curiosity to know more about the hellishness of war. I loved danger and was exhilarated by it."

Her mind flicked back to the previous summer in London when the Germans' pilotless V-1 missiles, which the plucky British called "buzz bombs" or "doodlebugs," rained down on the city. "Didn't I get quite a kick out of the buzz bombs, the blitzes?" she admitted. "Danger and adventure, they quickened the pulse and challenged me. I wondered why I was made that way."

It was a rare moment of introspection for Gertrude Legendre, who had spent most of her life on a quest for excitement with very little reflection about why she sought it. Born into an ultra-wealthy family that made its fortune in carpet manufacturing, she had bucked many of the constraints of proper society that strait-jacketed so many of her female peers. The striking brunette had made her introduction to society as expected and attended scores of teas, balls, dances and fancy-dress parties. She had also hobnobbed with celebrities on the Riviera in the 1920s, contributing to the "simple-minded nonsense" by riding a motorboat-drawn surf board while wearing an evening gown.

She was as comfortable on a horse as in a car, was an accomplished golfer and tennis player and a crack shot whose game ranged from quail to elephants.

In truth, Gertrude was most comfortable when she was roughing it, sleeping under the stars in the wilds of Wyoming, tramping alongside a line of pack animals on a mountain trail in Iran, crawling through thorn bushes after a snarling lion in Africa or gliding down a river in Indochina with two pet monkeys along for the ride. In 1928 she talked her father into financing an expedition to East Africa so she could collect specimens for New York's American Museum of Natural History. She took along Morris and Sidney Legendre, two insanely handsome brothers from New Orleans, to audition for the role of husband. Having settled on Sidney, she married him in September 1929 just a few weeks before the stock market crashed — which no doubt wiped out some of the guests who had presented the couple with lavish gifts. Her family was largely spared the financial devastation, and, with her father's help, she and Sidney bought a 250-year-old rice plantation in South Carolina for their home.

Medway had been a wreck when they bought it, the house as difficult to reach through the undergrowth as Sleeping Beauty's castle; indeed, when Gertrude first saw the house from horseback in 1929, she said, "It reminded me of one of Arthur Rackham's drawings." Yet they had reclaimed it, bringing the house into the twentieth century with indoor plumbing and electricity and adding a tennis court. At Medway six months of the year, they enjoyed a privileged lifestyle of hunting, fishing, picnic lunches, leisurely cocktail hours and formal dinners, often entertaining family and friends.

Much as the Legendres loved Medway, they seldom stayed there for long, even after their daughters were born. A distant and disinterested mother, Gertrude largely delegated their upbringing to hired staff and private schools. Travel had brought the couple together and their feet seemed to perpetually itch for more of it. Even as they reveled in their plantation lifestyle, before long they would be writing letters, ordering supplies and Sidney would be setting up their tents in a practice safari camp on the lawn.

Gertrude mulled over the highlights of the expeditions she and Sidney had taken together as she sat in the bombed-out German village, wondering what the Nazis were going to do with her. "I had met the challenge of 12,000-foot mountains to secure a shot at a fleet ibex on a rocky peak. There was the time Sidney and I had hunted the rare Abyssinian nyala for the American Museum of Natural History, which meant weeks of ordeal. Had we not taken the swirling rapids of the headwaters of the Mekong and cut our way through unexplored jungles of French Indochina to capture new specimens?" That had been followed by a trip across the blazing sands of Southwest Africa to procure a group of twisty-horned antelope known as kudu, mounted and on display at the Philadelphia Academy of Natural Sciences. She bagged a Kodiak bear in Alaska, a 600-pound tiger in French Indochina and an elephant in Uganda. "There was a driving power within me to test my resources and satisfy my craving for excitement," she thought. "But was it enough to explain away this folly?"

Her reverie didn't last long. Practical needs claimed her attention. She stood up, dusting off her wrinkled olive drab uniform, and returned to the house to check on the injured men and rummage about for food. In the upstairs rooms that American soldiers had occupied shortly before, she found some loaves of bread, bags of flour and sugar and a couple of dozen bottles of wine. Two of the German soldiers set up a portable brazier and together they prepared a dinner of pancakes.

As Gertrude wolfed down the sugary pancakes and swigged from a wine bottle, she started to laugh. Soon she was telling her companions about a fall day at Medway, a day like this one, "a little nip in the air. Made you feel wonderful." Next, she described the deer hunt they had been on and the picnic they had enjoyed under a clearing in the pine trees: oyster soup and casserole of quail baked with mushrooms and bacon, "with lots and lots of rich white butter sauce," sweet potato pie with marshmallows, deep-dish apple pie with cinnamon, washed down with beer, bourbon and hot coffee.

She walked over to the bleeding driver and put a cigarette between his lips. "He was such a nice-looking boy," she thought. "In September, at home, his mind would have been full of rabbits, squirrels and football." And then her mind turned to escape.

Gertrude would spend six months as a prisoner of the Germans, the first American woman in uniform captured on the western front, and the one held the longest. She was spared the severe treatment that awaited many POWs — torture and death from disease and exposure for some, near-starvation for most, but it required all the survival skills she had perfected on her four expeditions, as well as the social skills honed at a thousand cocktail parties, to keep mum about what she knew and bring her home safely.

To fully understand what got her into such a predicament and how she got herself out, it's best to start at the beginning of her fabulous life.

Gertrude was ten months old in this photo portrait, sent to her godmother.

1

Gilded Age Girl

———— • ————

When Civil War Gen. William Tecumseh Sherman led his forces into South Carolina early in 1865, he promised to exact a terrible revenge on the state that had been the first to secede from the Union. "The devil himself couldn't restrain my men in that state," he said. He sent one of his most destructive subordinates, Maj. Gen. Hugh Judson Kilpatrick, a man who reveled even in burning down churches, to attack the town of Aiken and level its textile mills. In preparation, it was said, Kilpatrick spent $5,000 of his own money on matches.

But he met his match, so to speak, in his Confederate counterpart, Gen. Joseph "Fightin' Joe" Wheeler. The Battle of Aiken was one of the last southern victories in the war. Kilpatrick and his men turned tail for the state capital of Columbia, forty miles away, where they assuaged their vanity — and used up some matches — by burning much of the city to the ground. Today, the walls of the State House are studded with bronze stars marking places the Union cannon balls hit.

In the decades after the war, the Yankees returned to Aiken under decidedly different circumstances. These Gilded Age visitors came in droves, filling the town's hotels and boarding houses, even building their own out-sized "cottages" as they had along the cliffs of Newport, Rhode Island. They were armed not with cannons and matches but with golf clubs and polo mallets. By the late 1880s, Aiken's moderate climate and ideal conditions for outdoor activities earned it the sobriquets "Newport of the South" and "Sports Center of the South." The cash-starved Aikenites were happy to cater to the northern visitors who formed the Winter Colony.

Gertrude Sanford Legendre's family was among their number. She was born in Aiken on March 29, 1902, the third and last child of John and Ethel

Sanford of Amsterdam, New York. Named for her maternal grandmother, Gertrude Ellen du Puy, she was from the beginning called Gertie, which is how she will be known henceforth in this book. A button-eyed baby with full lips and curly dark hair, she joined an older brother, Stephen — nicknamed Laddie — and sister, Sarah Jane, known as Janie. The Sanford siblings all made their marks in the world. Laddie became an internationally ranked polo player and Janie married an Italian diplomat and advisor to Benito Mussolini. Gertie's mark was different. She lived a life of adventure that spanned the twentieth century.

The Sanford parents were second cousins — their grandfathers were brothers — thus Ethel was a Sanford before and after she married. Descended from an English couple who came to Massachusetts eleven years after the *Mayflower*, their money was made in manufacturing. John's came from carpets loomed in New York; Ethel's — though nothing was left of it after a lifetime of bad investments by her father — was from tacks produced in Connecticut.

Ethel's father, Henry Shelton Sanford, was a celebrated diplomat, President Lincoln's first ambassadorial appointee, who was stationed in Brussels during the Civil War. He cut a fine figure there, with a full chestnut-colored beard, his well-made suits accessorized with a stovepipe hat and gold-headed cane, and he entertained lavishly. According to the writer Christopher Dickey, Sanford operated as a sort of rogue CIA agent in Europe, supervising Lincoln's secret service there. He spent a million dollars in the early years of the conflict on war materiel and supplies, cornering the European market on saltpeter, a key ingredient in gunpowder. He was so reckless, Dickey said, Lincoln finally ordered him to cease and desist some of his activities.

Other accounts of his diplomatic career are much kinder, but the fact remains that Henry Sanford made so many enemies in Congress that he was thwarted in his later years when he tried to obtain new diplomatic posts in Europe. He wound up serving as an agent for King Leopold II of Belgium in his effort to colonize the Congo, even recruiting the noted explorer Henry M. Stanley to establish trading posts there. He also served as the king's lobbyist in Washington, winning recognition of the African colony from the Congress. Leopold was successful, to the detriment of eight to ten million Congolese who perished under his brutal rule. Shortly before Sanford's death in 1890, he realized he had been duped by the wily king and died bitterly disillusioned by Leopold and deeply in debt, according to historian Adam Hochschild.

A small city in central Florida near Orlando is named Sanford after Henry, who in one of his many failed business ventures established a citrus empire there. Although initially successful, the Florida groves fell victim to freezes and Henry's inattention as he spent most of his time in Brussels. In a letter, his wife likened Florida to "a vampire that... sucked the *repose* & the beauty & the *dignity* & cheerfulness out of our lives." She might be chagrined to know her husband was a posthumous inductee into the Florida Citrus Hall of Fame.

Gertie believed she got her adventurous spirit from her maternal grandfather, Henry Shelton Sanford.

Gertie devotes the first pages of her autobiography *The Time of My Life* to admiring words about this grandfather, noting that "people say I inherited my sense of adventure" from him. Like most grandchildren who are indoctrinated in family history, she probably had no idea of the darker side of Henry's life. Indeed, the city of Sanford continues to venerate him in its local history museum, which contains a scaled-down version of his 2,800-volume library, his Civil War general's uniform (which was given to him, along with the rank, in honor of donations he made to the Union cause) and one of his black tail-coats. Displayed in the library is a portrait of Henry's beautiful wife, for whom Gertie was named.

Gertie's mother, Ethel, who had spent her girlhood in Europe and never lost her continental accent, was just nineteen in 1892 when she married forty-one-year-old John Sanford. He was completing his second — and last — term in Congress, a Republican representing the district that encompassed Amsterdam, where his primary interest was perpetuating tariffs that protected the carpet industry. He had met and won his bride, according to an account in the *New York World*, during a visit the previous year to Belgium. (The wedding write-up headlined "Orange Blossoms Galore" described a small ceremony attended by family and close friends at a Sanford church. Among the gifts was a "massive silver cup given by the 2,500 work people" at the Stephen Sanford & Sons Carpet Company.) Ethel's mother received many letters of regret about missing the ceremony, including an especially gushing one from Caroline Astor — the New York social arbiter known as *the* Mrs. Astor — who was vacationing in Algiers. "Where will the married couple live? I hope in New York," she wrote.

By then the bride's widowed mother was so strapped for cash that she had reluctantly settled at the Florida home, Belair, to escape creditors in Belgium, and the bridegroom reimbursed her for the expenses of the wedding. There is the whiff of an arranged marriage about the match, although the young bride and her middle-aged groom seemed to get along well at first. Letters to "Dear Jack" from Ethel have an almost pleading nature as she sought his time and attention. He wrote to his mother-in-law of his admiration for the way she sat in her saddle. Still, their interests were vastly different. Ethel was cultured and mannered — she spoke French at home — primarily interested in music, literature and intellectual conversation. John was a tough businessman whose life centered on the breeding of race horses at his family's Hurricana Stud Farm near Amsterdam and the carpet company founded by his grandfather, in that order. "Mother and Father were so different that in later years there was less companionship," Gertie wrote tactfully in her autobiography. According to Gertie's younger daughter, Bokara, in these later years the couple stopped speaking and communicated by leaving notes for each other in the elevator of their New York mansion.

But that was far in the future. Gertie recalled a happy childhood where the family spent summers at the New England shore, fall and Christmas in Amsterdam and migrated to Aiken for the winter and early spring. Although modern Aiken is dotted with the same chain restaurants and retail stores as the rest of America, the charm of its turn-of-the-20th-century self is not hard to find. The serpentine wall hemming in Hopelands Gardens on Whiskey Road, the roads "paved" with sand in the area where thoroughbreds still live in stables run by champion trainers and the charming Willcox Hotel, restored to its former glory, are reminders of what the Sanfords saw when they arrived more than a hundred years ago. By the time of their marriage, John was a frequent visitor to Aiken, and the news of his nuptials was greeted warmly.

If young Gertie went looking for a role model in that Aiken of old, she need have looked no further than the Winter Colony's matriarch, Louise Eustis Hitchcock. "Loulie" Eustis was a wealthy but sickly orphan when her aunt, Celestine Eustis, brought her to Aiken from New Orleans in 1872. The little girl not only recovered her health but also became an avid sportswoman, the first of her set to reject the side saddle. When she married Thomas Hitchcock, heir to a banking fortune, in 1891, she introduced him to Aiken. He was equally smitten with the place, and soon rich Yankees with surnames including Whitney, Mellon, Vanderbilt and Astor had joined the Hitchcocks there.

Thomas Hitchcock and a friend, William C. Whitney, bought an 8,000-acre tract of woods that they set aside for hunting and riding. A 2,100-acre portion of Hitchcock Woods remains in use today, the country's largest urban forest. Hitchcock started a golf club and Whitney built a polo ground. Louise Hitchcock, eventually dubbed "the Mother of Polo" by *Time* magazine, started a prep school for boys where the sport was part of the curriculum. "Sometimes I wished that girls were allowed," Gertie recalled. "The boys got to learn how to play polo and the bigger girls in town played against them. I had to content myself with bicycle polo."

The families wintering in Aiken and its grand hotels — most of which burned down without the help of the Union commander's matches — had all the leisure money could buy. "Both the men and the women, having inherited extraordinarily large fortunes from their daring and rapacious ancestors, seemed determined to amuse themselves in a life-threatening manner," observed John Seabrook in a *Travel + Leisure* article on Aiken. "The ideal of the Winter Colony was to play three sports a day — polo in the morning, followed by a game of golf, and then a hunt late in the day, preferably after dark, when the riding was at its most hazardous." Both W.C. Whitney and Thomas Hitchcock lost their wives in riding accidents in Hitchcock Woods. Louise Hitchcock, who had once said she took "infinite pleasure in training vicious beasts," was paralyzed in a fall the day after Christmas 1933 and died a few months later at age sixty-seven. Her ashes were interred at her home, Mon Repos, in Hitchcock Woods.

The sort of hectic activity practiced by the members of the Winter Colony was a signature of Gertie's lifestyle. Many years later, her husband, Sidney,

A three-generation portrait shows Stephen and Sarah Jane Sanford, Gertie's mother and father, John and Ethel, and their first child, Laddie.

complained in a letter that by living in as isolated a place as Medway, they had to find their own amusements and invite constant rounds of company to keep her occupied. This created a problem as she had too much energy and he had too little so that "after I was whipped from a morning's ride, you were just limbered up for an afternoon of tennis or quail shooting." For the youngest member of the Sanford family, hunting and tennis were still ahead. Gertie's memories of Aiken were of "ponies, picnics, costume parties… the fun of playing marbles with the Hitchcocks." Tommy Hitchcock, oldest son of Louise and Thomas, would often figure in the lives of Gertie and Laddie.

In the summers, Gertie's father rented a "huge, rambling home" in Newport or Bar Harbor, Maine where they could enjoy the cool breezes and the seashore. They always concluded the summer with the annual racing season in Saratoga Springs. Gertie recalled that when they were small, she and her siblings were driven to the Saratoga races in a surrey, complete with fringe on top, pulled by a pair of chestnut horses named for Janie and Laddie. Her heavy-set father, his balding head shaded with a Panama hat, a cigar clenched between his teeth and field glasses slung around his neck, "was forever studying the racing form," she wrote in her autobiography. "I heard so much race talk during my life that it finally became a murmur in the background that I no longer listened to or retained."

Gertie kept voluminous albums throughout her life. The one assembled from her early childhood years contains pictures of her baby self, bundled to the eyes, a nurse holding her beside a wicker carriage, and a formal sibling portrait in Amsterdam, with Laddie in a sailor suit and Gertie and Janie in starched dresses with wide sashes and patent leather Mary Jane shoes, big bows perched on their heads. In Aiken, she was photographed with Janie, both dressed as Indians, their dolls strapped to papoose boards. In a later photo, taken at Old Fort Johnson in Amsterdam, she wore fringed buckskin and a wig with long braids, her skin darkened with makeup.

Gertie had a thing for Indians and uninhibited play, as expressed in a letter she wrote to her mother in New York from Plainfield, New Jersey when she was twelve:

Dear Mamma!

We are having a lovely time here!

Today we played like wild Indians with five boys and one girl beside ourselves, we had great funn [sic] we tied to [sic] boys to a tree and see how quickly they could get ontied [sic] anyway.

Today (this morning) we went to the new house and picked a lot of flowers.

I hope you will come on Sunday this letter will reach you to [sic] late most likely.

<u>*Love*</u>

Gertrude

(excuse the writing I am at a rickety table)

She developed a life-long love of costume parties, throwing a New Year's Eve masquerade for years at Medway in which she is best remembered dressed as an Indian princess in white buckskin. Photos in her albums show Gertie masquerading as everything from a chorus girl to a gypsy to, horrifyingly, in her teen-age years, as a white-sheeted member of the Ku Klux Klan, her identity disclosed in her handwritten caption.

Laddie, Janie and Gertie wore their Sunday best in this formal portrait.

Although she never met her maternal grandfather, Gertie's paternal grand-father, Stephen Stanford, was a vivid presence in her childhood. "I remember Grandfather Stephen as being tall and straight, dressed in a frock coat, four-in-hand tie and Panama hat. He often carried a green umbrella," she recalled. "I was always a little afraid of him." Her fear may have been due to a childhood misadventure when she broke an umbrella stand in the hall, drawing the ire of her grandfather. She ran upstairs, fearing a spanking.

A graduate of West Point and a one-term Republican member of Congress representing Amsterdam, Stephen Sanford was described by the family biographer, Alex M. Robb, as "ramrod straight physically, mentally and every other way." He had built up the carpet company started by his father in 1842, introducing new product lines and, during the Civil War, producing blankets for the Union Army. After Gertie's Yale-educated father John and his brother Will joined the business, it was renamed Stephen Sanford &

Sons. Then in middle age, Stephen stayed in shape by using a chinning bar he had installed on the front porch, and it was rumored that he had gone a round with heavyweight boxing champion John L. Sullivan. Stephen was a ruthless businessman, and competitors as well as employees sometimes suffered from his profit-driven actions. He once said, "Business is sordid, but there is pleasure in it when you win."

The hard-driven businessman sometimes suffered from bouts of dyspepsia, or heartburn. Advised by his doctor to find a recreational diversion, he established Hurricana Stud Farm in the 1870s. It became his consuming passion, and by the 1890s he was shelling out small fortunes for good horse flesh. The stallion Potomac set him back $30,000, close to $1 million in current dollars. (Unfortunately, Stephen did not live to see a Hurricana horse, George Smith, win his stable's first and only Kentucky Derby in 1916.) John and Will were just as passionate about thoroughbred horses as their father, and the love of all aspects of equine sports was passed along to Laddie and, to a lesser extent, Gertie and Janie. Stephen Sanford bought his grandson a Shetland pony "almost before he could walk," according to Alex Robb. (Young Stephen's nickname was also the name of this first pony.) All three children spent long days at the farm and at race tracks, especially Saratoga, while taking riding lessons wherever they lived.

Stephen Sanford was, without question, the leading citizen of Amsterdam, the proverbial big fish — make that a whale — in a small pond. He did not share John's penchant for travel and society, was far more involved in the business than his son, and was content to stay in Amsterdam and environs with his wife Sarah Jane. When John and his family were not in Aiken or traveling to some other distant destination, they shared the big house Stephen built on Church Street in Amsterdam. (John's brother Will, who died unexpectedly in 1896, at age forty-two, never married.)

But Stephen's life was coming to an end, and the ties to Amsterdam were loosening for John and his family. New York, with all its bustle, culture and high society, would soon be the main stage for their family life.

2

Everyone Seemed to be Dancing

——— · ———

W hen Stephen Sanford died in 1913 at age 87, he left his son John an estate valued at $40 million, more than $1 billion in current dollars. Fortunately for John, the federal inheritance tax was still a few years off. Unfortunately for him, the federal income tax, enabled by the Sixteenth Amendment of the Constitution, was ratified shortly after Stephen's death. The scandal of factory working conditions unleashed by the Triangle Shirtwaist Company fire in New York in 1911 resulted in that state's first serious effort to address workplace safety, which also affected corporate earnings. The family's wealth, though considerable, steadily diminished over time. However, that time was far in the future, and a million dollars went a long, long way in 1913.

Like other ambitious and socially mobile men, John Sanford purchased a home in New York, on 49th Street. *The* Mrs. Astor had died in 1908, but at last her wish that the John Sanfords would live in New York came true. The move no doubt pleased his culture-loving wife. Ethel had done her duty as the doyenne of the leading family of Amsterdam, raising money for charitable causes and the like, but life in a small factory town surely was stultifying for Gertie's cosmopolitan mother.

The family's horse interests also began taking them to Europe on an annual basis. Gertie made her first trans-Atlantic crossing at age eight. "How I dreaded those trips by sea!" she remembered. "Six or seven seasick days aboard the *Olympic* or the *Mauritania* there and back. It's ironic that I sailed in every great passenger ship of this century and was always miserable." Gertie's postcard collections from those summer jaunts show sights familiar to most European travelers today. They toured museums and cathedrals, the battlefield at Waterloo, and marveled at the Eiffel Tower, then the world's tallest structure. They also visited the last place Ethel had lived prior to her marriage, the Chateau Maillard in Belgium. But the most memorable European trip in Gertie's childhood was the one in the summer of 1914, when she was twelve.

"Americans watched the growing crisis almost with indifference," wrote historian William E. Leuchtenburg. "When after weeks of gestures and counter-gestures, war came, it seemed like a bomb dropped from the sky into a pleasant country picnic." The Sanfords were among some hundred thousand traveling Americans caught by surprise on July 28 when Austria-Hungary declared war and attacked Serbia. John Sanford was seeing to budding horse interests in Maisons-Laffitte, a suburb of Paris, with his entire family and various servants along. As tensions grew in Europe, the Sanfords were still planning to travel to Le Touquet on the French coast, where they had rented a house. Within days of Austria-Hungary's declaration, Germany, Russia and France joined the war.

Gertie recalled that day in an interview late in life: "And war was declared and the people in the garden all put down their rakes and all went down to the village of Maisons-Laffitte. I remember bicycling down to see what the excitement was all about; there were big posters up, like '*Guerre est declarée*' and everybody was fearfully emotional about the whole thing — very excited — and the bells were ringing."

The Sanfords, still not believing the war was serious, packed people and luggage into two cars and headed for Le Touquet: "I remember Father and Mother saying: 'Oh, it isn't true; it isn't going to amount to anything.'" In Le Touquet, officials urged them to cross the English Channel, and they drove on to Calais.

"Everyone wanted to cross the Channel at the same time," Gertie wrote in her autobiography. "As we made our way through one of the many checkpoints set up along the coast, a French general stopped us and said that he needed our car. When we protested, he went away and came back with all sorts of official looking papers authorizing him to requisition the Rolls and our chauffeur. I remember watching them drive away and wondering if I would ever see Bidell [the chauffeur] again."

England was in the midst of a three-day banking holiday, sending thousands of stranded travelers into a panic. In London, a resourceful engineering firm executive named Herbert Hoover sprang into action. He offered his services to the overwhelmed officials at the U.S. Consulate and made short-term loans from his own funds to many of his countrymen. His response to the panic and his efforts toward Belgian war relief that followed launched Hoover's political career, leading to his election as president in 1928.

The Sanfords stayed on in England with friends, as the racing season in Saratoga had been canceled due to the war. Several weeks later, Gertie was walking down a street in Piccadilly when she came upon Bidell and the Rolls. Bidell explained that after the French general released him, he crossed the Channel and went driving around London until he happened upon Gertie. "I shouldn't have been surprised to see him," she recalled. "Bidell always found his way home."

The four years of war that followed curtailed international travel, and the Sanfords focused their attention on American homes and watering holes. Following his father's death, John expanded and remodeled the Church Street home in Amsterdam, but the family was spending more of its time in New York and the children, who had been taught at home by French governesses and tutors, began attending boarding schools. Like most good upper-crust boys, Laddie went to prep school. He entered St. Mark's School in Southborough, Massachusetts, which, with its competing schools Groton and St. Paul's, funneled its graduates into Harvard, Princeton and Yale. Upper-crust girls enrolled in corresponding finishing schools.

Janie and Gertie, although eighteen months apart in age, started Foxcroft School in Middleburg, Virginia in 1916. The focus under its founder, the indomitable Charlotte Haxall Noland, was on character development and horseback riding, or, as the school's motto states, *mens sana in corpore sano* (A healthy mind in a healthy body). Foxcroft girls were not then expected to go to college, and the first graduate from each class to give birth to four children was presented with a commemorative cup.

Foxcroft accepted only twenty-two students in the freshman class, and initially the Sanfords were told there was only room for Janie. "I have always hated favoritism, especially when it doesn't benefit me, so I wrote Miss Charlotte a very determined letter offering to sleep in a bathtub if need be. She found room for me," Gertie recalled.

She loved Foxcroft, later sending her daughters Landine and Bokara there, and adored the headmistress, who she remembered seated on her horse in her "elegant sidesaddle habit," with her white hair and white stock. "Miss

The headmistress of Foxcroft School, Charlotte Haxall Noland, was a towering figure in Gertie's life.

Charlotte was a woman of exceptional character and she cared deeply for each of her girls," Gertie wrote. "The presence of someone like that in your early life is felt forever... She valued discipline, commitment and loyalty, and she knew how to have fun."

Gertie's father sent a mare to Foxcroft for her to ride. It did not go well. "I made the mistake of thinking she was a buggy horse and hitched her up and started out on a little drive around the school," she recalled. "Things were fine until she caught sight of a fence and then there was no stopping her. She was a jumper and she tried to take the fence, buggy and all! She cleared it, but the buggy didn't; somehow I survived, but I sent the mare back to Father."

Naturally, Foxcroft students went fox-hunting, as well as coon hunting and "beagling" with packs of beagle hounds. Gertie also took up basketball, playing on an outdoor earthen court dressed in full below-the-knee skirts, black stockings and white sports shoes. But it wasn't all fun and games. Miss Charlotte, Gertie wrote, "believed we should be aware of and involved with the world outside school. For the war effort, she piled us into a jitney and drove us all over the state to perform skits and sing songs to raise money for war bonds."

In 1918, when the war was over and Gertie was halfway through Foxcroft, the family made a huge leap in Manhattan real estate ownership. John Sanford bought a four-story, twenty-eight-room, eight-bath mansion at 9 East 72nd Street, just off Central Park, with Fifth Avenue as the cross street. "This Beaux Arts style residence has a magnificent limestone facade, mansard roof and intricate detail," gushed a real estate agent at the time of its most recent listing in 2010. Although it had been almost fifty years since she had been inside the house, Gertie had vivid memories of this childhood home when she wrote her autobiography. The house's huge front hall had a large, marble mantle and fireplace and opposite the fireplace was a wide, circular carpeted staircase leading to the ballroom above. The ground floor had an oak-paneled library and a small card room where dinners for four or six were served. An elevator took the Sanfords to the upper floors, with their bedrooms and baths and her mother's sitting room. The house would be the site of Gertie's wedding reception in 1929.

A huge house required an extensive staff. Gertie had fond memories not only of Bidell, the chauffeur requisitioned by the French general, but also the butler, Frale, who "looked like a Kewpie doll" and "seemed always able to fix things." Gertie and Janie shared a car and a chauffeur named Kane, who delivered them to dressmakers, restaurants, plays and, as they got older, speakeasies, waiting in the car until they were ready to go home. "Kane was a saint," Gertie said. There was a cook named Mary, who served the family for fifty years, but Gertie reserves her fondest words and praise for Rose Brind, who began working for the Sanfords when the girls were at Foxcroft, primarily looking after "the sewing and pressing of Janie's clothes and mine." Rose became Gertie's personal maid in 1924 and stayed with her until her death, handling every request and crisis, including a cook who "went berserk and

The imposing Sanford mansion at 9 E. 72nd Street, near Central Park, today belongs to the emir of Qatar.

began chasing his wife all over the house with a carving knife."

The move to the Upper East Side came on the eve of the Roaring Twenties, and even with Prohibition looming, the city was caught up in a time of celebration. "New York felt like the center of it all," Gertie wrote. "Every week a new musical would open and every night we could choose from an assortment of theater tickets left on the marble-top table in the front hall."

Ethel Sanford was in her element during those years. Gertie remembers how proud she was to be seen with her mother when they went to the opera in formal dress, their hands encased in long, white kid gloves: "She was naturally elegant, with an almost regal bearing, but never haughty. Her eyes were a clear blue and her features well defined and regular. She used to sweep up her short, curly chestnut hair with combs and always wore pearl earrings and a pearl choker on her neck." Ethel's husband was not a fan of opera. "Father hated it and seldom went," Gertie wrote.

The Sanfords entertained at home on a large scale, often including their children in their social affairs. "On Friday night, mother organized dinner dances for us that we called 'Businessmen's Dinners' because they broke up early, at midnight," she remembered, "but there was always a live band and plenty of dancing in the ballroom." Gertie described this period as a time of constant dancing. "Everyone seemed to be dancing then — tea dances, dinner dances, fancy balls… In the Bois du Boulogne [in Paris], we danced in full evening dress under necklaces of Japanese lanterns. People believed in having fun and didn't apologize for it." Occasionally Mrs. Sanford hired celebrated musicians, including the pianist Arthur Rubinstein and the lyric soprano Lucrezia Bori, to perform private concerts for her guests.

But the after-dinner entertainment that had the biggest impact on Gertie had been provided by a different sort of celebrity some years before, and she was an uninvited guest. In the summer of 1914, prior to their truncated trip to Europe, the Sanfords rented a home in Newport for the summer. It was a time of parties, each millionaire trying to out-do the other with his guest of honor. This particular evening, the Sanfords' guest was the famous big-game hunter Paul J. Rainey. He had just returned from Africa and was showing his films of lion hunting.

The children were sent to bed, but Gertie couldn't sleep. When she heard the dinner party breaking up and the guests resettling themselves in the living room, she sneaked to the head of the staircase and peered through the banister slats. "There it was: Africa in jumpy, badly lighted, black-and-white images against the far wall. I may have had a poor seat, but that evening changed my life. From that moment on, I knew that I would go to Africa someday."

First, she cut her teeth on an elk.

3

Every Inch the Successful Huntress

——— • ———

To modern-day sensibilities, Gertie's obsession with big game hunting seems strange and even distasteful. Only five percent of Americans to-day do any kind of hunting at all, and voices in the animal rights movement have called into question both the morality and mental state of anyone who would kill a living creature for sport. The disappearance of once-abundant exotic species has also led to a large-scale re-thinking of trophy hunting of the sort Gertie indulged in throughout the 1920s and 1930s. The 2015 bow-killing by an American trophy hunter of Cecil, a black-maned lion that was being studied by naturalists in Zimbabwe, caused world-wide outrage. The lion's death resulted in legislative action in multiple countries, the banning of transport of trophy animals by forty airlines and the creation of songs, art and a children's book, as well as a Cecil the lion Beanie Baby. The Minnesota dentist who killed Cecil received death threats, though he was not charged with a crime and went back to his practice once the furor died down.

This was not the world in which Gertie began to hunt big game in 1920.

Many people in rural America still hunted for food, supplementing their diets with deer, rabbit and other small game. Since the latter nineteenth century, American sport hunting among the elite had been considered a character-building antidote to the soft living enabled by their wealth. The only thing even slightly unusual about Gertie's enthusiasm was that she was a woman, though she certainly wasn't the only huntress out there. Delia Akeley, married to the explorer and naturalist Carl Akeley, was shooting elephants in Africa while Gertie was still playing bicycle polo in Aiken.

By far the best-known sport hunter in the world in the first decades of the twentieth century was Theodore Roosevelt, the former president. Although Roosevelt's sparing of a bear on an unsportsmanlike hunt in 1902 had inspired the toy Teddy bear, he was a passionate big-game hunter up until his death in 1919. The rapidly dwindling buffalo was the object of his first major hunt in 1882 in the Badlands of the Dakota Territory, Roosevelt declaring that he had to get there "while there were still buffalo to shoot." He got his bison trophy, along with mule deer, black-tailed deer and elk. Of the latter, he bragged that he shot one just for the antlers, fully aware that in "a few years it will have ceased entirely to be one of the common game animals on the plains."

By the latter 1880s, Roosevelt changed his tune somewhat and worked at different levels of government to create wildlife refuges and national parks as habitat for beleaguered species. He formed the Boone and Crockett Club in 1887 expressly to work for conservation legislation. Nevertheless, he took down another buffalo bull in 1889, exulting in his kill. Writes Roger L. Di Silvestro, author of *Theodore Roosevelt in the Badlands*, "The irony of killing a breeding bull in a shrinking bison population that he and his colleagues were trying to save apparently was lost on him."

After his presidency, in 1909, Roosevelt headed to British East Africa — present-day Kenya, Tanzania and Uganda — on an eleven-month-long safari with his son, Kermit, in partnership with the Smithsonian Institution. Although J.P. Morgan was said to have quipped, "Every American hopes that every lion will do his duty," the big cats were no match for TR and his guides. The father and son bagged more than five hundred big-game animals, including seventeen lions, eleven elephants and nine giraffes. Henry Fairfield Osborn, then the president of the American Museum of Natural History, said the trip was "by far the most successful expedition that has ever penetrated Africa." The museum, located across Central Park from Gertie's Manhattan home, came to figure large in her life, as did Osborn.

Roosevelt wrote about his exploits from the bush in a series of articles serialized by *Scribner's* magazine, and they were published together in a book, *African Game Trails*, in 1910. "Following the enormous publicity generated by Roosevelt's expedition, sportsmen from all corners of the globe began arriving in East Africa and safaris were rapidly becoming big business," wrote Brian Herne in his book *White Hunters*. Paul J. Rainey also added to the excitement with his films of lion hunts that had so entranced young Gertie.

Rainey conducted his own safari with the Smithsonian in 1911-12. This resulted in the silent movie *Paul J. Rainey's East African Expedition,* replete with scenes of "native bearers carrying the hunting gear, wild animals at the water holes, white hunters playing with monkeys and lots of dead animals shot by hunters," Herne wrote. The newly crowned King George V was among the many British fans of the movie, which was shown daily for almost a year in that country. It was also popular in New York and New Orleans, the home of Gertie's future husband, Sidney Legendre.

Paul Rainey inherited a fortune comparable to John Sanford's from his father, an Ohio coal mining company owner. Although his primary residence was in Mississippi, where his spread included a private polo field, extensive stables and an air-strip, he also owned a cattle ranch in Kenya. To ranchers such as Rainey, lions were such troublesome predators that they were regarded as "nothing more than dangerous vermin," according to Herne. Using horses and hounds on his hunts in 1911, Rainey and his friends killed 120 lions. Even for the time, though, that was considered excessive.

By the time Gertie graduated from Foxcroft in 1920, conservation efforts in the United States had allowed some of the big game in the West to recover their numbers. That year, she joined Janie in coming out — the preferred term to making their debut — but eschewed the round of debutante parties that summer in favor of a hunting trip to the Grand Tetons in Wyoming. She was invited by a man named Tom Evans, who she described as "an old friend." John Sanford consented and bank-rolled the trip on the condition that his long-time personal secretary, Dr. Henry Coffin, accompany them. "Although he wasn't much of a hunter, he loved the woods and had been a forester in his youth," Gertie wrote of their chaperone.

They set out in the summer of 1920, traveling by train and hired car to Jackson Hole, where they bought their hunting licenses. "Jackson Hole was a dusty frontier town consisting of a post office and a couple of houses," Gertie recalled. "On our way out of town, heading for the Tetons, we got lost and had to wake a couple of campers asleep under the stars to ask the way to the J.Y. Ranch. I remember a row of log cabins facing the lake in the moonlight and the black twin peaks of the Tetons soaring up at the far end, and the stillness."

Their hunting guide was "an eager young cowboy in leather chaps and Stetson hat" named George. Not to be outdone, Tom Evans stuffed his pants into leather boots laced to the knees and tied a kerchief round his

Gertie, her friend Tom Evans and their guide, George, looked ready for action on her first major hunting trip, to the Grand Tetons.

neck, while Gertie bought sheepskin chaps and a ten-gallon hat. "We were quite a trio!" she wrote.

They traveled into the mountains in a pack train, Gertie retaining strong memories of "the tinkle of the bell on the lead pony, the smell of spruce, the cold nights under the stars, the log fires and the warm sleeping bags." She reveled in it all, but especially the day she shot and killed her first elk. George spotted a group of five elk through his field glasses, far off on another ridge. They tracked the animals, coming as close as they dared, then settled down to wait.

"Even the waiting was a thrill," Gertie wrote. "There I was sitting on a log beside a game trail on a ridge in the middle of the Wyoming mountains on a beautiful afternoon. I held the gun tightly, in a ready position, across my knees. The faint scent of gun oil mingled with the scent of the surrounding woods." Although she had been shooting birds since childhood, Gertie may have never shot a large mammal before that day.

When the elk came in sight, Gertie fired off a shot at the bull, who stumbled and plunged into the brush. They soon found him lying on his side. "It was not a particularly large animal and it had neither great points nor heavy horn, but it was my elk, my first, on my first real hunt — shot with a bullet through the heart," she said. Although she could not bear to watch George disembowel the elk, when they returned to camp with her trophy secured to one of the pack ponies, Gertie was "filled with pride and the exultation of success. In my black and white chaps, my checkered lumberjack shirt and wide-brimmed Stetson with its beaded band, I strode into camp — all five feet five of me, every inch the successful huntress."

The unremarkable elk became the first of more than 150 trophy heads in Gertie's collection. The big-game bug had bitten her, causing a fever that would not wear off until she was in her fifties, laid down her guns (except for bird shooting) and turned her mind and resources toward preserving animal species rather than killing them off. Over the next seven years, Gertie took hunting and fishing trips to Alaska (where she bagged a Kodiak bear), Canada and wilderness areas in the continental United States, sometimes with Laddie, sometimes with Tom Evans and Henry Coffin. Images stuck in her mind, like the cold evening in Canada when her guide blew a moose call on his birchbark horn: "There was a crash of branches and the crackling of twigs, and by the edge of the lake a moose was etched in the fading silver light. Such moments one doesn't forget."

Gertie's other travels during that time included trips to polo grounds and watering holes in Europe, usually in the company of her sister Janie and their maids. On a crossing on the *SS Lapland*, they met the married film stars Mary Pickford and Douglas Fairbanks, and took pictures of them playing shuffleboard on deck. The only indication in her albums that the world had undergone a great upheaval, with the killing of almost seventeen million people and the toppling of monarchies across Europe, were some pictures of a battlefield in France, an overturned German tank at Verdun and an American cemetery. The girls kept in touch with their mother by letter, sometimes writing separate notes on the same piece of stationery. Ethel's letters to them were affectionate, sometimes offering "motherly advice," but she seemed comfortable with the idea of her daughters traveling without her, as long as they were chaperoned by staff and stayed in the best hotels or with family friends.

Gertie had her portrait painted during one of these European trips by the celebrated Irish society painter Sir William Orpen, who had a studio in London. His other subjects included Winston Churchill, President Woodrow Wilson and Sir Neville Chamberlain. In the oil portrait of Gertie, her dark hair is bobbed and parted on the side, and she wears a loose blouse in a striking pattern of blue and aqua. Her left hand is on her hip, and her facial expression is direct and challenging. Writing of the portrait later, Gertie describes herself as "a young, confident woman looking less like me than I remember." Nevertheless, she chose this portrait for the jacket of her autobiography.

About this time, a lesser artist drew a pencil portrait of Laddie, but it got much wider circulation, appearing on the cover of *Time* magazine. In March 1923, his horse Sergeant Murphy became the first American-owned steed to win the Grand National steeplechase race, having its eighty-third running in England. *Time* described the course as "the most hazardous four miles known to the racing turf."

The fall of 1924 brought another momentous event for the Sanford family when England's Prince of Wales, the future Edward VIII, came to dinner. The prince had traveled to the United States to attend the bi-annual international polo match between the U.S. and Great Britain, held at the Meadow Brook Club on Long Island. (Tommy Hitchcock, the Sanford siblings' friend from Aiken, played on the victorious American team.) "Everyone that summer was giving parties for the Prince of Wales," Gertie recalled. "Each tried to outdo the other." The Sanfords had leased The Chimneys, the forty-four-room Long Island mansion of a wealthy men's clothing merchant, and entertained the prince and members of the British International polo team on the evening of September 28 at a dinner-dance.

"When he came to our house for dinner, he was small and polite and charming, but seemed weak — which everyone thought but never dared to say," Gertie wrote. Perhaps her memory was colored by his abdication twelve years later to marry the American divorcée Wallis Warfield Simpson.

A few nights later, with other guests at dinner, someone entered Mrs. Sanford's bedroom and absconded with jewels valued at more than $50,000, according to accounts in the *New York Times*. The jewelry, including gem-encrusted necklaces, bracelets and combs and ropes of pearls, were mostly

Gertie had her portrait painted in her twenties by the celebrated Irish society painter Sir William Orpen.

uninsured because the Lloyd's of London policy covering them had lapsed a few months before. Investigators questioned the Sanfords' seventeen servants and finger-printed their handyman. The *Times* pointed out that an even larger jewelry heist had happened at the Long Island home of another wealthy couple where the prince had been entertained a few weeks earlier. There seems to have been no connection or any arrests made in either crime. Perhaps jewel thieves were on the prowl because so many valuable items had been taken from safes as hostesses gilded themselves to impress the prince and his retinue.

The loss was greatly overshadowed just six weeks later when Ethel Sanford died at The Chimneys at the age of fifty-one. (One of her obituaries was headlined "Hostess to Prince Victim of Cancer.") Gertie wrote, "It seemed that she was sick only that month, but perhaps it was longer. She was too brave to let on."

In a short manuscript titled "Egypt and the Nile 1924," Gertie wrote, "Mother's death in 1924 was a sad milestone of my life. I was twenty-two at the time and Father decided that Janie and I needed to go away on a trip that winter." In January 1925, he sent them off with his secretary, Henry Coffin, to visit Egypt, Palestine and Syria. Also along on the trip were Gertie's friend from the Wyoming hunting trip, Tom Evans, and two female friends, Peggy Thayer and Millie Smith, with their mothers. Peggy Thayer had lost her father in the *Titanic* disaster; her mother was a survivor of that ill-fated journey.

The travelers floated down the Nile, visiting pyramids, tombs and temples. Much as tourists do today, they had their photographs made sitting on camels in front of the Sphinx. In Luxor they were treated to a most unusual experience. The tomb of Tutankhamen had been discovered late in 1922 by the British archaeologist Howard Carter, and the party had a letter of introduction to him. He allowed them to enter the tomb, which still held its riches.

"The treasures were piled high, one on top of another to the ceiling. We saw the golden throne, the funeral couch and the mummiform coffin, but nothing had been yet touched or removed. It was a strange feeling to be present at such a momentous time, and we were grateful to Howard Carter for the privilege to see it," she wrote. In her autobiography, Gertie described the so-called pharaoh's curse on the archeological expedition, which claimed the life of its benefactor, Lord Carnarvon, in 1923. "The legend of the curse still persists," she concluded darkly.

Later, a *New York Times* columnist made the snarky observation that after Ethel's death "the Sanfords have become social nomads, grazing in the social pastures of Palm Beach, Paris, London and the continent." It could be argued they were doing that before, but certainly Mrs. Sanford's death removed a paperweight that had pinned down the family in New York. John bought a place in Palm Beach and concentrated more of his time on Laddie's polo career and his own golf game. He eventually gave his mansion in Amsterdam to the town, where it still serves as the city hall. He owned the Manhattan mansion until his death in 1939, but he spent less and less time there.

The family's love of equine activities and other sports brought them together. Gertie and Laddie were at the racecourse in Saratoga in August 1927 when they ran into Peggy Thayer, now Mrs. Harold Talbott. An airplane manufacturer from Dayton, Ohio who would later serve as secretary of the air force, Harold was also a polo player and, as Gertie recalled, "lean and wiry and rather handsome in a flashy way." Peggy "was one of those twenties top-drawer charmers — beautiful, intelligent and a good sport." The announcement two years before of their engagement in the *New York Times* was headlined "Margaret Thayer, Big Game Hunter, to Wed." Their invitation that day to the Sanford siblings to join them on a safari to Africa was quickly accepted and earned the blessings of their father.

Gertie's journal about their trip, which began in December 1927, gives full, breathless voice to three months of constant thrills. She was truly in her element from the time she stepped on the ship at the Bay of Naples bound for Mombasa until she departed Africa via boat, train and plane in a breakneck attempt to reach Liverpool in time for the Grand National, where Laddie's horse, Bright's Boy, was a contender. She was sad about leaving Africa but was already planning a return trip.

On the journey out, the party crossed the Atlantic by ocean liner, arriving in Italy on December 7. They then boarded an Italian ship for the eighteen-day trip via the Suez Canal and the Red Sea to Mombasa, on the coast of Kenya. Although Gertie claimed to have spent the trip "sick as a dog," she seems to have been well enough to drink iced beer and champagne, sing around the piano, grill other passengers about Africa, watch silent movies accompanied by music played on a Victrola cranked by one of the waiters and get so rowdy at a Christmas eve party in the bar that the ship's doctor gave her a stern lecture. "I got Pilsner beer poured all over my hair," she wrote. Laddie, who by then was almost thirty years old, handed out Teddy bears that squirted water through their noses, just to get things going. "He was always the life of the party," she commented approvingly.

They boarded the train in Mombasa on Christmas afternoon, riding in the colonial governor's private car — stocked with champagne on ice — thanks to a connection Harold Talbott made. The next morning, Gertie saw her first giraffe, thirty feet outside the train window. "He loped away with a very superior expression — very 'high hat' is the word," she wrote. For the rest of the day, she was astonished to see "hundreds of game animals undisturbed and unafraid of the railroad."

Arriving in Nairobi, they found the British residents consumed by social events — dances, polo, horse races and tennis. In between all the activities, the four hunters managed to get measured for custom bush shirts, which Gertie described as "the 'bees' knees' in safari kit, made of sun-proof light wool, khaki-colored material, shaped like a tunic with a belt and huge pocket." Harold bought two trucks and two sedan cars, and Gertie and Peggy shopped for provisions and got their hair clipped almost as short as the men's.

They also met their white hunters, or safari guides, two of the best-known men in that fledgling business. She and Laddie shared O.M. Rees, a South African, while the Talbotts used A.J. Klein, an American who had worked for Paul J. Rainey. The guides hired native gun bearers, skinners, servants and dozens of porters. Each of the four had a personal servant, or "boy." Gertie said hers, Hassan, looked exactly like the singer and comedian Eddie Cantor, who often performed in blackface. "Hope he makes me laugh. I'll think I'm at the Follies!" As it turned out, Hassan was meticulously attentive, setting up her tent, washing her underwear and even putting toothpaste on her toothbrush.

Her gun bearer, Simba, looked nothing like a Broadway performer. He "wore a wig of baboon hair on his head which gave him a very savage look," she wrote. "He was tall and lean, with a long face and keen eyes." He had an especially keen eye for the animal for which he was named, the lion.

Before departing for their first camp, the Sanfords spent some time at Rees's home, where they met two other white hunters, including Denys Finch Hatton, immortalized in the book and movie *Out of Africa*. Gertie was disturbed by all the "friction and jealousy" among the hunters. "This is a big country and should have room for everyone to hunt over," she wrote.

They departed on New Year's Day and drove sixty bone-jarring miles before stopping for lunch. Afterward, they saw their first game: ostriches, pigs, giraffes, gazelles and impala. Gertie wrote excitedly that "one can see across the plains for miles and miles, and everywhere game, as far as the eye can see." The plains were black with zebras, wildebeest, water bucks, elands and steenboks.

They set up camp almost three hundred miles from Nairobi on the Serengeti Plain. By then, both Talbotts had shot Thompson gazelles, or tommies, for the cooking pot, and Gertie and Harold got in one of the trucks to chase down and kill two hyenas. "It was great sport," she wrote. It was also illegal. Regulations in colonial Tanganyika specifically prohibited pursuing game in a motor car or plane.

Their first big hunting day was January 3. All rose before dawn in order to beat the worst heat of the day and began by removing the doors and windshields of the trucks "and stripping them for action," Gertie wrote. They chased an impala going thirty miles per hour for ten to fifteen minutes, and a cheetah "gave us quite a run for over twenty minutes." Her first trophy was a topi, an antelope known for its speed. They also filmed movies as they chased, shooting footage of galloping giraffes and zebras, and lion prides resting amid the rocks.

The white hunters advised them on the best trophies to seek, dissuading them from shooting at young lions that did not have manes, lionesses and horned animals that were not sufficiently spectacular, or *misouri*. At one point, the Sanfords came upon a lioness with "two little, tiny, baby cubs. We were frightfully tempted to shoot the mother and carry away the cubs"— also prohibited by regulations — "and raise them on a bottle." Rees talked them out of it, telling them cubs were "the very devil of a job to raise."

The Talbotts' hunter apparently didn't intervene when they got the same notion after coming upon a mother rhino and her little *toto*. Gertie blithely wrote, "The Rhino was over a hundred years old, and the idea of crating a baby Rhino back to America was too tempting to resist." Harold killed the mother, which Gertie estimated weighed two tons.

The scene she describes is heart-rending. "The little *toto* stayed close by its mother while the skinner cut off her head and then they caught the little one and put it in the back of the Chrysler and brought it home." They taught the baby, which Gertie refers to as Peggy's "new plaything," to drink milk from a beer bottle, and kept it in a cage of saplings the native men built. It traveled with them back to Nairobi in late January, where it stayed while they continued into Uganda to hunt elephants. Gertie said at that point the baby rhino had stood the trip well. That was her last mention of it. Where did it wind up? And what did Peggy Talbott plan to do with a two-ton "plaything"?

The party spent four weeks hunting lions, cheetahs, zebras and antelopes of various kinds. For the most part, it was like shooting fish in a barrel, a matter of accuracy rather than strength, endurance or cunning. With her Springfield .30-06 rifle, Gertie was usually successful when she identified a trophy animal, once boasting in her diary, "I cracked him with one shot." Again and again she marveled at the seemingly endless quantity of game. "It would probably take three to four or even six weeks in America to collect as many head as we had in one morning's hunt," she wrote. Usually she described the hunting as thrilling, and several diary entries were headed "red letter days" because of the variety, quality or challenge of the hunt. But she didn't always feel good about their activities.

A few days after the Talbotts shot the female rhino, Gertie and Laddie unexpectedly came upon a lone bull rhino and killed it. She wrote in her journal, "It wasn't as exciting as I either expected or hoped for; in fact we both felt almost sorry at killing such a huge, happy beast who didn't seem to be disturbing anybody and looked so peaceful and harmless." Sixty years later, when she published *The Time of My Life*, Gertie omitted any mention of the rhinos and her thoughts about kidnapping the baby cubs and killing their mother. By then she was heavily involved in the conservation movement and had made provisions to turn her South Carolina plantation into a wildlife preserve.

By the time they left for Nairobi, the party had bagged thirteen lions, five of them Gertie's trophies. While stalking the lions had been more challenging than hunting other game, only the last of hers had put any of them in danger. They were aided by some Maasai tribesmen, who had seen a lion with one black foot and one white one, with a black mane "the length of their spears." Hunting with Laddie, Rees and their native staff, she tracked and shot the lion, but did not kill him, as they could hear his roar nearby. With Rees in the lead, they proceeded, single file and bent double, into a tunnel of thorn bushes. "Then, in an instant, there was a roar, a charge and shots. All I saw was a great halo of yellow ruff coming down on us. Rees fired both barrels of his Holland & Holland and the lion fell ten feet from us — his neck broken. For several minutes, we just sat there silently, unable to move. It wasn't until later that we felt the thorns that had pierced our clothing and torn our flesh."

Killing a lion was cause for great celebration back at camp, and Gertie loved her evenings there, watching the spectacular sunsets, sitting around the fire, drinking whiskey with quinine to ward off malaria and listening to records on the Victrola, hand-cranked by Hassan, then retiring to their tents and rolling into sleeping bags on their cots. "Outside, the mosquitoes, as big as moths, used to bang against the canvas and netting. Nothing could wake me except maybe the grunt of a lion or the eerie, mocking laugh of a hyena."

Gertie loved being away from "the world of cement walls and streets and city noises." She wrote, "Camp life was the great thing — living out in the open for weeks; getting up at dawn and hurtling across the country like mad men in our rattling trucks... Being out in the middle of the Serengeti was like being at sea with nothing but the empty, flat horizon for hundreds of miles."

The only other humans they saw were African tribesmen. She was both fascinated and repelled by the Maasai, nomadic herders who had roamed the plains for centuries with almost no change in their culture. "They carry spears, wear few clothes, just a cowhide and wear tremendous loop earrings of different sizes and shapes in their deformed ear lobes which hang way down to their collar bones, a great many bracelets and anklets, and safety pins in their hair. They are filthy people," she wrote in her journal.

At one point, she filmed movies of a group of Maasai women, elaborately turned out in "brass rings (principally)," with babies on their hips, but lamented, "... it was a filthy process, as I was forced to shake hands with each of these dirty blacks that had not seen water in all their lives, in connection with a bath." The Maasai women apparently found Gertie just as exotic and strange, as they "laughed hysterically... apparently much amused at my appearance."

Again, the version of the encounters presented in her autobiography is more positive and does not mention the hygiene of the Maasai. The world changed, and Gertie changed with it.

At the end of January, the party broke camp and returned to Nairobi in preparation for the last leg of the trip, an elephant hunt in Uganda. Gertie sent the first half of her journal to Janie, asking her to have it transcribed. In her accompanying letter, she insisted it was "the greatest thrill in the world seeing all this game," but admitted that it was hardly a challenge to shoot animals from a car and expressed some disappointment that the African big game hunter was not quite the creature of "iron courage, strength and endurance" that she had imagined. She said she wanted to plan another hunting trip to Alaska with the Talbotts so they could appreciate the contrast when they were hunting under "hardships, and all kinds of difficulties."

The second part of their adventure provided plenty of both. Uganda was the best place to hunt elephants — the last trophy on their lists — but getting to the hunting grounds involved a boat journey of hundreds of miles on the Nile through waters teeming with hippos and crocodiles. The mosquitoes and the heat and humidity were fierce, and an outbreak of deadly sleeping sickness kept them confined to the boat, even when they spotted elephants.

At one point, they met a tribal chief — comically attired in gray flannel trousers and a khaki shirt, accessorized by a gold watch chain and a hat five sizes too small — who asked them to shoot a hippo for his hungry village. Laddie obliged him, and they watched, somewhat horrified, as the villagers hacked the hippo to pieces, eating some of the meat raw.

The Talbotts decided to try their luck elsewhere and the group split up. Finally, after days on the Nile, Gertie and Laddie found a herd of thirty to forty elephants and Gertie got a shot off Rees's .350 Rigby that felled a big bull with huge ivory tusks. She hit him right in the heart. As with the hippo, the natives crawled all over the five-ton animal, eating meat raw while they sawed off the tusks. The tusks weighed sixty-nine and seventy-four pounds. In her autobiography, Gertie wrote, "having found our elephant, we decided to bring this expedition to a close."

Only they didn't. Laddie wanted an elephant, too, and got one. Its tusks were slightly smaller, but the siblings happily posed for pictures with their ivory trophies. Gertie wrote about it in her contemporary journal but omitted mention of the second elephant in her autobiography. The devastation of the elephant population in Africa was well underway by then. The early explorer and naturalist Herbert Lang estimated that, between 1913 and 1923, approximately 630,000 elephants were killed, primarily for their ivory. Piano keys were overwhelmingly made from ivory then, and the U.S. was the dominant ivory importer for uses ranging from corset buttons to combs. Plastic replaced ivory for most consumer uses in the 1950s.

By the time the siblings got their elephants, food and tempers were growing short. "We have no food in the chop boxes, only two very fine elephant tails and a bit of salt and chewing gum," she wrote. They discovered the cook had been stealing hippo meat, and the hungry native staff were on the point of mutiny. Gertie lashed out at the "boys" in her journal: "They are a hopeless lot, and the more one has to do with them the more one hates and despises them. They are a lazy, sullen lot. They have no guts, and no will to do anything. Selfish to the n'th degree." One wonders what the Africans'

Gertie and her brother Laddie show off tusks harvested from the elephants they killed on their first African safari.

opinions were of the Americans at this point.

When the Sanfords reconnected with the Talbotts, they found them looking thin. It was early March. The party headed toward home, entrusting their trophies to the white hunters, who handled shipment to America. As they said their good-byes to Africa, Laddie played a tango on his ukulele.

"For me, the atmosphere of Africa had delivered its magic in a very real way," Gertie wrote in her autobiography. "I knew that I would repeat this experience. I knew that I would also hunt in other countries and that future trips would have a different purpose. Perhaps I could collect for a museum."

But before that could happen, she had some serious partying to do.

4

The Roaring Riviera

— • —

Americans filled the streets and cafés of Paris in the years after the Great War, but it was a different sort of crowd than the Gilded Age tourists of Gertie's childhood. Some of the names of those who lived in Paris are familiar as writers, artists and their patrons: Gertrude Stein and her consort Alice B. Toklas (who arrived before the war), John Dos Passos (who stayed on after being stationed as a soldier in Paris), Ernest and Hadley Hemingway, Scott and Zelda Fitzgerald. In 1921, an American couple arrived in Paris seeking a freer life than they could expect in a country whose new president promised "a return to normalcy." They were Gerald and Sara Murphy, the human embodiment of the Spanish saying, "Living well is the best revenge."

Fitzgerald immortalized the Murphys — at least superficially — in his novel *Tender Is the Night*. (He dedicated the book to "Gerald and Sara — Many Fêtes.") Sara was the heiress of a Cincinnati ink manufacturer; Gerald the son of the owner of the Mark Cross luxury goods company in New York. When they arrived in France, they were in their thirties and had three small children. They spent their first years in Paris, reveling in the thriving arts and literary scene, "an infinite roll call of modernism," writes Amanda Vaill in her joint biography of the couple, *Everybody Was So Young*. Their friends included the Spanish painter Pablo Picasso and the Russian composer Igor Stravinsky. Gerald, who had not found his calling at his father's business or in studies in landscape architecture, began to paint and discovered he had a gift for it. Over eight years, he produced ten large canvases in a style that is today seen as a pre-cursor to 1960s Pop. One, measuring six feet square, depicted the inner workings of a watch.

In the summer of 1923, the Murphys joined their friends Cole and Linda Porter for a vacation at the sleepy village of Cap d'Antibes, a few miles down the Riviera from Cannes. They were enchanted. Gerald extolled the hot, dry air during the day and the cool evenings, and described the water as being "that wonderful jade-and-amethyst color." At the time, the season on the Riviera ended in late April, when the English and German visitors packed up and went home. Locals couldn't imagine why anyone would want to lie in the sun in the sultry summer heat — tanned skin was not yet in vogue — and the lone hotel, the Hotel du Cap, always closed when the tourists left. But the hotel's owner, Antoine Sella, agreed to stay open as an experiment, and Gerald and Cole cleared a section of a nearby beach of stones and seaweed to create a haven for sunbathers. Their friends, and later friends of friends, began to join them at Cap d'Antibes.

The Hemingways came, and then the Fitzgeralds; poet Archibald MacLeish and his singer wife, Ada; the critic Alexander Woollcott and the writers Dorothy Parker and Robert Benchley. Playwright Philip Barry and his wife Ellen, a portrait painter, had a home in Cannes called Villa Lorenzo and the Murphys bought their own place in Cap d'Antibes, which they named Villa America.

"Sara and Gerald were lovers of art and Gerald was a good painter in his own right, so I was delighted when they invited Janie and me to spend a week with them at Villa America in Antibes," Gertie wrote in her autobiography. This was the summer of 1928, and by then the place had lost most of its artistic mystique and was a playground for the young and beautiful rich. "I never thought of myself as belonging to any special milieu that summer," Gertie wrote, and she was right. The magic was fast disappearing, and the 1929 stock market crash and personal disaster would affect many of the Riviera's denizens. But that doesn't mean Gertie and Janie didn't have a blast in 1928. What made it even better was that Gertie had fallen in love — with two brothers from New Orleans.

"[T]he main event of that summer was meeting Sidney and Morris Legendre," she wrote in her autobiography. Her father rented Osterly Park, an enormous Georgian country house near London. Laddie was playing polo and squiring his sisters around at parties, while becoming infatuated with the gorgeous — and married — Edwina Mountbatten. A friend introduced Gertie to the Legendre brothers, who were in England because Morris was on a Rhodes Scholarship at Oxford. The brothers were inseparable, so Sidney came along to keep Morris company.

Gertie said the highlight of the summer of 1928 was meeting the handsome Legendre brothers, Morris, left, and Sidney.

"They were tall and handsome and different from anyone else I had ever met," Gertie wrote. She said she was "immediately smitten by both of them." Morris had sandy hair and blue eyes, while Sidney's hair was dark and curly, and his eyes were also dark. Gertie's oldest daughter, Landine Manigault, has traced the Legendre family history and is delighted to claim a relationship with Marie Laveau, the New Orleans voodoo queen.

The Legendres were the youngest children of prominent New Orleans attorney James Gilbert Legendre and his wife, Cora Jennings Legendre. They were Creoles, the highest tier of New Orleans society, and lived in Audubon Park, a private street of twenty-eight homes adjacent to the Tulane University campus. It was developed as a millionaire's enclave in the late nineteenth century and remains so today. When the former Legendre home, a classic Queen Anne-style dwelling with seven bedrooms, sold in 2014 for $5 million, it set the record for residential real estate sales in New Orleans for the first half of the year.

There were six children: brothers Hennen, Armant, Morris and Sidney, and sisters Katherine and Edith, known as Fifi. Their mother died suddenly at age forty-five, probably of the same heart ailment that would carry away two of her sons at around that same age. Sidney was just ten years old when she died, Morris a year older. Their father did not remarry, and sister Katherine took over as the mother of the children left at home. She told Gertie that they were so wild and uncontrollable that "the only way to keep the brothers out of trouble was to hide their clothes and shoes so they couldn't leave the house. Sometimes even that didn't work."

All four Legendre brothers graduated from Princeton, where they starred on the gridiron, and Sidney had been the light heavyweight boxing champion. Morris delayed graduation so that he and Sidney could be in the same class, 1925, and subsequently they traveled together by three-masted schooner to more than thirty countries in Europe, the Middle East and the Pacific. They were adventurers of the first order and handsome and charming to boot. No wonder Gertie was smitten.

Somehow, Gertie tore herself away from the beguiling brothers, accepting the Murphys' invitation to stay at Villa America in June. There, she and Janie knew most of the crowd, including their old friend Ellen Semple Barry, whose playwright husband Philip found the Sanford siblings so inspiring he wrote a hit play about them called *Holiday*.

"The Murphys were charming — perfect hosts and lots of fun," Gertie wrote. "Gerald used to wear silly clothes and costumes because he was amused by them. He couldn't care less about fashion." He liked the striped boat-necked shirts and tight knit caps worn by French sailors; soon expatriate men and women both were wearing them. Sara was never seen without her signature rope of pearls: she even used them to accessorize her bathing suit. The actress and interior decorator Elsie de Wolfe, also known as Lady Mendl — she's mentioned in Cole Porter's song "Anything Goes" — was one of the few who eschewed sunbathing. She wore white opera gloves when she swam to prevent sunburn on her arms.

Gerald and Sara were doting and loving parents to their children, and affectionate and imaginative hosts to their friends. Gertie and Janie were among the many who enjoyed a morning snack of cold sherry and sweet biscuits served on the beach, just as Fitzgerald wrote about his fictionalized Murphys, Dick and Nicole Diver, serving their guests in *Tender Is the Night*.

One afternoon, Gerald challenged Gertie and another friend, the writer Almet Jenks, to swim almost two miles up the coast to the villa of Charlie Brackett, a movie director and producer. Gertie wore a black woolen bathing suit "that got heavier by the minute, and Gerald wore striped trunks with a bathing cap." Cheering them on, Ellen Barry and Sara Murphy followed the swimmers in a small boat, playing songs such as Cole Porter's "Fifty Million Frenchmen Can't Be Wrong" on the Victrola.

Charlie Brackett greeted the exhausted swimmers in semi-formal attire — tail coat, top hat and swim trunks — and presented them with medals made of bottle caps. They spent the remainder of the afternoon dancing on the patio and drinking Black Velvets.

Gertie was having a marvelous time. She wrote, "The only thing missing on the Riviera were the Legendre brothers and that was easily fixed." She badgered Antoine Sella, the owner of the Hotel du Cap, into giving the boys free rooms in return for their services as lifeguards. ("He insisted that there was no need for lifeguards, but I persisted, and I am used to getting my way.") Once they arrived, Gertie and Janie rented a fourteen-bedroom Belle Epoque mansion on the grounds of the Hotel du Cap called Villa Les Cèdres. It had previously belonged to the exploitative King Leopold II of Belgium, her grandfather Sanford's one-time patron. When it went on the market for $117 million in 2017, it was described as "the most expensive house in the world."

Pictures taken that summer show bright young things at the prime of their lives, the young men muscular and trim, copying Gerald Murphy's striped-shirt-and-French-sailor-cap style, the women baring their long, tanned legs and wearing broad-brimmed hats to shade their eyes from the sun. Gertie was photographed on the beach, wearing a short, light-colored dress, a scarf around her neck, hat cocked rakishly. Sidney appeared as an Adonis in short, tight-fitting bathing trunks with a striped belt.

One of their new friends was the comic actor Harpo Marx, the silent member of the Marx Brothers team. Gertie had a Renault convertible for hauling her crowd from place to place, and sometimes Harpo joined them: "I can still see him sitting on the canvas cover, with his feet and harp on the seat, playing our favorite tunes. He was almost always silent, but he was the first to join in our silliness and he had plenty of mischief of his own. I remember once in Maxim's at Juan-les-Pins, he wrapped himself up in a

Sidney, ready for the beach, exchanged his services as a life guard for a hotel room on the Riviera.

Spanish shawl and danced around the room with a chair, gazing at it as if it were the most desirable woman in the world."

Much like Laddie Sanford, Morris Legendre was the one who got a party going. When they went out in the evenings, Morris and Sidney wore short, white coats that Gertie called monkey jackets which "made them look like waiters." She recalled another night at Maxim's when Morris "rushed up to our table and told us to go to the bar and he would meet us there in a minute. We knew better than to question him. A few minutes later, he ushered a party of eight to our now-empty table and joined us at the bar where he ordered champagne for everybody." Morris had been mistaken for the maître d' and had been tipped handsomely for finding the guests a table.

Morris asked a local carpenter to make surf boards, like the ones he and Sidney had used in Hawaii, except shorter and broader, so they could be pulled by a motorboat. They dubbed their creations "free boards." They began by just standing on the boards, swinging way out to the right or left of the motorboat, but soon they were expanding their repertoire to include tricks. Morris would sit in a chair on the board, and Gertie would climb up on his shoulders. "We must have been quite a sight," she wrote. "Some of the swimmers thought us a nuisance. I knew that we made life miserable for Somerset Maugham, who hated waves and the sound of the engine. Crazy show offs, he called us." She allowed that he was the only writer really working that summer, but he "was a complainer and not very likable."

Her expertise on the free boards led to the most spectacular event of the summer. That evening, Gertie and Janie threw a party in their empty swimming pool, which they festively decorated with Japanese lanterns. Among the guests was Elsa Maxwell, who had journeyed from Monte Carlo to attend. Maxwell, an American, had devised a living for herself by organizing imaginative parties for wealthy people. She is credited with inventing the scavenger hunt.

"While the party was in full swing, someone challenged Morris and me to ride the free boards in our evening clothes," Gertie wrote. Morris accepted for them, and they climbed down the rocks to a waiting motorboat, managing to get on two free boards without incident. "The moment that the lines were taut, the engines roared, and we took off in a sheet of spray and foam, swinging way out to the sides to impress our audience."

Unbeknownst to them, the entire challenge had been a set-up. An English director was on hand to film the scene, and his spotlights illuminated the water as the cameras captured the action. "Now, there was nothing I liked better at that age than to show-off and be the center of attention," Gertie wrote.

"This was my chance. We circled the harbor twice, waving and showering the night with sparkling fans of water until Morris made a sharp turn and fell." He tried to convince her to join him in the drink, but Gertie had other ideas. "Like hell I will!" she shouted and got the driver to tow her board close to a large swimming float. She stepped off the board onto the float "bone dry and slightly incredulous. The audience went wild!"

Elsa Maxwell tried to persuade them to repeat the performance in Monte Carlo, "but I knew better than to tempt fate twice," Gertie wrote. Thanks to the film, there was proof positive for years that Gertie had actually accomplished the amazing feat. "Then it was lost, and we all began to remember that night differently — each memory perfectly true and exactly how it happened, of course."

That summer Philip Barry was putting the finishing touches on his play *Holiday*, which premiered on Broadway in November. It was twice made into movies, most notably with Katharine Hepburn and Cary Grant in the leads in 1938. The plot revolves around Johnny Case, who has fallen in love with a young woman named Julia Seton while vacationing at Lake Placid. He has proposed marriage and she has accepted, but he has no idea she is the youngest child of a spectacularly wealthy banker who lives in a mansion on Park Avenue. She has no idea that he isn't interested in money or society but wants to earn just enough to take a long holiday and see the world.

The other siblings are the brother, Ned, a weak drunk under his father's thumb, and the oldest, Linda, a free spirit who is obviously much better suited to Johnny than her shallow and materialistic sister. Of course, it takes two hours for them to come to that conclusion. Barry based the character of Johnny's friend Professor Potter on Gerald Murphy.

Some of Gertie's traits are obvious in the free-spirited and fun-loving Linda, but the other two siblings aren't as close a match with Janie and Laddie. Janie put off marriage until she was in her late thirties, when she made the unconventional choice of wedding an Italian diplomat, and Laddie, though a heavy drinker, was hardly a weakling dominated by his father. According to Gertie, he could do no wrong in John Sanford's eyes. Nevertheless, Gertie was proud that she and her siblings had inspired a hit by a marvelous playwright she counted as a dear friend.

Her thoughts on other authors weren't as charitable. "Being a good writer often has nothing to do with being a good person," she concluded in her autobiography chapter on the roaring Riviera. "In fact, the opposite is frequently the case. I don't do somersaults at the mention of Hemingway or Fitzgerald; they were drunk most of the time. What they wrote is left to personal taste, but as far as company is concerned, I've had the good fortune to have known far greater men…" When she returned to Antibes the following summer, she was in the company of the Legendre brother she had chosen. Sidney proposed there, and they looked forward to a September wedding.

For other members of the colony, though, the fall of 1929 brought disaster. The stock market crash that October wiped out fortunes that fueled their lavish parties. That same month, the Murphys' younger son, Patrick, was diagnosed with tuberculosis; he died before his sixteenth birthday, as did his brother Baoth. The Fitzgeralds left for Paris, where Zelda Fitzgerald's schizophrenia became more and more apparent. (Gertie described her simply as "charming and sweet and distant.") Beginning the following spring, she spent the rest of her life in and out of mental institutions, while Scott succumbed to a life of chronic alcoholism. Hemingway's second marriage proved no more successful than his first (or third). His posthumous memoir, *A Moveable Feast*, stuck a knife in the back of the Murphys, who had never done anything but support him, sometimes with generous loans.

For Gertrude, though, the time of her life was only getting better. She was already planning a return trip to Africa.

5

The Queen of Sheba's Antelope

—— • ——

The American Museum of Natural History was founded shortly after the Civil War with the support of a group of nineteen New York worthies with gold-plated names, Theodore Roosevelt Sr., J. Pierpont Morgan, William E. Dodge and Joseph Choate among them. Its exhibits, based at the Central Park Arsenal, were wildly eccentric at first, including collections of stuffed birds, fossils and "a life-size tableau of a lion attacking an Arab on a camel." By the time Gertie was old enough to visit, it had become a museum of distinction, having opened an impressive new building across the street from Central Park at West 77th and 81st streets, with an ambitious building plan that would eventually fill the entire block. The cornerstone was laid in 1874 by President Ulysses S. Grant, and the building was dedicated three years later by President Rutherford B. Hayes.

The museum not only exhibited a vast collection of specimens of animal life and relics of human civilization, it was also a major player in the so-called "golden age of exploration" that lasted from 1880 to 1930. As the museum's official history states, "During this time, the Museum is involved with expeditions that discover the North Pole; explore unmapped areas of Siberia; traverse Outer Mongolia and the great Gobi [desert]; and penetrate the densest jungles of the Congo, taking Museum representatives to every continent on the globe." Gertie would lead one of twenty-eight museum-sanctioned expeditions in 1928-29.

Even as she partied on the Riviera and free boarded in her evening gown, Gertie was talking incessantly about making another trip to Africa, this time as the leader of a scientific expedition. She did her homework, discovering that the Field Museum in Chicago had a display that the New York museum lacked, that of a rare African antelope, the mountain nyala. Its habitat is in

Gertie's father John Sanford favored her brother Laddie, but he bankrolled her first expedition.

a remote area of Ethiopia, a country which Gertie preferred to call by its ancient name, Abyssinia (as we will call it here), and it is sometimes nicknamed the Queen of Sheba's antelope. Nyala would be a valuable addition to the ambitious Hall of Africa that had been started by the master taxidermist and explorer Carl Akeley. The hall was to include as its centerpiece a collection of elephants Akeley had shot and mounted, surrounded by twenty-eight dioramas featuring other African animals.

Back home in New York, Gertie plucked up her courage and wrote a letter to Henry Fairfield Osborn, the president of the museum, asking for an appointment. "He was a charming man with white hair and a kindly face that registered shock when I told him what I proposed to do," she recalled in her autobiography. "I'm not sure whether it was the proposal or the fact that I was a woman that shocked him more."

Shock indeed! Though there had been woman explorers before — among them Akeley's wife, Delia, who had saved his life after he was attacked by a rampaging bull elephant — they were generally the spouses of exploring men. Here was a twenty-six-year-old "society girl" suggesting that she might lead an arduous and dangerous expedition herself! Gertie made her case, giving her background in hunting and detailing the large and sometimes dangerous animals she had shot. She recalled, "I know that I sounded boastful, but I wanted to convince him."

Osborn listened, then presented Gertie with a hard, cold fact: No matter her credentials and abilities, she would have to come up with $30,000 just to create the diorama. Not only would she have to bring back the animal skins and bones for mounting, she would need to procure other flora and fauna to create a realistic representation of the nyala's habitat. Accurate photographs were needed so an artist could paint the diorama's background. The cost of the expedition itself was not included in the price tag.

"I can still feel the despondence that I had felt that afternoon when I left the museum," Gertie recalled. Perhaps she walked home through Central Park as she brooded over this setback, or perhaps she slumped into the backseat of the Rolls as Kane drove her home. She was not disheartened for long; the cost was a roadblock, but she wasn't about to be stopped. Gertie did what any rich girl would: she approached her father.

John Sanford could be an intimidating figure, and Gertie was resigned to the favoritism he showed her brother Laddie. Cleverly, she asked if he would give her a present of equal value to a string of polo ponies, something he not infrequently bestowed on her brother. Mr. Sanford didn't seem to hear her at first, so she plunged on, detailing her plan to travel to Abyssinia on behalf of the museum. To her surprise and relief, he agreed, saying he believed "in museums with mounted groups for the public to enjoy. If I give Laddie presents, I will do so for you, too."

Gertie was elated and moved ahead with the second part of her plan: including the Legendre brothers in the expedition. "When I telegraphed them in England that fall, they were pretty surprised," she remembered. But they were more than game to join her after Morris completed his studies at the end of the fall term.

If Henry Fairfield Osborn had been shocked at the idea of a young woman leading an expedition, one can only imagine his reaction when he learned Gertie planned to bring two attractive bachelors with her. Even for the liberated 1920s, it was a very forward move. The museum agreed to supply a naturalist named T. Donald Carter, who was a decade older, to accompany them and see that the animals were properly collected and preserved. It was his first trip to Africa. It was also the first African trip for the Legendre brothers, though they had participated in a scientific expedition in Southeast Asia after their graduation from Princeton.

In 1928 Africa was still very much dominated by European powers, having been carved up and claimed by the French, the British, the Belgians and the Italians. The Germans had lost their colony in southwest Africa after World War I. The only independent, self-ruling nations were tiny Liberia, established as a colony for freed American slaves after the Civil War, and Abyssinia, a kingdom that had rebuffed efforts by Italy to colonize it in 1896. Its regent was Ras Tafari, a forward-looking leader who would ascend to the throne as Emperor Haile Selassie in 1930.

While Gertie had felt she was prepared for a do-it-yourself safari based on her experience in British East Africa, Abyssinia was a challenge. "It was all new, the opening up of this unknown country, which was primitive and completely unprepared for hunting expeditions," Gertie wrote. They purchased all their supplies in the United States, ordering custom-made tents and a luxury that especially pleased Gertie: a portable toilet. "It was the greatest invention of all; it made camp life almost civilized." The long list of foodstuffs they ordered included a mysterious item called "pencil soup." All the supplies were shipped to the east African port of Djibouti.

Gertie departed from New York in December 1928 — whether Carter was with her at this point is unclear, but it's reasonable to think he was — and met the Legendre brothers in Paris at the Hotel Ritz bar, a popular rendezvous for expatriates. Austrian-born and New York-trained Frank Meier was the Ritz's genial and gifted head bartender, famous for both his vast knowledge of cocktails — his book *The Artistry of Mixing Drinks* contained recipes for more than three hundred drinks — and his connections to everyone who was anyone. Meier gave them a letter of introduction to a friend named Chambard, who he said was Ras Tafari's French chef. "He promised me that if we went to the palace, we would have a very special meal by his friend," Gertie recalled. She was somewhat dubious. "The whole thing seemed a little far-fetched, but we took the letter. We should have known better than to doubt Frank's word."

From Paris they traveled by train to Marseilles and by boat to French Somaliland on the horn of Africa, arriving in the city of Djibouti at Christmas. A bumpy, three-day, up-hill train trip took them to the capital, Addis Ababa, at 6,000 feet above sea level. They arrived in early January. The city's streets were unpaved, and the four were warned to carry big sticks to ward off hyenas and wild dogs if they ventured out at night. Gertie was impressed with the beauty of the Abyssinian people, "tall and elegant looking, with sharp, chiseled features." The men wore white leggings with white cloaks, were generally bare-footed, and carried spears. The women were wrapped in white, filmy fabric. The Americans stayed at the city's one hotel, the Hotel de France, and connected with the U.S. State Department's representative, Addison Southard. An invitation to dine at the palace was soon proffered.

"The evening was like a page out of *The Arabian Nights*," Gertie wrote of their evening eating French and Abyssinian dishes off gold plates — Frank Meier's friend, Chambard, was indeed the chef — and drinking a potent honey wine called *tej*. "It went straight to my head like champagne." In a joint article she and Sidney wrote for the museum's journal *Natural History*, they described walking between a double line of guards, passing through an anteroom and colossal doors, to the throne room, where the royal couple waited for them "on a magnificent tiger skin." Ras Tafari was not tall, but he had great presence. He spoke perfect French, which gave Gertie an edge — she had been put out when required to walk in behind the men! — and he was astonished when she told him she had shot five lions in Kenya. She gloated, "He'd never heard of a woman hunting."

His queen had more prosaic interests. After dinner, she peppered Gertie with questions about American fashion, finally inviting her to sit down for a lengthy chat. Without even thinking about it, Gertie sat in the nearest chair — which happened to be Tafari's throne. He seemed to find it highly

Morris, Sidney, Gertie and Donald Carter display the horned skulls of nyala procured for the museum.

amusing, signaling his approval the next morning by sending over a beautiful silver mule in embroidered velvet harness and saddle as a gift. It joined the caravan, but never carried a load or its intended rider. Gertie preferred to walk.

There were several more dinners at the palace, for the four Americans learned that in Abyssinia, "no one knows the meaning of hurry. Tomorrow is as good as today and, when there is work to be done, a great deal better." Even with diplomat Addison Southard's help, lining up some sixty mules and almost as many load men, skinners, trackers and personal servants proved harder than expected. Just as they were ready to depart with the caravan, "everything happened that could happen; the mules bucked off their loads; the men holding them let go of the ropes and all the mules ran away, distributing the luggage over the country-side as they went." It took until early afternoon to get them reloaded and on their way, and then Gertie and Sidney had to return to the city and crash a funeral in order to exchange paper currency for the appropriate silver coins accepted in remote areas.

What followed were four months of adventures and misadventures. Carter lost forty pounds, Gertie's skin turned bronze under the sun and the Legendre brothers' hair grew long and wild. They soon learned that the local guides were fearful of bandits and kept directing them to villages where they could meet women and find food and liquor. Fights sometimes broke out among men from different tribes. Morris Legendre oversaw the payroll and regularly fined the men for infractions ranging from neglecting their mules to leaving camp without permission. After one especially egregious incident in late March, he had the men affix their thumbprints to a document in which they promised not to desert the expedition "or give any trouble of any kind."

Eventually, though, their efforts paid off. Carter shot two blue-winged geese, which were peculiar to the high plateaus, and a friendly chief, Pasha Tasama, came to their camp for dinner. He sent his own son the next day as a guide and with his help they reached the Arusi Plateau and began to spot mountain nyala with their distinctive lyre-shaped horns. Carter, describing the habitat and habits of the nyala in his book *Hoofed Mammals of the World*, hints at the difficulty of shooting one. They fed on giant heather above the timber line in the early mornings and late afternoons but disappeared into forests of "almost impregnable bamboo" at other times. "They were remarkably sure-footed and when frightened could gallop over the rocky terrain with amazing speed."

Finally, after a full day of tracking and a cold night spent on a mountain top, Morris shot a bull. "It had a forty-inch spread — a beauty!" Gertie wrote. "After that, the rest of the museum group was easier to complete." Their specimens included another small bull, some does and a fawn. In addition to the nyala, they collected samples of the grass, heather and other vegetation, took dozens of photographs and Carter wore himself out collecting and skinning other specimens. His eventual haul for the museum totaled more than three hundred mammals and a hundred birds.

At this point, someone had to make a trek back to Addis Ababa with the nyala skins before they spoiled while the others continued collecting. The Legendre brothers flipped a coin and Sidney lost, departing with a small number of mules and men while the others journeyed on. Things got progressively worse. "The whole trip was a tough one — heat, rock cliffs the mules couldn't climb, thorn trees, lava slopes, flies, mosquitoes, anything else you can imagine," Gertie wrote. One night they were wined and dined by another friendly chief who traded them seven monkeys for a bottle of cognac. After Sidney rejoined them, there was a smallpox outbreak and then malaria took down most of the native men as well as Carter. Early rains mired them in mud and cost the life of a pack horse. Their men were exhausted, and the food supplies were running low. They decided to turn back.

Sidney's month-long absence had helped Gertie discern which of the Legendre men suited her best. She had always liked Morris, recognizing how similar they were. She was impressed by his organizational skills, and the way he always rose to a difficult occasion. She wrote, "But then, suddenly, Sidney was gone, and I missed his humor and the thoughtful quality he had about himself, some unknown side of him that he protected. Maybe it was that vulnerable quality that is so attractive to women, especially in strong men. Maybe that was all it was. But Sidney was also gentle and not afraid of his gentleness. He was a perfectionist, with all the disappointment that brings in life."

When they finally got back to Addis Ababa in mid-May, Morris and Carter re-fitted their pack train and headed out together to do some more collecting in another part of Abyssinia. Gertie and Sidney stayed with the Italian ambassador while they sold the remaining equipment. Then they decided to depart Abyssinia on their own. Perhaps with tongue slightly in cheek, Morris wrote to an official at the museum, "Gertrude Sanford and Sidney Legendre unfortunately were unable to join [us], finding it imperative to return to France at once." Gertie recalled, "Sometimes things happen to you and you say 'yes'… We sailed to Antibes together and I rented Villa Les Cèdres again, and we knew that we were in love." Gertie's dutiful maid, Rose Brind, was waiting for them at the 18,000-square-foot mansion, with household staff in place, a stocked ice box and her mistress's bathing suit laid out on the bed. It was quite a contrast from living in a tent!

When they returned to New York, they told her father of their plans to marry. His response: "That's fine, my children, that's fine. Now, let's all go and see Laddie play polo at Meadowbrook."

6

Jungle Trail Leads to Altar

———— • ————

Gertie's fame had preceded her to New York — and almost everywhere else in the United States.

In February 1929, a news release went out — it's not clear who sent it — accompanied by pictures of her with some of the lions she had shot on her first safari. Newspapers ran them with thrilling captions such as, "Society Girl Shoots Lions," "Lion Tamer" and "Nice Kitty." The accompanying article about her mission for the American Museum of Natural History described her as "an experienced hunter and a dead shot," listing some of the large animals she had bagged in Tanganyika. Gertie's picture appeared in newspapers across the country; she filled an album with the nearly identical clippings.

In late August, when John Sanford announced his youngest daughter's engagement, it became evident that her trophies also included a very handsome and presentable fiancé. The wedding was set for Tuesday afternoon, September 17, at St. James' Church on Madison Avenue, just around the corner from the Sanford mansion. It was a delectable jewel of an Episcopal church, with glowing stained-glass windows and an elaborate gilded wood altar, the result of a recent makeover of what had been a simple Romanesque structure into a Gothic Revival masterpiece. Her wedding would be one of the few occasions in her life when Gertie darkened a church door except as a sight-seer.

As is the custom with most brides-to-be, Gertie went with Sidney to meet his family in New Orleans, and immediately took to the whole clan, describing them as "irresistible and each one so different." Katherine, the older sister who had practically raised Morris and Sidney after their mother's death, was "a marvelous woman," who eventually married into the socially prominent Philadelphia Biddle family. Gertie enjoyed an afternoon of drinking bourbon

The wedding party included, from left, Hennen Legendre, Janie Sanford, Armant Legendre, Gertie and Sidney, Morris Legendre and Laddie Sanford.

with "all the society belles who had pursued him." It was something like an Irish wake. "I'm sure that they never figured out why Sidney had chosen me," she wrote.

In her autobiography, Gertie gives a fond description of the love of her life: "My Sidney was tall and dark, and he parted his thick, curly black hair just to the left of center and plastered it down. In photographs, he stood tall and straight, always rather elegant." Her head barely cleared his shoulder. She loved his sense of humor, the way he "could pull your leg with a perfectly straight face, which made you think twice before breaking into a smile." But she also recognized his attributes that sometimes put them at odds during their marriage: "He was moody, often brooding and worrying about things ... When he felt like it he could entertain everyone, but when he became bored with the dinner conversation or the weekend guests, he grew sullen and quiet."

Headstrong and domineering, Gertie certainly brought her own deficits to the union, and as by far the wealthier partner, she could prevail over her more passive husband. In one of his books, Sidney admitted, "I am not what you call a vital person."

But those discoveries still lay ahead. For the present, she was a young woman madly in love with her husband-to-be, and the emotion appeared to be both reciprocated and enduring. Writing to Gertie in the mid-1930s when she had just departed for a short trip, Sidney confessed to leaving the station before the train pulled out "because the tears were streaming down my face so that I was ashamed of the porter seeing me." In a follow-up letter, he confessed to keeping a telegram from her under his pillow. "It was about as good as being able to hold onto your nightgown." At this point, he was hardly a besotted bridegroom; they had been married at least five years and had a child.

The short notice of the wedding date and the absence of a mother to oversee the festivities did not prevent Gertie from planning the sort of affair over which New York society writers drooled. She had her gown made by Herman Tapé, a leading New York dressmaker, choosing white satin and the mid-calf length popular at the time. The rather simple design, with long, tight sleeves and a high, scooped neck was highlighted with old rose point lace and seed pearls at the neckline, with similar detailing on a tight cap to which her grandmother's bridal veil was attached. Gertie later joked, "It was the height of fashion in 1929 and looks for the world like a bathing cap today." She carried a bouquet of white orchids and lilies of the valley as she walked down the aisle on her father's arm to the bridal chorus from Wagner's "Lohengrin." Or, as most people think of it, "Here Comes the Bride."

Sister Janie served as maid of honor, and there was a flower girl and six other attendants, including Peggy Talbott, her long-time friend and companion on her first safari. The bridesmaids processed in twos, with each pair in a different pastel-colored dress with handkerchief hemlines: peach, wild rose and autumn brown.

Morris stood as his brother's best man, and Hennen and Armant Legendre and Laddie Sanford served as ushers, wearing cutaways, silk ascots and white carnations. "I must confess that I was rather proud of myself," Gertie gloated. "After not caring much for beaux, I was surrounded by the best-looking men of our generation." Nevertheless, in all the photographs the wedding party looks as humorless as people standing before a firing squad.

While its account of the wedding began with a portentous sentence about the union of "[m]embers of two distinguished families," even the *New York Times* couldn't resist a sub-head about the nuptials of "Explorers and Big-Game Hunters." New York's other papers were less circumspect. One picture of the wedding party was captioned "Jungle Trail Leads to Altar," while the *New York Telegram* smirked, "… an expedition into dark and perilous Abyssinia is regarded as fine preparation into an expedition into marriage."

The *Telegram* went on to describe the bride: "Miss Sanford, horsewoman, student, explorer, beautiful but 'not too modern' daughter of an old American colonial family, makes decisions quickly." An impartial observer would not have described Gertie as beautiful, but she had a puckish and arresting face: a wide, bright smile with a tiny gap between her front teeth, high cheekbones, a pointed chin and snapping brown eyes. Certainly, anyone in conversation with her would be too entranced by the lively stories coming out of her full-lipped mouth to give an objective description of her appearance.

The wedding guest list was peppered with the names of the socially prominent and well-to-do: broker and attorney Hugh Auchincloss, who would eventually become stepfather to both author Gore Vidal and First Lady Jacqueline Kennedy Onassis; childhood friend Tommy Hitchcock, by then one of the country's leading polo players; Ellen Barry and her playwright husband Phillip, whose Broadway play about Gertie and her siblings, *Holiday*, had closed in June after a respectable 229 performances; illustrator Charles Dana Gibson, originator of the iconic Gibson Girl; and a heavy sprinkling of Astors, Biddles, Vanderbilts, Cushings and Whitneys.

The ceremony at St. James' Church was followed by a reception at the Sanford mansion, which was sumptuously decorated with ferns and flowers. Gertie had a fifteen-foot orange tree placed in the stairwell, perhaps a nod to her maternal grandfather's pioneering efforts in Sanford, Florida, perhaps merely the popular tradition of orange blossoms for a bride. Guests partook of a lavish luncheon, and an orchestra played in the ballroom. "Mother would have approved," Gertie wrote wistfully.

But the bride herself was eager for the whole thing to be done with so she and Sidney could escape. "All I can remember wishing for was an end," she wrote. "I couldn't wait to throw my bouquet over the stairwell and dash out the front door where Kane was waiting at the wheel of the Rolls." They spent their wedding night in New York before heading by train to Chicago and Seattle, bound for a hunting trip into the Cassiar Mountains of British Columbia and Alaska. Along the way, who should turn up on the boat traveling up the Stikine River but Morris and Laddie, who were taking their own hunting trip. Everyone else on the *Hazel B* was a prospector or a trapper.

"We stalked sheep and goats through snow drifts and were tent-bound for several days in a blizzard," Gertie remembered. And in coy shorthand that leaves everything to the reader's imagination, she added simply, "It was glorious."

Back in New York, what was happening was far from glorious. The year had been marked by wild upswings and downturns in the stock market. The Dow Jones average had peaked at 381 on September 3, but a little over a month after Gertie's wedding, it suffered a crash that reverberated around the world. Over four days, beginning on October 24 — Black Thursday — and ending on October 29 — Black Tuesday — a tremendous sell-off brought the Dow Jones average to 230.07. It would continue to decline over the next three years, bottoming out at 41.22 in mid-1932. Among the many people wiped out was Gertie's Riviera friend Harpo Marx. He said he had "liquidated every asset I owned except for my harp and my croquet set."

Writing in her autobiography almost sixty years later, Gertie observed, "Who would have thought that the Great Depression was just beginning? Fortunately, Father had very little money in stocks." Which was not quite true.

Unknown to anyone except himself and possibly Laddie, 78-year-old John Sanford had been negotiating for months for a merger with the Bigelow-Hartford Carpet Company. He was ready to semi-retire. He seldom used his home in Amsterdam, spending most of his time in New York and Palm Beach, where he had taken up golf with a vengeance. Laddie had no interest in the carpet business other than the money it earned that enabled him to play polo and live the high life. The merger would create Bigelow-Sanford Carpet Company, the largest manufacturer of woven floor coverings in the country.

Ironically, the agreement was completed on Black Tuesday. Sanford accepted $16 million in stock in the merged company and retained $4 million in cash and securities of his Stephen Sanford & Sons company. The sticking point was the valuation of Bigelow-Hartford shares. That company's negotiators set the value of preferred stock at $150 per share and common stock at $85 to $94. Sanford insisted on a blended evaluation of $100 per share, and prevailed. He was smart to stick with the lower figure. By May 1930, common stock in Bigelow-Sanford had declined to 59 ½. By December 1930, it had fallen to 32 ½. The company recorded a loss of more than $600,000 that year, and more than a million dollars in 1932.

All this is to say that Gertie's father was still rich — just not as filthy rich as before. The people who had worked for him were in much worse shape. Showing his ruthless side, he made no provision for his executives, believing they should have saved from the generous salaries he had paid them before the merger. Only two kept their jobs and they were soon shunted aside. Like Herbert Hoover, who had begun his presidency in March 1929, the merged company's executives thought the crash heralded a recession that would soon right itself. As the Depression deepened, wages in the mill in Amsterdam were cut, followed by layoffs.

In 1933, Franklin Roosevelt's New Deal and its National Recovery Administration brought with it a forty-hour work week and a minimum $14 per week wage in the carpet industry. John Sanford, the rock-ribbed Republican, was not a fan. Writing to Sidney during the Roosevelt Recession of 1937, he complained taxes had gotten so high that a friend of his had to dip into his principal. "I am afraid I am now getting near that situation," he groused. "God knows where we are drifting to in this country." Yet throughout the Great Depression, he continued to play golf, breed thoroughbreds and throw lavish parties with Janie, and Laddie continued to play polo and hob-nob at fashionable watering holes at home and abroad with his movie star wife.

When Sidney and Gertie got back from their honeymoon, they went house-hunting in an area of the country that had been suffering long before the Depression began: South Carolina.

7

Mistress of Medway

———— • ————

Gertie had been a regular visitor to her native state throughout her life, usually spending time with other Winter Colony families in Aiken. At the same time Aiken had become a fashionable destination for the rich and horse-obsessed, coastal South Carolina had become a magnet for the rich and duck-obsessed. Not surprisingly, there was a good deal of cross-over.

Lowcountry rice growers had been among the wealthiest people in the country prior to the Civil War, overseeing vast plantations worked by hundreds of slaves. The war and emancipation, coupled with market changes, had slowly put an end to that way of life, even though many of the freed slaves stayed on the only land they had known to work as miserably paid hired hands. Nevertheless, their freedom had greatly changed the labor-intensive growing and harvesting of rice. Slaves had no choice but to stand in waist-high freezing water in the fall and winter and risk their lives to poisonous snakes, alligators and malaria-carrying mosquitoes in the summer. Freedmen could refuse and look for less dangerous work. In addition, nature conspired to bring an end to widespread rice growing with back-to-back hurricanes in 1910 and 1911 that decimated the Carolina crop.

Land that had been suitable for growing rice but not much else was highly attractive to water fowl, and northern hunters were amazed at the quantity of ducks and other game birds they found when they ventured to the Carolinas and Georgia in the late 1800s. As Virginia Christian Beach, author of *Rice and Ducks*, put it, they found "a mild climate and a banquet of birds." In a 1904 hunt, a man marveled at seeing what he estimated were several hundred thousand ducks in one day. Others described "black clouds of ducks," rather as Gertie had described the beasts thundering across the African plateau. Many hunters leased former plantation land, obtained shooting rights and formed private hunting clubs, often inviting friends to join them on hunting trips. Among the most enthusiastic visitors was President Grover Cleveland. In a visit in 1896 he and his fellow hunters shot down more than four hundred ducks.

The wealthiest and most enthusiastic hunters bought their own plantations as hunting preserves. They restored the derelict plantation houses on the property or built new ones and there emulated the lifestyles of the British aristocracy with their country houses. Their wealthy friends came, saw and conquered — this time with cash in hand — to the extent that between 1880 and 1940 more than a hundred former plantations changed hands as part of what Beach calls "the second Yankee invasion."

Among the most prominent plantation owners on the South Carolina coast was New York financier Bernard Baruch. Like Gertie, he was a native of the state, born in Camden in 1870, but he had spent most of his childhood in New York, where he worked on Wall Street and became a millionaire by age thirty. Baruch was the highly respected advisor to seven U.S. presidents and international figures such as Winston Churchill, entertaining celebrities of all stripes at his Hobcaw Barony in Georgetown County, an hour up the coast from Charleston. Baruch was Jewish, and though his daughter, Belle, was Gertie's contemporary and an internationally acclaimed horsewoman, Gertie was prone to the anti-Semitism common in her WASP social class, as was Sidney. The only hint of social interaction between the families is a photograph of Bernard Baruch given to Laddie's wife Mary in 1942, inscribed "to Mary Sanford with affectionate regards."

Gertie and Sidney visited the Lowcountry as guests of another wealthy northern couple who had created a lovely second home in Berkeley County. Benjamin and Elizabeth Kittredge, a generation older than the Legendres, had bought Dean Hall plantation in 1909. She was a Charleston native and, like the Sanfords, they had been Winter Colony residents of Aiken. The Kittredges refurbished and modernized the 1827 plantation house, then transformed 170 acres of their property into the magnificent Cypress Gardens. When Gertie and Sidney visited Charleston during their post-honeymoon travels, the Kittredges gave the young couple a warm welcome. Their son, Ben Jr., was their contemporary and a long-time friend.

"In those days, you could ride for hours in open and forested country," Gertie wrote. On one of those rides with Ben Jr., carrying a picnic lunch

At the time the Legendres first saw Medway, it was in derelict condition, looking to Gertie like Sleeping Beauty's enchanted castle.

packed on the horses, they came upon Medway: "It stood derelict in a grove of live oak trees several hundred years old. Its brick walls were faded to a soft pink. All anybody could tell us was that the house was over three hundred years old." When they spread their picnic lunch on the ground, members of the Gourdine family, the descendants of slaves who had lived at Medway since colonial times, ventured out of their wood frame houses to stare at the couple.

For Sidney, it was love at first sight. Medway had put him under its spell. "I don't think Sidney really considered any other place after seeing Medway," Gertie wrote, describing themselves as "rash and romantic." It would be a long and frustrating love affair for Gertie's husband, who was both a romantic and a perfectionist and knew little about what it would require to reclaim and maintain the plantation house and grounds. Back at Dean Hall, they enthusiastically talked with their hosts about Medway, and Ben Jr. declared, "What fun it would be if you bought Medway and we all lived like neighbors here, shooting and fishing and enjoying life in the Lowcountry."

Gertie and Sidney inquired about the property, which belonged to the

Stoney family, one-time rice planters who were using the shell of the house as a hunting lodge. Believed to be the oldest standing masonry building in the state, it had no modern conveniences, including heat, light and indoor plumbing, although materials advertising its sale said it was "one of the most interesting and best-preserved old houses in this section." The asking price for the house and 1,000 acres of surrounding land was $100,000.

The plantation on the Back River has a long and colorful history. Built around 1692 by South Carolina's first Dutch immigrant, Johan van Aerssen, its name was derived from the original name of the Back River, the Meadway River. His widow, Sabina, married Landgrave Thomas Smith, later a colonial governor of South Carolina who is buried on the grounds. Under its next owners, the house burned in 1703 and a new, smaller one was erected on its foundations (which made it 226 years old in 1929, not 300, as Gertie had been told.) The property changed hands a number of times over the next 130 years as financial ruin and personal tragedy plagued its owners. Around 1833, Medway was purchased by the Stoney family, whose primary crop was rice, cultivated by slave labor. By the eve of the Civil War, the Stoneys owned more than a hundred slaves, who not only grew and harvested rice but also made hundreds of thousands of bricks from clay mined on the property. Many of these bricks were incorporated into Dean Hall (which was since moved to Beaufort County) as well as buildings in Charleston.

This prosperous but exploitative way of life ended with the Civil War, emancipation and natural disasters, including an earthquake that severely damaged the Medway house. The last members of the Stoney family who called Medway home were Captain Samuel Gaillard Stoney and his wife, Louisa, who labored for twenty years to reclaim and replant the gardens and grounds. Mrs. Stoney's particular interest was the gardens, and she was responsible for having seven hundred flowering azalea bushes planted on the grounds. After Captain Stoney's death in 1926, the family struggled to maintain Medway, with his son, Sam Stoney Jr., being heard to pray, "Lord, please send us a rich Yankee." His prayers were answered when Gertie and Sidney arrived.

Gertie made a list of reasons for and against buying Medway on the back of an envelope. The "for" list included its central location (supposedly between New York and Florida), the rarity of the house and "need a home." The "against" list included insufficient funds, their lack of knowledge about plantations and "too big a responsibility — too young. May exceed our income limit due to children, upkeep, etc." Against all reason, the "for" side won. The newlyweds traveled through Georgia and then joined John Sanford in Palm Beach, where they put the case to him for buying Medway. Just how much resistance he gave is hard to determine. In her autobiography, Gertie wrote, "Father didn't even try to argue." In an interview she gave to Virginia Beach for her book *Medway*, she said John Sanford thought they were "crazy" to want to live in the South Carolina Lowcountry, which he considered an unhealthy place. Nevertheless, he gave in, and with his backing, they closed the deal in the spring of 1930. Eventually, the Legendres increased Medway's holdings to almost ten thousand acres.

For the next ten years, their starry-eyed romance with the plantation would be consistently frustrated by the reality of owning it. Writing in his plantation diary in the spring of 1937 about what he called "the curse of the Carolinas," Sidney groused, "If you have anything in your blood that demands neatness or efficiency, the Lowcountry is the worst place in the world for you. In a short time, you will have high blood pressure, and an attack of nerves as a result of battling futilely against the iron will of Southern 'Yes mams' and laziness."

Their original focus was on the house, because it was uninhabitable. Gertie and Sidney rented a house on Church Street in Charleston, making daily trips to Medway to oversee an army of workers. They hired a Charleston architect to plan the renovations, and a landscape architect to develop the garden layout. The basic floor plan of the house remained unchanged, and they tried to give it the feeling of a colonial home, which was further carried out in the furniture and decorations they chose. Indoor plumbing was installed, and the home was wired for electricity, although Berkeley County, like most rural areas of the country, did not have power. That would come almost a decade later with the New Deal and the Rural Electrification Act. In the meantime the Legendres installed a generator, but it failed at strategic moments, sending Sidney into a cursing frenzy.

When they finally moved in, Gertie was overjoyed to reopen their wedding presents — oceans of silver, china and bric-a-brac — all given to them in the innocent weeks before the stock market crash. "How lucky we were," she remembered. The haul, listed on five typed legal-size pages, included eighteen antique silver goblets, seven clocks, eight Cartier cigarette boxes and a sterling silver "muffineer," a server with a pierced dome for keeping muffins hot on the table. There were twelve place settings of her china and a full set of silver in the heavy and elaborate English King pattern from Tiffany's, a gift from Sidney's brother Morris.

These gifts were just the beginning of the home furnishings the Legendres needed for their five-bedroom abode. Soon truckloads of furniture, bedding and linens began arriving from New York. A shop called the Salon de Trousseau sent imported linens, most of it monogramed, including seventy-two guest towels and hundreds of cloth napkins. Oak furniture was delivered by Macy's, which also sent a man from New York to sew and hang drapes on site. Wall-to-wall carpeting was installed in several rooms, courtesy of the Bigelow-Sanford Carpet Company. Gertie wanted a comfortable house, where the dogs could jump on the furniture without anyone making a fuss. Among her papers, along with records about the dogs' rabies vaccinations, is an advertisement for a product called Dog-Tex, which claims, "Eradicates Liquid Dog and Cat Stains." No doubt it was employed regularly at Medway.

Through the years, the Legendres repurposed some out-buildings at Medway and tore down others. The small smoke house became Sidney's private study, and the bricks from the old rice mill formed a wall around the kitchen garden. The slates from the mill roof repaired the stable roof. When the Legendres bought an adjacent plantation, Pine Grove, its lovely antique cypress paneling was installed in Medway's living room and the master suite.

From the beginning, Sidney was determined to make Medway a working plantation rather than just a hunting preserve for wealthy Yankees. The presence of the African-American Gourdine family was integral to his plan. Like Bernard Baruch, who employed the former slaves and slave descendants who lived at Hobcaw Barony, the Legendres offered jobs in the house and on the grounds to the Gourdines and their kin. (Indeed, it was a condition of the sale.) A ledger dating from 1931 shows female house workers earned a day rate of sixty cents or so, while the men who labored outdoors earned up to $1.25 — a relatively good wage, as the average agricultural worker in South Carolina during the early years of the Depression could expect $3 a week. Anyone who killed a poisonous snake earned a handsome bonus of one dollar.

The symbiotic relationship between the Legendres and the Gourdines would last for decades; Doris Walters, Gertie's long-time private secretary, said the 1990s was the first time any of the house staff was white. Sidney hired whites as overseers, and his heart was nearly broken when the top man, who was paid a princely $165 a month and provided with a house, turned out to be cheating him and had to be fired. Both men were teary-eyed at the exit interview. Sidney made many references to "pouty" Negro employees and the slovenliness of the "white trash" supervisors, but he apparently kept his feelings fully in check. Mrs. Walters, who came to work for Gertie in 1964, said the old staff who had worked under Sidney remembered him with great affection, adding with a grin, "They thought he was a demi-god."

The Legendres had no background in farming, but that didn't stop Sidney from trying. The inventory of farm equipment by 1933 totaled almost $3,000, along with livestock valued at more than $2,000. That year they were the proud owners of six horses, three sheep and a ram, two mules, fifteen ducks and two peacocks, as well as twenty dogs — among them Gertie's beloved spaniel, Clippy — and a monkey and a Gibbon ape brought home from an expedition to Indochina. Nevertheless, the combination of inexperience, uncooperative employees and the Legendres' long absences in the summer growing and harvest seasons — when they escaped the heat, humidity and swarming insects for cooler destinations or took off on expeditions — seemed to doom every enterprise. Crops rotted in the fields, a bull proved so belligerent it had to be sold for a pittance, and the flock of chickens Gertie envisioned as making Medway look like a farm in Normandy and providing fresh eggs for their breakfast table ascended "up to heaven at the rate of about three a day," Sidney wrote. "By the end of next month, we will not be bothered with them anymore. All that will be left will be the chicken house."

The struggle Gertie and Sidney faced with their environment is one that was familiar to anyone living in the South prior to the advent of air-conditioning and effective pesticides. The oppressive heat began in late May and got worse by the day. Every outing left their clothes covered with ticks, and they spent hours picking parasites off their dogs. Yet Sidney characterized their most intransigent foes as mold and decay. "These twin brothers appeared to have taken the plantation in their clammy arms and held it there until the place took on the characteristics of this ghastly pair," he wrote in his plantation diary. Returning one fall, the Legendres found the cars sitting on their flat tires, as Sidney put it, "like a chicken setting on her eggs" and the Cadillac lying against one wall "like a tired soldier that had run countless leagues to tell his general that the battle had been won and then in doing so dropped dying into the arms of a companion."

Gertie and Sidney adored their cocker spaniel Clippy, one of many dogs they kept at Medway.

Fortunately, the couple did not have to depend on farm income to pay their bills. Earnings from investments and Gertie's trust fund kept them in style, and though they peevishly haggled over bills from local providers of goods and services, they were sitting pretty even in the depths of the Depression. Sidney's assets at the end of 1934 totaled more than $220,000, and Gertie's more than $3.5 million. Their joint assets, including Medway, totaled another $352,000. In current dollars, their total combined net worth topped $76 million.

Examining their annual income is even more enlightening. In 1933, it exceeded $86,000. In comparison, the average income reported on tax returns from South Carolina that year was just over $2,500 — a figure that is almost meaningless because less than 1 percent of the state's residents were required to file a return. Beyond cold statistics, the heart-rending reports of Lorena Hickok and Martha Gellhorn, both investigators for the New Deal's Federal Emergency Relief Administration, documented the pitiful plight of South Carolina's poverty-stricken textile workers, sharecroppers and farm hands. (Three out of four South Carolinians worked in agriculture.) In

1933 Gellhorn wrote of "houses shot with holes, windows broken, no sewerage, rats," and of textile workers so weak with hunger they could not stand through their shifts, of people suffering from malnutrition, rickets, anemia and pellagra. Arriving in Charleston in February 1933 after an exhausting and dispiriting six weeks in the South, Hickok was glad to try some of the local corn liquor: "I took one drink of it — and wondered what had kicked me behind the ear!"

In addition to farming, Sidney tried his hand at commerce. He and Morris, who lived with them at Medway off and on until his marriage in 1938, invested in a Charleston grocery store and a chain of movie theaters, the nearest of which was in Summerville, about twelve miles away. They renamed it the Jungle Theater, displayed some of their hunting trophies on the walls and prior to the main features ran shorts of Gertie's lion hunt in Africa with the Talbotts and the free boarding feat on the Riviera. Considering that the movie *King Kong* made its debut in 1933 and the *Tarzan* franchise starring Johnny Weissmuller was popular throughout the Depression years, they chose an alluring theme for their theater. Morris, who Sidney readily conceded was the better businessman, was the managing partner, but Sidney stopped in from time to time to be sure the staff was on the job. Gertie loved having Morris at Medway, writing that there was constant laughter as the brothers "suffered from an interminable case of one-upmanship that resulted in endless jokes and exaggerated stories."

For all its frustrations, living at Medway was a deeply satisfying experience for Sidney and Gertie. "Medway has always meant much more to me than its storied history," Gertie wrote. "It's more of a feeling about the place, a sense of remoteness and serenity… It is home, if ever there is such a thing." Just as she kept albums and photos about each of her expeditions and her travels in the United States and abroad, Gertie kept Medway albums filled with pictures of visitors, parties and family gatherings. She processed some of these photos herself in her Medway darkroom.

When not venting about the litany of crises he was expected to address, Sidney wrote poetically about the beauty of Medway. After one awful day, when the last straw was a malfunctioning radio, Sidney left the house after dinner and walked over to his office to write. "It was fairy land," he recounted in his diary. "The giant oaks threw the moon onto the ground in a series of intricate patterns, and the fire flies lit up the lawn with their sparkling light.

Sidney and Gertie seemed to give little thought to their daughters, Landine, left, and Bokara.

The old house sat there and dreamed of its three hundred years of existence, and the people that had lived, fought, loved and died inside its walls."

Sidney's diary, which covers the spring of 1937 until Pearl Harbor in December 1941, is full of descriptions of social visits, picnics and convivial dinners at other plantations, fishing trips up the Cooper River, horseback riding, tennis matches and affection for his dogs, but he makes only a few references to the two daughters Gertie bore during the first eleven years of their marriage. Landine was born in 1933 and Bokara in 1940. Sidney wrote with amusement in 1937 about Landine bossing around the black children on the plantation who he said were "wonderful playmates for her as they, unlike white children, never try to get into trouble but rather keep her out of it." Of Bokara, born on their eleventh wedding anniversary, he wrote that "her tiny sweet smile always forces me to laugh," but he was in the navy, stationed in Hawaii during most of her baby years. In his diaries, letters and other writings, he devotes many more paragraphs to his dogs than his children.

Likewise, in her autobiography, Gertie devoted less than a page to her daughters. She explained the origins of their unusual names: She and Sidney wanted a French name that began with "L" for their first-born, and Landine (pronounced LawnDEEN) was the one they chose from about sixty Sidney looked up at the New York Public Library. Bokhara was a place in exotic Turkestan they had wanted to visit, but Gertie thought the spelling was too long for her daughter's name and dropped the "h". "Of course, full names rarely last," Gertie observed, "especially in the South. Everyone calls her Bo or Bo-Bo now." She described Landine, who was fifty-four at the time she wrote the book, as "bright and willful and argumentative," with "Morris's fair coloring and Sidney's dark moods." Bokara, who was forty-seven at the time, she described as "short, vivacious and unpredictable," with "Sidney's dark looks and my zest for life."

Neither daughter has much positive to say about the woman they called "Mummy." Landine Legendre Manigault said she did not read *The Time of My Life* or Gertie's World War II memoir, *The Sands Ceased to Run,* and has no plans to read this book. Bokara wrote an autobiography with scathing words for Gertie shortly before her death in 2017 called *Not What I Expected*; it wasn't on Landine's reading list either.

"Affection didn't enter into my world," Landine said matter-of-factly of her childhood during an interview at her home in Connecticut. Like many children of the wealthy upper class at that time, she and Bokara were raised mostly by nannies and governesses, and often separately from their parents and each other. Landine had a series of French governesses she describes as horrible and cruel. One warned her that if she got out of bed at night, the animal skins on the floors at Medway would come to life and eat her. Another tied her spread-eagled to her bed, giving her only the choice of face down or face up. Landine attended a day school in Aiken for some years, living in a boarding house with her governess. Once, she recalled, she asked her mother why she had given birth to her if she did not want her. Gertie replied, "Perhaps if you had been a boy."

Landine has more positive feelings about her father, recalling a time when he engaged her in making hors d'oeuvres for dinner guests in the kitchen and then sent her into the living room to pass their creations around. The guests devoured the snacks, never dreaming that their basic ingredient was dog biscuits. "He had a lovely sense of humor," said Landine, who keeps the Simon Elwes portrait of Sidney, shotgun over his shoulder, in her book-stuffed library. Bokara, in her autobiography, recalled only "the maroon velvet sleeves of his dinner jacket, which appeared at my eye level when I approached his chair to say good-night on the occasions I was invited to visit my parents at their home at Medway plantation."

What is clear from Sidney's writing prior to World War II is that the two things which mattered most to him in the world were his wife, whom he clearly adored to distraction, and the opportunities to escape civilization and live on his wits in rough and wild terrain. These were in perfect concert with Gertie's feelings about him and their periodic travels into the unknown. In the fall of 1931, with Medway at last livable, the Legendres packed up and left for nine months for what was then called French Indochina on another expedition for the American Museum of Natural History. Over the next seven years, trips to southwest Africa and Iran would follow. They left Medway in the arms of mold and decay, and little Landine with her governess.

8

From Indochina to Iran

———— • ————

The American Museum of Natural History on New York's Central Park West attracts some five million visitors a year. On the steps, they pass a heroic equestrian statue of Theodore Roosevelt, wearing a "crown" of thin spikes meant to discourage pigeons from landing on his head, and enter a giant rotunda covered in murals celebrating his achievements. After buying tickets, many visitors wander into the Akeley Hall of African Mammals.

The hall does what its namesake, explorer and master taxidermist Carl Akeley, intended and died trying to accomplish: enable people who would never see Africa first-hand to experience some of its natural splendors. A large grouping of elephants, from bulls to babies, forms the darkened room's centerpiece, while ranged around it on two levels are twenty-eight lighted dioramas displaying exotic beasts in representations of their natural habitats. Gertie and Sidney's mountain nyala draw their share of attention as visitors stare at (and are stared at by) the two bucks, a doe and a fawn. Many visitors pause to snap a photograph with their phones, sometimes arranging their children in the shot.

Few pay much attention to the handsome brass plate at the base of the display frame that bears the names of Gertrude Sanford and Sidney and Morris Legendre or wonder who they were. Such casual visitors would probably be astounded to know that the animals and artifacts on display in the museum are the tiniest tip of the iceberg of the specimens it has in storage: more than forty-one million items that are augmented at the rate of 44,000 per year. Most will never go on display but are studied by research scientists from all over the world.

Gertie and Sidney added hundreds of specimens to that total during their expeditions in the 1930s. The nyala were not on display in 1931 — the Afri-

Small visitors pose at the exhibit of mountain nyala Gertie, Sidney and Morris procured for the American Museum of Natural History.

can hall would not open for another five years — when Gertie suggested to Sidney that they mount a collecting expedition in French Indochina — five countries that include today's Vietnam, Cambodia and Laos. They contacted Donald Carter, the museum naturalist from their 1928-29 trip to Africa, who joined them outfitted in shoes with five thicknesses of sole and a skin-tight suit. By the time they returned home nine months later, he had lost forty pounds and the suit hung in folds. In Sidney's words, the jovial Carter was "the gyroscope that kept our tempers on a level keel and the work of collecting going steadily ahead."

The French had colonized much of the peninsula between India and China in the late nineteenth century, attracted by the region's rich natural resources. Chief among these was rubber, initially used for carriage and bicycle tires, then for automobile and truck tires. France's Michelin Corporation, with its mascot Michelin Man, Bibendum, was a major operator of rubber plantations in Indochina.

With tongue only slightly in cheek, Sidney wrote in his account of the trip,

Land of the White Parasol and the Million Elephants, that Gertie had been the one with the "urge to push through uninhabited jungles, cross uncharted rivers and issue [forth] with memories of strange lands and stranger people… She proved to be the only member of the expedition who never called it quits." Gertie wrote simply, "Indochina was a long trip, but so beautiful and varied that I loved every minute of it. Our modes of transportation changed constantly; we went from train to caravan to *pirogue* [dug-out canoe] and horseback, and the trip ended on elephant back."

Inveterate traveler Martha Gellhorn, in the preface of her memoir *Travels with Myself and Another*, observed, "The only aspect of our travels that is guaranteed to hold an audience is disaster." If disaster is indeed the measure of attention, the accounts Sidney and Gertie wrote of the expedition are beyond riveting. Sidney slipped while trying to shoot a wild goat and tumbled to the bottom of an embankment. He came down with fever and severe dysentery. Gertie's pack pony lost its footing on a bamboo bridge and fell into a river. (Fortunately, she was not riding it at the time.) The couple got separated from the rest of the expedition while traveling down the Mekong River and wandered around in the dark for hours until they found a native tribesman who let them sleep on the floor of his hut under a flea-infested blanket. Other choice accommodations shared with Donald Carter included a building where the ceiling fell in on them and what turned out to be the village morgue, stacked high with coffins. In that gloomy setting, they consumed a meal of boiled monkey, while Sidney imagined the coffins were whispering to each other, "Which one will it be, the woman, the older man or the younger one — or shall we take all three?"

In many remote villages, Gertie was the first white woman the native people had ever seen, and she drew tremendous curiosity from the other women, just as she had in Africa. They were especially amused to see her dressed like one of the men, in trousers and boots. At the Armistice Day celebration in a town in southwest Vietnam, she learned that some of the tribal chiefs had traveled three days just to see her, having been notified of her presence by drum signals. They poked and prodded her body, giggling, and closely examined her dark, wavy hair. They were most fascinated by her tiny emerald wristwatch, and amazed when they noticed the hands move.

While Gertie later admitted she can't imagine why she brought her emerald jewelry with her, the other major nod to civilization was their hand-cranked

Sidney read at the campground with a rhesus monkey he dubbed Trompé — "deceived" — on his back.

Victrola and a stack of records. Their native staff and children they met became fans of the crooning of Bing Crosby and Hawaiian music, and Gertie and Sidney attracted quite an audience one morning when they performed a tango, she in overalls and he in his striped pajama bottoms. They were so surprised to hear American voices in the crowd that he dropped her on the floor; the voices belonged to a pair of missionaries who invited them to dinner that night. They all came down with food poisoning.

On another occasion they were invited to attend a Feast of Rice in a native chief's bamboo hut. Wanting to dress presentably, Gertie had her pleated dress and Sidney's suit cleaned and pressed by their cook. When they got the clothing back, Sidney's suit had been folded and pressed into squares the size of a handkerchief and the cook had forgotten the pleats of Gertie's dress were vertical. He had ironed them in horizontally, all the way to the neck. Sidney looked like "an elongated checkerboard" and Gertie like "the Michelin tire man's wife." In the end, it didn't matter. The festival consisted of much singing and dancing by the women, followed by pelting the guests with unhusked rice. Gertie remarked dryly, "It was believed that the more they danced and the more rice they threw, the better the harvest would be. From the looks of our clothes, the harvest should have been abundant."

All through the months, they were collecting specimens, some of which they shot themselves, many others brought to them by native people in return for payment. (Akeley had used this method of collecting in his early travels in Africa as well.) It freed up their time to hunt for larger specimens and enabled Carter to focus on skinning and preserving the findings. He worked almost around the clock, drawing unstinting admiration of Sidney for his industry. Occasionally a specimen proved too much for them to handle, such as the twenty-foot boa constrictor that curled itself around the leg of their hut and looked menacingly at Sidney when he approached it. Two other would-be specimens, a rhesus monkey and a baby gibbon ape, became pets for Gertie. Sidney dubbed the monkey "Trompé" — "deceived" — and the Gibbon "De Trop"— "too much". Gertie's name for the gibbon was the more prosaic Gibbie. Their hijinks enlivened camp life in ways both positive and negative, as when Gibbie went into a Buddhist temple and ate all the food that had been left as offerings. He came home from the trip with them and continued to wreak havoc at Medway for years, regularly stealing rolls of toilet paper and festooning the trees.

As in Africa, the Legendres hired native men as porters and personal servants. Language and cultural barriers caused misunderstandings that enraged Sidney and tickled Gertie, like the time her husband asked for bacon for breakfast and the cook presented him with a grey mass of cooked pork — the bacon supply for the month. On one occasion when the *pirogues* they had ordered mysteriously disappeared, Sidney told the man responsible that he and Gertie were siblings of the president of France and the governor general of French Indochina. The *pirogues* soon reappeared.

Both Legendres wrote admiringly of the beauty and colorful costumes of the native people, though the heavy gold jewelry worn by the royal family of Laos had proved fatal to the king's three wives and four children who drowned in the river when their boat overturned. The ruler, who received Sidney and Gertie in his palace, presided over the Kingdom of the White Parasol and the Million Elephants, which gave Sidney the title of his first book.

They also suffered through social engagement with the Europeans living in Indochina with their ubiquitous cocktail hours and social clubs. Sidney joked that any time two white men arrived in the Orient, they immediately started a club. A few days of social intercourse with the expatriates had them itching to get back into the jungle.

They spent the final weeks of the expedition hunting on elephant back, which Gertie adored, in search of tigers. "The secret to tiger hunting is patience — not my strongest suit," Gertie wrote. She spent days sitting inside a blind called a *boma*, with the smelly carcass of a water buffalo outside as bait. Her vigil would begin at 2 a.m., when she was escorted on foot an hour and a half from camp and installed in the *boma*, where she stayed alone until dusk, peering out a tiny peephole. She could not smoke, and it was too dark to read. The heat was stifling, and ants crawled all over her face and hands. Her patience finally paid off on the fourth day.

Sidney was late going to the *boma* to claim her, and on the way, he heard two gunshots. "What did that second shot mean? Had Gertrude only wounded the tiger with the first, and tried to stop his charge with the second?" He began to run, arriving at the *boma* to find his wife calmly smoking a cigarette while sitting on a six hundred-pound tiger. The following day, they left for Saigon and home, with a side trip to Bali.

The Legendres returned to Medway, having their first rude awakening about how much decline can occur at a South Carolina plantation during the absence of its owners. Soon afterward, Gertie became pregnant, and gave birth to Landine in June 1933 at Doctors Hospital in New York. Franklin Roosevelt had been elected president during their time in Indochina, his New Deal was in full swing, and nobody in the Sanford or Legendre households would ever have anything good to say about him.

They traveled regularly, visiting John Sanford in Palm Beach to play golf and tennis and hob knob, and spending time there with Laddie and his wife, glamorous Hollywood actress Mary Duncan, whom he had married in a private ceremony in 1933. They vacationed in Ireland, Mexico and South America, and went shooting in Hungary, but they did not mount another collecting expedition until 1936. That fall, Sidney's book about their Indochina travels was published by Dodd, Mead. The Kirkus Review described the book as a "[m]ost interesting and amusing travel story. The author has a fine sense of humor and almost no scientific dignity, to mar the story-telling quality of his narrative for the layman… Appeals largely to men and the few women interested in such adventure."

The world in 1936 was rapidly changing, being shaped by both the Depression and the dictatorships that would soon plunge it into an all-consuming war. In the fall of 1935, Italy's fascist dictator Benito Mussolini had sent an Italian army into Ethiopia, deposing Gertie's beloved emperor, Haile Selassie. The United States was staying neutral in the rising conflict but had condemned Mussolini's actions; the League of Nations imposed economic sanctions. The Ethiopian royal court was operating in exile in London, where Gertie and Sidney called on the emperor in September 1936. By then, Janie Sanford was romantically involved with a polo-playing Italian diplomat, Mario Pansa, a close advisor to Mussolini. (It was said that he schooled Mussolini in the social graces, such as how to properly use a knife and fork.) Meeting up with her in Paris in October, Gertie recounted in her journal, "Her mind was at sea as to her marriage plans — she was beginning to feel a little uncertain as to the prospect of Mario Pansa as a husband. She talked of sailing home in November — and I was very glad to hear it." But Janie got over her jitters and married Pansa a few months later.

The finances of the American Museum of Natural History were so strained by the Depression that it had closed some of its exhibit halls and suspended all its exploration activities. The Legendres instead agreed to collect specimens of kudu and gemsbok along the Okovango River in Southwest Africa (present-day Namibia) for the Philadelphia Academy of Natural Sciences (the present-day Academy of Natural Sciences of Drexel University). It took almost a year to obtain permission for the safari from the Union of South Africa, which since World War I had been governing the former German colony under a mandate from the League of Nations. "It was nothing like the rich, colorful trip up the Mekong four years before," Gertie wrote. "The Okovango trip was a journey of survival and thirst. The land was primitive and savage, and its people were its product." Sidney seconded her, writing, "Why game or human beings should want to live in such a dreary, burned-out land was beyond my comprehension."

Gertie and Sidney traveled halfway around the world by ship, prop plane and train. In Nairobi she reconnected with A.J. Klein, one of the hunters of her first safari, spending the night in his home and listening to tales of hunting and hunters "all equally exciting and hair-raising." A train traveling five miles per hour — Gertie was thankful to have a copy of the enthralling new novel *Gone with the Wind* to pass the time — brought them to Johannesburg, where they toured a diamond exhibit and descended into a gold mine. By November they reached the Southwest Africa capital, Windhoek, a city consumed by hatred. The British and Germans loathed each other;

the Afrikaners, native whites descended from Dutch Boers who spoke a tongue called Afrikaans, hated the British and Germans. Within the white community there was a hierarchy with civil servants at the top and railroad people at the bottom. A notch below the whites were the "colored" population, the offspring of interracial couples, and below them were the tribal blacks, who had issues with each other. The specter of Nazism was rising within the German community, which wanted its colony in the fold of the Third Reich. Hitler Youth groups had formed, and a boastful German farmer assured the Legendres that war was inevitable and the only solution was for France to become a colony of Germany.

They had arrived toward the end of the dry season, the only time when the bushland was accessible for hunting, and the heat was terrific. The Europeans they met in Windhoek couldn't believe Sidney would take his wife into the dangerous bush, to which he invariably replied, "I am not taking her; she is taking me." Gertie added, "It was easy to shock people with so little imagination." But if Gertie loathed the heat and insects of a South Carolina summer, she was totally miserable in the dry furnace blast of Southwest Africa where temperatures exceeded 100 degrees by 10 a.m. and black flies swarmed over everybody and everything. Sidney writes of her exploding with temper about delays and problems, and quotes her saying, "Of all the God-forsaken countries, this is the worst."

The museum's naturalist, genial and even-tempered Harry Lance, joined them a few days after their arrival. Eventually they cobbled together a small expedition party with a mountain of an Afrikaner man named Williams as their primary driver; a rather sinister German assistant named Van Furrin; Cornelius, a black cook from South Africa; and a tribal youth, Johannes, to help out around camp. (Terrified of snakes, Johannes spent most of his time on top of the truck. Gertie called him "the human goat.") Later a colonial administrator loaned them his tribal tracker, Rubens, and they picked up a rag-tag retinue of natives who worked for the meat from the specimens they shot. In late November they departed from Windhoek in two new Ford trucks shipped from America and Williams's springless 1928 Chevrolet touring car, which had lost its roof. Williams, a gentle giant, dressed for the great occasion in a tiny feathered hat and short-shorts that barely covered his huge, hairy legs. Sidney likened him to "King Kong dressed up for a Tyrolean party."

After days of driving through the desert and digging the vehicles out of sand and ant bear holes the size of subway entrances, they finally reached the Okovango River, where Gertie and Sidney each took a turn bathing while the other kept a rifle trained on a nearby crocodile. To avoid the worst of the heat each day, they woke before dawn and hunted until 9 a.m., then rested in camp until 5 p.m., when they resumed hunting until dark. Their efforts were hampered by problems with their guns, which had been improperly sighted in America, incompatible ammunition and Sidney's propensity to leave the safety on and his poor marksmanship. He confessed that he could kill anything at five yards, but an animal more than a hundred yards away would only die by accident. However, after a successful day's hunt, Gertie admitted to mixed feelings: "We went home feeling a little sad from shooting so many lovely animals who were so happy in the open plain," she wrote in her journal. Her consciousness about the rights of animals was slowly awakening, but it would take decades for her thoughts to be translated into actions.

They managed to catch radio signals from time to time, including a news broadcast on December 11 that flabbergasted Gertie: Edward VIII, the King of England, who had been a guest at her parents' home when he was Prince of Wales, had abdicated the throne to marry the American woman Wallis Warfield Simpson. "Amazing to think that a man can give up his country, his people, his life's work, duty, etc., etc., all for the [love] of this hard-boiled, twice-divorced harlot — Mrs. Simpson," Gertie wrote in her journal.

The Legendres had contact with several of the local tribes and both wrote extensively of their customs and rituals in their journals. Sidney's resulting book *Okovango Desert River* is illustrated with photographs, the most astounding being profiles of the men, women and children of the bushmen, who consumed an all-meat diet. Whenever they had a major kill, they stuffed themselves until their stomachs protruded like they were all in an advanced state of pregnancy.

Despite the trials and tribulations, their specimen collecting went well, with the one exception being a kudu bull with its prized spiral horns. Returning to Windhoek after almost a month in the bush, they were given permission to hunt in a park five miles outside town, where Gertie finally bagged a large kudu buck and they could at last depart. They continued around the world by boat plane, with stops in Australia, South America and the West Indies before landing in Florida, where they spent the winter in Palm Beach with

Gertie's father, brother and sister-in-law. In February, Janie married Mario Pansa at Mr. Sanford's mansion, with three-year-old Landine serving as a flower girl. The small ceremony was followed by a lavish wedding brunch for 250 guests.

That June, the second movie version of *Holiday* was released, starring Katharine Hepburn in the role of Linda Seton, the free-spirited heiress modeled by playwright Philip Barry on Gertie, and Cary Grant as Johnny Case, the self-made man who initially falls for her conventional younger sister, Julia. (Hepburn and Grant had previously starred in the screwball comedy *Bringing Up Baby*, and would team up again in *The Philadelphia Story*, another vehicle based on a Philip Barry play.) George Cukor directed the comedy of manners, which film historian Jerry Vermilye describes as "[l]iterate, amusing, thought-provoking, and often quite moving… a vintage film that admirably stands the test of time…" Contemporary critics praised the film, and it garnered an Academy Award nomination for best art direction, but audiences weren't impressed. Hepburn had a reputation as box office poison at the time, and apparently Depression audiences weren't attracted to the story of a wealthy man wanting to take an extended "holiday" from working to see the world.

Like Johnny Case, the Legendres were ready for more travel and adventure. Gertie wrote, "Travel for Sidney and me was like pushing back the canvas flap of a circus tent." In the fall of 1938 they traveled to Iran, which had been called Persia until 1935, again collecting for the American Museum of Natural History. As their plane out of Amsterdam climbed into the skies, Sidney wrote in his unpublished memoir *Persian Paths*, "I felt intoxicated with a sense of freedom… I turned to speak to Gertrude, my wife, but her eyes were already closed, their long lashes sweeping down to her high cheek bones, down to a face so strong, so Mongolian in character that its counterpart might have ridden beside those Iranian conquerors of old."

Reza Shah Pahlavi had risen through the ranks of the Persian army and was elected shah in 1926; he was dragging the ancient kingdom into the twentieth century with hands of iron. His role model was Kemal Ataturk, who had transformed Turkey from a backward Ottoman caliphate into a secular nation after his election as president in 1923. In Iran, Pahlavi neutered the power of the Islamic mullahs, banned the traditional brimless hat for men — which enabled them to place their foreheads on the ground when they prayed — and liberated women from their chadors and veils. He built

Gertie and Sidney's Iranian visas were just the beginning of the permits they had to procure.

railroads, schools and hospitals, and ejected foreign powers and influence. But he also ruled by fear and terror, capriciously throwing people into prison, and had secret police reporting to him. It took a year before departure for the Legendres to get the shah's permission to collect rodents, birds and several large animals, among them the wild ass — thought by some to be extinct — the maral stag, and the ibex, a mountain sheep. But after they arrived in Baghdad and met up with George Goodwin, the naturalist from the museum, the shah's bureaucracy threw up one roadblock after another even before they could cross the border. Once in Teheran, they were assigned a member of the sinister "dark police" as escort.

Sidney quickly recognized a key characteristic of the Iranian personality: the refusal to take responsibility and its avoidance by making promises that are never kept. Gertie and Sidney's major concern as their expedition was delayed was with the weather because the northern region of the country where they needed to hunt would be covered with snow, its roads impassable in a matter of weeks. After one especially dispiriting day, Sidney thought a whiskey and soda might be the best way to revive his spirits, but Gertie had another thought, an "infallible one for all women, and not a bad one for men," Sidney wrote. "'Let's go shopping in the bazaar,'" she said. They proceeded to the bazaar with their "go-between," a French-Iranian called Monsieur Richard who helped them negotiate the purchase of a pair of pearl and ruby gold earrings. He also took George Goodwin hunting outside Teheran where he shot and killed a wild ass, one of the most important animals they sought.

Rather than discouraging them, the shah's constant rebuffs stiffened their resolve, and they decided at one point they would remain in Iran for up to two years seeking permits rather than going home empty-handed. (Neither Gertie nor Sidney expressed any concern about Landine, back home in America, who was then just five years old.) Gertie's natural impatience was stretched to the breaking point, and she chafed at dealing with underlings who declared their hands were tied or lied about passing along requests to the proper authorities. The breakthrough came when she wangled an audience with the second most powerful man in the country, the secretary of war. He served them the ubiquitous hot tea — Sidney said that at one lengthy meeting he drank thirty cups of tea and smoked two packs of native cigarettes — and slowly the barriers began to fall.

After more than three weeks of waiting for their permits, they were summoned by the minister of education, who asked them why they needed so many guns. Gertie burst out angrily, "One shotgun and a rifle for each of us is 'so many'?"

The minister handed her a list. "Over five hundred," he said. It turned out that someone had mistaken the five hundred shells they had brought for firearms and decided the Legendres had brought in an arsenal, obviously set on arming an insurrection against the shah. They set the minister straight and were able to leave for the hunt the next day.

Gertie and Sidney set out with George Goodwin, Monsieur Richard, and an entourage of drivers and staff in two trucks and a touring car, heading into the Alborz Mountains in northern Iran. Their local staff included chauffeurs and assistant chauffeurs, a cook, a waiter and a camp "boy." They soon discovered that while Richard was an amusing companion and a fairly effective go-between in the city, the knowledge about hunting grounds that he claimed turned out to be all braggadocio. Between his bum leads and the "expert" hunters assigned to them by various local officials, they managed to bag little beyond a wild boar, which Sidney had to skin and carry back to camp himself because their Muslim staff refused to touch pork. But while Gertrude had been notably short-tempered on their Southwest Africa trip, Sidney expressed nothing but admiration for his wife on this one.

Writing of the strengths she brought to the expedition, he said she spoke French fluently, which enabled her to communicate with Monsieur Richard, who spoke French and Iranian dialects but no English. He continued, "Gertrude had an excellent sense of humor, tremendous drive and was tireless. She could not stand inefficiency or foolishness and made no bones about telling the offender his error. This relieved me of this responsibility, and I was delighted because I dislike giving people the devil… Further she had a woman's intuition, sizing up situations and giving her decisions at once. This saved a great deal of time, because while I might be trying to reason out an answer in man-made method, she had already arrived at the conclusion. With the experience of four previous expeditions to back up her judgment she could be counted on not to make a mistake." He continued to marvel over her unflagging energy and her intolerance of the absence of it in others, writing, "She was like a husband who assumes his wife may suffer a little in giving birth to a child, but will never know just how much."

Responding to these compliments many years later in her autobiography, Gertie wrote that Sidney's sense of humor was their saving grace: "No matter what the problem, his humor surfaced and lifted us out of the gloom of flat tires, broken axles, bad food and missed shots." An evening at camp was like going to the well for Sidney, who wrote in Persian Paths, "There is nothing in the world that can match the physical satisfaction of making camp after an exhausting march. The shadows of the fire on the tent, the soft tinkling of the lead horse's bell as he moves from patch to patch of grass, the murmur of the men's voices as they push their vases of tea nearer the fire form a melody that soothes the soul. The wind becomes charged with cooking odors and you feel you have entered a different world, an ancient one in which the trivial has disappeared and only the necessities of shelter and food remain."

Their hunt continued for two months, taking them through forests and across the parched earth of the Turkoman desert with little to show for it.

The animals they sought proved elusive. Climbing high into the mountains in northeastern Iran, Gertie bagged a fourteen-point ibex ram and Sidney a maral stag. Their luck had changed, and they spent long stretches on the hunt, collecting more ibex and stag. One morning, camping just below the snow line, Sidney thought he saw a bear and raised his gun to shoot. Instead, he was astonished to see a snow leopard, "a spattered streak of creamy fur," Gertie wrote in her autobiography. "Immediately recognizing its rarity, he did not pull the trigger." It was revisionist history. In her expedition journal, she said the big cat disappeared before Sidney had a chance to shoot.

While their hunting luck had improved, the weather conditions had worsened. They were hit by a blizzard one night, and then came a deluge. At the village of Bojnūrd, Goodwin and the staff headed back to Teheran with all the equipment and specimens, while Gertie and Sidney proceeded into the Aladagh Mountains. In the holy city of Mashhad, which had been an important oasis on the fabled Silk Road, they got their first hot showers in months. They visited the famed bazaar and asked to see the huge Gohashad Mosque and the holy shrine of Imam Reza, a direct descendent of the prophet Mohammed. He was the eighth Shi'ite imam and had been martyred in Mashhad in the ninth century. The shrine was visited by 90,000 pilgrims a year in the late 1930s, undeterred by a massacre of devout Muslims there by the shah's men in 1935.

A bumbling secret police officer, wearing a felt hat and a wrinkled raincoat, became their surprisingly adept tour guide. The law had just changed to allow Europeans into the mosque, and the Legendres were the first to take advantage of it. "It was so cold I hated to part with my shoes and stand in my silk stockings on the tile floor, but we found out later how worthwhile it was to get a cold in the head in consequence," she wrote in her journal. "Never have I been so impressed by the beauty, symmetry and proportions of a building. This, combined with the atmosphere of religion and prayer, was a never-to-be-forgotten experience." She was struck by the sound of prayers, which "rose like the drone of a great organ," and the homage paid at the sarcophagus of Imam Reza. "We were privileged infidels to be allowed to enter a mosque, especially one with such a holy sanctuary," she wrote. The mosque had a museum, where the guide showed Gertie glass cases of animals carved in turquoise. Her offer to buy some of the pieces, made half-jokingly, was quickly accepted, and she chose several. The secret policeman himself handled the transaction.

They traveled on into the desert, sleeping in the houses of village chiefs, usually on the floor in rugs hopping with fleas. "I was used to it by then," Gertie wrote. Their hunt was again fruitless, and after spending two days under their car while rain pounded the mud around them, they gave it up. Back in Teheran, they got news from home: Morris had married Nancy Newbold, a woman from Washington, D.C. "We felt elated, yet disconsolate that he hadn't waited for our return," Gertie wrote. Sidney must have felt especially forlorn to miss such an important occasion in his brother's life. They were ready to go, but they found getting out of Iran was almost as difficult as getting in.

The secret police interrogated them and confiscated Gertie's film, censoring pictures they felt portrayed their country in a backward light. Customs officials examined every specimen — 550 birds and beasts — and charged them exorbitant customs fees. But they were finally cleared to leave in mid-December. With George Goodwin, the Legendres took a train to Baghdad where they feasted on English bread and butter, ham and eggs: "It was heaven," she wrote. Rain had shut down the airport for eight days before they arrived, and it didn't reopen for another eleven. After finally boarding a flight for Cairo, Gertie was elated. They sailed home on the Italian liner *Rex*, Sidney sporting a moustache and Gertie a fur-trimmed coat and stylish hat and gold hoop earrings when they disembarked in New York on January 12, 1939. In a *New York Times* interview, the credit for shooting the wild ass was given to Sidney rather than Goodwin. The reporter said Gertie "always accompanies her husband on his expeditions," a phrase that certainly must have gotten a rise out of "The Instigator."

During their time in Iran, Europe had shifted ever closer to war as Germany's demands for the territory in Czechoslovakia known as the Sudetenland resulted in intense negotiation with British Prime Minister Neville Chamberlain. In late September, while the Legendres were stuck in Teheran waiting for hunting permits, Chamberlain was meeting with the German dictator at the Rheinhotel Dreesen in Bad Godesberg, a place Gertie would come to know as a prisoner of war in 1944. A fateful meeting in Munich was ahead. Gertie and Sidney listened by radio to Chamberlain's speech in the House of Commons prior to his departure: "One could have heard a pin drop, the silence was so terrific," Gertie wrote in her journal. "He spoke slowly and deliberately, relating the sequence of events leading up to today's crisis and he ended by saying England was ready to fight if need be but as the last and final resort and effort was the meeting of Hitler, Mussolini, Chamberlain and [French president Édouard] Daladier today in Munich… The whole world awaits the outcome of this afternoon's conference at Munich. Tomorrow we will know whether it is peace or war." The next day, a call to the U.S. charge d'affaires provided them an update. Hitler had been given the Sudetenland without bloodshed. "War has been averted for the present, despite future problems and possibilities that may arise later to cause again serious trouble," Gertie wrote. "… It seems that Germany and England have agreed never to fight each other again."

The coming two years would tell the lie to Hitler's promises. Gertie skips over 1939, 1940 and most of 1941 in her two books, but they were sad and tumultuous years for the Sanfords as well as the world.

9

The Gathering Storm

— · —

Now in his late eighties, John Sanford was spending most of his time in Palm Beach. Son Laddie and his glamorous wife Mary also made their home there, and Laddie shone on the polo fields, much to the pleasure of his proud papa. John had given his home in Amsterdam to the city, which converted it into the city hall, but continued to operate his stud farm. The 1923 Grand National win represented the apex of the farm's racing glory, but its horses had won four American Grand National Steeplechase races in the 1930s. John relished his identity as a turf man, presented the Sanford Cup each year in Saratoga Springs and spent large sums on promising thoroughbreds.

On the morning of January 9, 1939, a fire broke out in the main stable, racing through the stalls and taking the lives of twenty-six terrified horses. Among them was Supply House, described by the *New York Times* as "one of the best steeplechasers in the country," and Sunport, for which Sanford had paid a reported $15,000 just the year before. The financial loss was estimated at $200,000, or more than $3.6 million in current dollars.

Gertie and Sidney arrived home by ship in New York from their Persian expedition a few days later, and traveled to Palm Beach to see her father and brother. They were regular winter visitors to Palm Beach and often sent Landine and her nanny for a stay when they were traveling. John also visited them at Medway. Between visits they kept in touch through chatty letters. John advised them on stock investments and shared news of his favorite pro golfers — "He appears to have no waggle at all" — and groused about President Roosevelt.

It was March before they reached Medway, Sidney reliving in his diary the thrill of the moment he "entered through the old brick gate posts that

The Legendres had an almost mystical connection with Medway and its house. They commissioned this painting from A.L. Ripley in 1940.

seemed to lean down towards me and welcome me home." The next sentences speak worlds about the Legendres' relationship with their pets versus their child. "And then as the car swung up before the half moon steps a ball of tan fur pushed open the door, high balled down the porch and sailed into Gertrude's outstretched arms. It was Clippy, her cocker spaniel. The one that had occupied ninety percent of our conversation at night in the tent, the original of the only picture that we had taken with us, the thing that we had missed the most."

Clippy would also cause the major trauma of that visit to Medway. He was bitten by a copperhead snake and almost died, triggering a plantation-wide snake hunt with bounties for every dead poisonous serpent turned in. Gertie's Medway albums includes several photos of farm workers displaying tremendous snakes they have killed, as well as more benign scenes, such as blonde-headed Landine and some of the young black children whose parents worked for the Legendres posing with their Easter baskets. Gertie took a close interest in the plantation children, providing a daily hot meal to them at their one-room school. When the school burned down in 1940, she built the two-room Promised Land School on part of the land.

By the summer of 1939 the Legendres were in Europe with Landine, Gertie's right-hand-woman Rose Brind, and Clippy, enjoying leisure activities at St. Jean de Luz, a picturesque fishing village in the Basque region of southwest France. Their villa overlooked the Nivelle River, and photos in the album Gertie kept show them playing golf and tennis, lazing on the beach at Hendaye and bicycling. In one photo Clippy wolfs down a croissant. In another, Landine models a traditional Basque costume. But by late August, ominous newspaper clippings joined the snapshots. The *New York Herald Tribune*, published in Paris, trumpeted the news on August 23 that "British Cabinet Summons Parliament for Tomorrow to Vote Emergency Laws, Reaffirms Its Pledge to Defend Poland." The headlines became more and more alarming, leading up to the horrific news published on September 2: "German Army Invades Poland Along Four Fronts; France, Great Britain Order General Mobilization."

Gertie's photos illustrate what the headlines meant to the people of France. Her hand-written captions say, "Putting up a machine gun at the Yacht Club at St. Jean," "General Mobilization Cannes, Horses are requisitioned" and "Everyone calm but sad." The Legendres packed up and crossed over the border into Spain, which in the wake of its civil war was described by Sidney as a "country of starving children, emaciated women and young boys dressed as soldiers." Before they could cross the border to Portugal, they were forced to put all the cash they had "in a box marked for the poor." Then they went to Lisbon, where they waited two weeks for the *Dixie Clipper*, the Pan-American boat plane that had made its maiden trip in June. Before they could get home, John Sanford died on September 26. He was eighty-eight years old.

John had gone to Saratoga Springs in August, where he had sold the remaining horses in his stable except for a favorite aging jumper named

Golden Meadow. His health had taken such a bad turn there that his physicians advised him to stay in his room at the Gideon Putnam Hotel rather than return to Palm Beach. He died of a heart attack in the company of his long-time trainer, Hollie Hughes.

Laddie and Janie were also abroad when they received word of their father's death. Laddie reached New York first and made funeral arrangements in Amsterdam. Janie was in Belgium with her husband, who was the first secretary of the Italian Legation in Brussels, and did not attempt to leave. Bad weather and a faulty spark plug that forced the plane to return to an airport in the Azores for repairs held up Gertie's flight, and she did not arrive in Amsterdam until the funeral was over.

Sidney wrote of his father-in-law, "What a wonderful man he was, the kindest, most generous, most delightful person in the world. A father that did everything for his children, an iron man with the rest of the world. It was a great privilege to have known him." Newspaper accounts said Amsterdam honored its favorite son with "one of the largest funerals in the history of the city," the body laid in a solid bronze casket covered with a pall of orchids and white carnations, "the latter being the favorite flower of Mr. Sanford." Mourners gathered for the service at the Second Presbyterian Church, and John was buried beside his late wife Ethel in the city's Green Hill Cemetery.

John Sanford had maintained an increasingly ceremonial title as chairman of the board of Bigelow-Sanford Carpet Company, and Laddie had a largely ceremonial seat at the board table. The chairman title was abolished after John's death, and though Laddie remained on the board, he paid no more interest to the carpet business than he had before. He didn't have to. John had provided for him handsomely in his will, leaving him two shares of the inheritance trust, $122,195 in stock and property in Palm Beach and Amsterdam. (In Amsterdam Laddie reactivated his father's stud farm as a racing stable, retaining Hollie Hughes as his trainer.) Gertie and Janie each received one share in the trust and some stock, and the siblings shared jewelry and personal effects.

Sidney watched what followed with a jaundiced eye. "His thought was that they would live together happily ever after," he wrote in his diary. "What a fatal error. They eye one another with distrust like wolves who have eaten their fill and yet will not permit one another to take one more bite than they themselves… Gertrude wishes a fair division and often sacrifices her own interests to keep peace in the family or to protect her sister's rights which due to her living abroad are at the mercy of her brother."

The Sanford mansion in Manhattan had to be emptied in preparation for sale, and the contents list is an eye-popping inventory of Gilded Age excess. A small sampling is the list of silverware, valued at more than $50,000 in current dollars, including seventy monogrammed teaspoons, a thirteen-piece sterling dresser set, and the Saratoga Cup. Gertie purchased thousands of dollars of furniture and other items from the estate and had them shipped to Medway. Her portion of the estate tax was over $55,000, or almost a million in current dollars. No doubt both her father and grandfather were rolling in their graves that the federal government could take such a bite.

The sad news for the Legendres continued in December when Sidney's oldest brother, Hennen, suffered a massive heart attack while lying in a hammock at his home in New Orleans and died. He was forty-six. Soon after, Gertie discovered she was pregnant again, and Bokara was born in New York City on September 17, 1940. She was given the middle name Hennen. A photo album contains pictures of a smiling, round-faced baby being held by her nurse, a gentle, middle-aged English woman named Violet Evans. Nicknamed "Mamie," she would be much more of a mother to Bokara than Gertie was. Sidney was enchanted with the new baby. "Bokara is a charmer," he wrote in his diary, reflecting philosophically, "Her hands are so tiny and yet so perfectly formed with the lines that show her life that one can only wonder who has thought out the intricacies of our world and the life upon it."

Sidney said Gertie recovered quickly from the birth, but she later developed a severe throat infection and left Medway for treatment in New York. She spent a week in the hospital, Sidney mourning her absence. "Medway without her is a dull, uninteresting place," he wrote in his diary. "A land of gray shadows and trouble. A plantation filled with annoying repairs and requests for the innumerable things that appear to be necessary when you employ thirty people. Without Gertrude's happy laugh and shining eyes, without the happiness that radiates from her person, life is a very colorless proposition."

The major effect of the war in Europe on the Legendres was to curtail their travels abroad. The dust jacket of Sidney's second book, *Okovango Desert River*, published on October 31, 1939, said he and Gertie planned to next collect and hunt in Afghanistan. It was not to be. They stayed close to home, and Gertie's contemporary photo album reflected it with snapshots of visits to Middleton Gardens outside Charleston, horse race meetings in South Carolina and Georgia, a cattle auction a few hours away in Orangeburg, and a beach outing at Sullivan's Island, with Landine sharing the shade of the striped beach umbrella with Clippy. Hordes of visitors came, to Sidney's consternation. After an afternoon when twenty Charlestonians had attended a dove shoot and picnic, with a different crowd expected for dinner, Sidney confessed, "People exhaust me. They leave me with few ideas and drag away my own so that my mind is only a mass of cotton wool after I have been with them all day." He noted in his journal on January 5, 1941 that it was the first day in a month when they had not had company. Their only exotic trip was taken with a group of friends, including photographer Toni Frissell, to Guatemala in early 1941. Gertie wrote an article about it that was published in an issue of *Vogue* magazine.

Sidney's never-ending quest for a competent overseer for the plantation and farm seemed to have finally hit pay dirt when he hired a man from New York. His own enthusiasm for farming reinvigorated by the man's ideas, Sidney went on an equipment and livestock buying spree, admitting, "I am affected by farming as a gambler who sees the turning wheel." In the summer of 1941, he and Gertie took courses at Cornell University to learn to better utilize their farm. Sidney's subjects were farm management, field machinery repair and electricity. Gertrude focused on nutrition and automobile engines.

On the way home in their new Cadillac, they talked of selling Medway and buying land in Virginia. Sidney listed the benefits over South Carolina: no fever, a more moderate climate, no ticks and mosquitoes. They could find a smaller place, one that was less expensive, which gave them a view of mountains and rolling hills. If finances became tight, the children could be educated locally rather than being sent away to boarding schools. But their minds were far from settled. Medway, he wrote, "depresses us, weighs us down, and then when we feel that it is all useless, it produces one of those days so startlingly beautiful, that our doubts are dispelled, and we promise one another that it is the most beautiful place in the world, and wonder how we could think of disposing of it."

They returned to Medway to find the place in shambles and their overseer no more successful than any of his predecessors. Angry and disheartened, they were having a quiet Sunday afternoon in the gun room, Sidney reading the newspaper and Gertie brushing Clippy, when the phone rang. It was Morris.

"Have you got your radio turned on?" he demanded. "Then turn it on, the Japs are bombing Honolulu and have sunk some of our boats."

As they listened, aghast, to the reports on the surprise bombing of Pearl Harbor that December 7, Sidney lay back in his red chair. "At last the whole world was on fire," he wrote in his journal. "I had known this date was coming and had been written on the wall for months. This was the end of plantation life. …How ridiculous my worrying about whether the planting for the quail had been done correctly. We were at war with Japan."

Gertie later wrote in her war memoir *The Sands Ceased to Run* that Christmas that year was "outwardly as gay and festive as it had always been," with a pine tree from their own forest decorated with tinsel and colored lights, toys for the children scattered about and Clippy gnawing on a new rubber bone. On Christmas morning, they followed the old plantation custom of giving envelopes of cash to the adults who worked for them and clothes and sweets to their children. But Gertie and Sidney keenly felt how the world had changed, and that their "pleasant and carefree life" would soon disintegrate "under the weight of outward forces."

In early 1942, Sidney and Morris enlisted in the navy, and initially worked out of the navy intelligence office on the Charleston battery. Gertie joined the Red Cross Motor Corps, where she took courses in first aid and mechanical repair, met and fed troops that were flooding into Charleston, and drove to Toledo, Ohio to pick up an ambulance. The men who had worked on the plantation began disappearing one by one, joining the service or being drafted. The overseer departed for a better-paying job in a defense plant. The three men who had failed to meet requirements for the draft planted a large victory garden and left the azaleas to the weeds. Then, in late spring, Sidney received orders to report to Washington, D.C. There was no question that Gertie would go with him, along with their daughters and some staff. He wrote a will, giving his interests in the theater business to Morris, forgiving the debts of both Morris and his brother Armant, and leaving to them all his stocks, bonds and cash. He left a thousand dollars to Rose Brind, and explained that the fact that "I make no other provision for my children who may survive me is not due to any lack of affection for my two daughters who are now living, or to any lack of a sense of responsibility to whatever children might survive me, but to the knowledge that other provision has been made for their future that is amply sufficient for their needs." Gertie

Morris, left, and Sidney enlisted in the navy and served throughout the war to-gether, mostly in Hawaii.

used the same language when she wrote her last will in 1997, as Landine and Bokara's inheritance was guaranteed by the family trust set up by her father.

They literally left Medway in mothballs. "The house looked desolate and bereft of life," she wrote. "But then Medway had known solitude before and could once again entertain the ghosts of bygone masters and mistresses."

In Washington, the Legendres rented a house in Georgetown and arranged for Landine to attend Foxcroft as a day student. Gertie had Violet "Mamie" Evans to look after baby Bo, and Rose Brind to oversee the household and sometimes do the cooking when she could not find local help. Knowing it would be just a matter of time before Sidney was shipped overseas, she began looking for a job that would support the war effort. She tried the Red Cross — presumably for overseas work — but was turned down. The Library of Congress, which was a crucial resource for intelligence research, turned her down because she did not have a college degree. Then someone suggested she apply to a new intelligence agency that was headed by a Wall Street lawyer named William J. Donovan, the most decorated American soldier of World War I. His agency had been created by President Roosevelt through executive order a few months before Pearl Harbor as the Office of the Coordinator of Information or COI. Working there would change the course of Gertie's life.

10

Member of the OSS

———— • ————

Prior to the war, even with the burgeoning bureaucracy of FDR's New Deal, the Washington metropolitan area held only about a million residents and maintained the façade of a genteel, rather sleepy southern city. The war had changed all that, and by the time Gertie and Sidney arrived in the spring of 1942, newcomers were pouring in. In the year following the attack on Pearl Harbor, 70,000 arrived, and the government employee ranks alone were growing by 5,000 people a month. The Legendres had to pay the unheard-of sum of $450 a month to rent a two-bedroom house.

"Life in wartime Washington was maddening to most people, but to me it was thrilling," Gertie wrote in her war memoir *The Sands Ceased to Run*. "It was a period of trial and change. Everyone seemed to be trying to fit somehow into the picture puzzle which was being formed for a nation suddenly plunged into war." The war strained every facet of the city's infrastructure, from housing to public transportation. Even the patterns of society changed. There was an escalation in social events, what Hope Ridings Miller, the influential society editor of the *Washington Post*, called "partying with a purpose," as people furiously networked to further the war effort — and, sometimes, line their own pockets in the process. For a Washington hostess, wrote Joseph Dalton in his biography of Miller, a high-ranking military figure was a prized guest of honor.

Not all the newcomers were hoping to be useful; some were wealthy people who found war-time Washington a more exciting place to be than their usual watering holes, especially with Europe off limits. President Roosevelt spent a press conference early in 1942 grumbling about these folks, whom he characterized as "parasites," threatening to take their twenty-two-room mansions and turn them into office buildings for the war effort. He jokingly suggested writing an article that could appear in a box in the Washington papers headlined "ARE YOU A PARASITE?"

Had Gertie not been determined to contribute to the war effort, she might have been relegated to the parasite class herself, but she was not solely motivated by patriotism. The job with COI, whose name was changed to the Office of Strategic Services in June 1942, was essential to her as she faced life without Sidney for the first time in fourteen years. He departed for Hawaii in August, a time she described as "Black Week." To make matters worse, their dog Clippy unexpectedly died, a heartbreaking event that she and Sidney bewailed in their letters for months. The madhouse of the OSS was a welcome respite from brooding.

"Wild Bill" Donovan — brilliant, creative, dynamic, reckless, autocratic, and combative — had been hand-picked by Roosevelt to head America's first spy organization. One of his Wall Street law partners described him as "a rosy-cheeked, smiling gentleman with a voice as soft as the leaf of a shamrock, a shining light in his blue Irish eyes, and a punch in each hand like the kick of an army mule." He needed that kick as he had plenty of enemies to fight just in Washington, never mind the Axis powers. The army and navy already had intelligence operations, and J. Edgar Hoover became one of Donovan's worst enemies because he wanted his Federal Bureau of Investigation to handle intelligence worldwide; the FBI was already covering Central and South America. But Roosevelt always kept his hands on the reins of his government, and he relished having a spymaster who reported directly to him. By creating the COI and OSS, he gave Donovan "all the authorization he needed to build his empire, with millions from FDR's secret, unvouchered funds hidden from congressional scrutiny," wrote historian Nelson D. Lankford.

And build it he did. With almost half a million dollars in seed money from FDR, Donovan began hiring staff — including the president's eldest son, James — and taking over Washington real estate. The nerve center of the OSS was a former Public Health Service property near the State Department at 25th and E Streets. Donovan worked out of room 109 in the East Building, which came to be known as "the Kremlin." The campus included another substantial old building and two so-called temporary wood-frame buildings that had been thrown up on concrete pads. One of these flimsy and unpleasant structures, Q building, housed the office where Gertie worked.

William "Wild Bill" Donovan was tapped by President Roosevelt to create America's first intelligence agency.

Gertie was assigned to the cable desk under Secret Intelligence or SI, one of five branches of the OSS. It was headed by David L.K. Bruce, a Virginia gentleman lawyer who was unhappily married to the daughter of Andrew Mellon, the former treasury secretary and one of the richest men in the country. He and his new hire got along famously, and their friendship, like so many of Gertie's, would be deep and long-lasting.

Her days began at 9 a.m. and often lasted until after seven or eight at night, six days a week. The work was exacting, but once she got the hang of it, not difficult. She eventually had an assistant, a secretary and two stenographers, plus a messenger boy on her staff. "It keeps us all six busy for nine or ten hours every day," she wrote to Sidney. "It's far and away the most fun of my part of the office as you get all the red-hot news, all the dope, and it takes speed and action which suits me down to the ground."

Nevertheless, it was hardly a task to make the pulse pound; she'd much rather be driving an ambulance on the front, she confided. "I would be good at that I am sure, and wish it was what I was doing right now. You would really feel you were helping those poor guys in a big way and really doing something. This work is all remote control."

Donovan's empire grew by leaps and bounds. By the end of the war, the OSS had 21,000 employees worldwide, 4,500 of whom were women. Most of the women held clerical positions in Washington and elsewhere in the United States, serving as what Donovan characterized as "invisible apron strings" tied to every theater of war. They were essential to the success of the OSS and to victory, he insisted, but few reached the administrative level — or pay grade — of men. Gertie initially earned $150 a month, half the salary of a man with a comparable job.

In a letter to Sidney in October 1942, she unloaded about the way women were treated at her office. "What burns me up the most is the unbelievable lack of confidence in a woman's ability," she wrote. "It positively enrages me. Men cannot bear to have the world encroached upon by more efficient women. They hate to give way, they hate to admit they are good, they hate to give them power." Part of her rage was that she knew men were avoiding active service by taking jobs that could just as easily be handled by women. She spoke sneeringly of men with "cellophane commissions: You can see through them, but they keep off the draft."

Sidney responded approvingly. "Your tirade against men still makes me laugh," he wrote. "They are a dreadful race, I agree, and full of hot air."

The hundreds of letters exchanged by Gertie and Sidney beginning in August 1942 were a first in their marriage; before the war they had never been apart for more than a few days, just as they had never had real jobs. Many of the exchanges hinted at their passionate relations. When Gertie complained about her bedroom in Georgetown being cold, Sidney replied, "I would love to be in that cold bedroom with you. I know that for at least four days we would never get up. Just lie there and huggle and snuggle and let Rose bring us things to eat." They exchanged news about their children, family and friends, their social activities and, as much as they could reveal, their work. Sidney had a cushy assignment in Honolulu, where he and his brother Morris handled administrative duties under a captain in navy intelligence. They shared an apartment and filled their off hours with swimming, surfing, tennis and luaus. He often wrote to Gertie of the natural beauty of the island and urged her to consider living there after the war.

Gertie was more than willing — but she didn't want to wait. Unlike army wives, navy wives were not allowed to live in the same theater of war as their husbands, but Gertie was constantly dreaming up some scheme or another to enable herself to join Sidney. In some of her letters, Gertie poured out her heart to her "doodle ears" and "curly head," admitting that she sometimes cried at night from loneliness. She yearned for the sun and shore and him. By early February 1943, when she had seen the sun only three times since Christmas, she wrote, "I have now reached the point of feeling so sunk I could cheerfully cut my throat... There is nothing so gloomy in the world as this black hell hole, and those four filthy walls of Q building have got me down." But in that same letter she told Sidney that she had tried to wangle a post in India, where she would have done office work as well as intelligence gathering. "I was to take trips on the side and really get around and report back," she wrote. "I can't get into it all but you can piece it together and see what a swell chance it was for me had it gone through."

A few weeks later, she wrote an angry letter accusing Sidney of not wanting her to come to Hawaii at all and of not loving her as she loved him. He responded, lifting the lid off his frustrations about the balance of power in their marriage. "I do not know what our past life has meant to you, Gertie," he wrote. "In every way I have tried to do the thing that would please you, I tried to hunt on those damn horses, I gave up all ideas of business, I went on expeditions, we toured Europe in motor cars until I thought my back would break and I was so happy to do it because those things pleased you. Now because our country is at war and I am trying to do my best out here and have been unable to get you out you say I do not love you. It is all beyond me and I seriously wonder who I have been married to, is it someone who is so selfish that she upbraids me the first time I cannot accede to her wishes because it is beyond my power."

Chastised, she asked his forgiveness in a subsequent letter, explaining that she was tired and nervous when she had written. She shared a cute scene of Bokara playing dress-up in her bedroom and moved on to other subjects. Bokara, now two and a spunky little devil who reminded her parents of

Gertie's father, was living with Gertie in Georgetown but spent most of her waking hours with her nanny. Landine was living in Middleburg, Virginia with her French governess, attending school and enjoying some activities at Foxcroft, but Gertie saw her frequently. She had written Sidney in detail about their Christmas together, when Landine got everything she asked for and Bo spent three hours carefully unwrapping every gift in her stocking. Nevertheless, Gertie sometimes found the children exasperating, writing to Sidney "I wish Bo was a boy… but there it is. She won't have to go off to war anyway." Of Landine, Gertie wrote, "She is a funny kid, craves affection but acts all wrong so much of the time. Very lazy, spoiled and never seems to have the right attitude about so many things. It's quite annoying, I find." Sidney replied that Landine had many of Gertie's sister Janie's personality traits, which was probably what she found most irritating about her, and had probably spent too much time in Palm Beach as a small child. He urged Gertie not to make the same mistake with Bo.

Gertie filled many evenings by giving and going to dinner and cocktail parties, the proliferation of which were legendary in war-time Washington. (When the words "dinner party" are used as a search term in the Gertrude Sanford Legendre Papers' digitized correspondence file, they turn up in ninety-seven letters.) She rubbed elbows with generals and became great friends with Sir John Dill and his wife, even taking them to Medway for a short vacation. (Field Marshall Dill was the highest-ranked and most influential British army officer assigned to Washington, where he developed a close relationship with U.S. Army Chief of Staff Gen. George C. Marshall.) She reveled in discussing the war with such highly placed authorities and bragged that at a dinner she gave for Gen. Donovan — "General Hush-hush" in the society columns — and Oveta Culp Hobby, director of the Women's Army Auxiliary Corps, she also had two British air marshals and two colonels at her table.

As a guest at another dinner party, she was seated between Harry Hopkins, FDR's most trusted and versatile aide, and young Nelson Rockefeller, who controlled propaganda for Latin America for the White House. (He was one of many thorns in Donovan's side.) Gertie described Hopkins as not attractive "but easy to talk to" and Rockefeller as delightful. She was amused when Hopkins's new bride, Louise, failed to recognize Secretary of the Navy Frank Knox when he walked by. "I did not believe there was a soul who did not know Knox," Gertie wrote to Sidney. "He is exactly like his pictures."

In addition to socializing in Washington, Gertie distracted herself and recharged her emotional batteries with days and weekends visiting friends in the Virginia and Maryland countryside, occasional trips to New York and a few vacations at Medway. The place was a mess, she wrote Sidney, but she continued to be in awe of its natural beauty and questioned how they could ever give it up. Clippy now lay in a grave in the flower garden under a head-stone describing him as "A FAITHFUL FREIND AND A CHARMING COMPANION." Gertie was always poking fun at herself for being unable to spell. Whether it was her fault or the mason's, the stone was never changed.

Part of Gertie's disenchantment with her job in the winter of 1943 was the absence of Col. Bruce. He had gone to London, where he was placed in charge of OSS operations in Europe. In April, during a heart-to-heart talk with Donovan about her role in the war, he suggested she transfer to London. It was closer to the action, the mail service from Hawaii was dependable so she could still keep in touch with Sidney, and she would be working for Bruce again. With Sidney's support, she began seeking the transfer, though she continued researching avenues to join him in Hawaii.

By late June the transfer was falling into place. She got the children settled with Mamie at Watch Hill, Rhode Island for the summer and made plans for them to go to New Orleans to live with her sister-in-law Olive Legendre in the fall. (Olive's husband, Sidney's brother, Armant, was also in the navy.) To simplify staff and save money, she dismissed Landine's governess, a move that distressed both her daughter and "Mademoiselle," reasoning that Mamie could look after both girls. The irreplaceable Rose Brind would be based at Medway and trouble-shoot as needed in New Orleans and New York. Gertie spent a final week at Watch Hill with the children, writing Sidney that both girls were "bursting with health and spirit."

On August 16, 1943, all her arrangements were in place and she boarded a Portuguese ship in the Philadelphia harbor for England. Gertie would be one of just nine hundred OSS women who served abroad; future celebrity chef Julia Child was another. A third, less-known but crucial woman was Evangeline Bell, daughter of an English mother and American father, a graduate of Radcliffe, proficient in five languages, who had worked for the OSS in Washington. She had gone to London in 1942 with the first head of OSS operations there, William Phillips, as his secretary. She now filled the same position for Bruce — who was in the process of falling madly in love with her — while pulling double duty in the department that created false documents for OSS spies. Bell's proficiency in languages made her a major asset in that department, where the tiniest mistake on a faked passport could mean summary execution for a spy. She and Gertie would become great friends, and Gertie watched the burgeoning love affair with approval, even though she was acquainted with Bruce's hypochondriac wife, Ailsa.

The trip overseas was not without incident. The ship made a twelve-day crossing, then the women flew out of Lisbon on a blacked-out flying boat, making a wide circle around England to avoid the English Channel. "We had a nasty moment over the Irish Channel when one of our engines dropped into the choppy waters below," Gertie wrote in *Sands*. They made an emergency landing in Southampton, where a Royal Navy WRNS — the British version of the American navy's Women Accepted for Volunteer Emergency Service or WAVES — picked up Gertie and her five female co-workers in a motor launch.

Gertie was immediately struck by the prevalence of women at work on the docks: "Women in overalls, girl 'grease monkeys,' and apprentice workers swarmed about and over the big flying ships as mechanics' assistants. A typical English gesture, I saw a tea wagon pushed forward and steaming cups handed up to the crews. They sipped their tea with a free hand as they kept on with their work. That was my introduction to the 'All Out' devotion to duty which claimed the British people," she wrote. She was mightily impressed and would continue to be during her entire year in England. Arriving in London, she wrote to Sidney that the city didn't look much different from their last stay there in 1939 and "everything has been swept clean" from the devastating Battle of Britain when German incendiary bombs had killed 20,000 Londoners and injured tens of thousands more. The attacks during the most intense period destroyed about two million homes across Great Britain plus thousands of other buildings.

Gertie's duty in London was the same as in Washington, setting up and managing the cable desk, this time in an office in Grosvenor Square. As the American nerve center in London, it had become the source of many jokes, including a conversation said to have taken place among FDR, Joseph Stalin and Winston Churchill about how they would divide up the world after the war. The punchline, relayed to Sidney in a letter, was Churchill's plaintive

In London, Gertie presided over the cable desk at the OSS headquarters in Grosvenor Square.

plea to FDR, "You promise to give Grosvenor Square back to the British when the war is over?"

As in Washington, Gertie wanted to rent a house where she could entertain. For a time, she camped out in the apartment of David Bruce and Tommy Hitchcock, Bruce's close friend and a man she had known since her childhood in Aiken: his mother was the Aiken matriarch Louise Hitchcock. Tommy was a celebrity on the polo circuit, where he was considered the No. 1 ranked player in the country if not the world. Besides that, he was an accomplished pilot, an Army Air Force colonel and the air attaché to the U.S. Embassy. However, she didn't want to impose any longer than she had to on their "bachelor hospitality" — though neither was, technically, a bachelor — and was delighted to find an apartment available at 80 Park Street, a five-minute walk from her office. On top of that, she procured a cook, a dour Swiss woman called Mademoiselle Renaud: "sixtyish, stocky, extremely neat, primly spinsterish and all-work-and-no-play." Their relationship was definitely one of oil and water, but Gertie tried to overlook Mlle. Renaud's "sullen antagonism and constant complaining" because of the amazing dishes she created with the heavily rationed ingredients she had to use, supplemented by weekly food boxes from America.

Not that Gertie was affected by rationing as much as the British people. She repeatedly assured Sidney that she was eating very well. She had PX privileges and could afford to buy expensive "gray market" goods, as her pay had been increased to $375 a month, which she supplemented with a $1,000 monthly stipend sent from her bank in New York. In addition, Gertie's highly placed friends and guests were always thoughtful to provide hard-to-find commodities, from a cut of meat to a bottle of whisky to an almost unheard-of piece of citrus fruit. When she gave a dinner in honor of U.S. Rear-Admiral William A. Glassford in the summer of 1944, he presented her with two lemons. "We fell on those two lemons like hungry wolves — we smelled them, carved them, squeezed them, sucked them, and what rind was not slivered for cocktails was used to make a pitiful dab of marmalade," she wrote in *Sands*.

Author Lynne Olson in her book *Citizens of London* observed that with few exceptions, "the American notables in Britain lived in a walled-off world of cocktail parties and black-market restaurants, with virtually no idea of what life was like outside their comfortable cocoons." The Eighth Air Force commander, Gen. Carl "Tooey" Spaatz, was especially well known for his lavish parties, and he was a particular favorite of Gertie's. "I think Spaatz is tops," she wrote to Sidney.

It wasn't only the American "notables" who fared well in England. The British took to complaining that the soldiers and sailors pouring into their country in preparation for the invasion of the continent were "overpaid, over-sexed and over here." The cheeky American retort was, "You're underpaid, undersexed and under Eisenhower."

In her letters to Sidney, Gertie mentioned spending free time with Ben Kittredge Jr., their good friend and the son of the couple who owned the plantation adjoining Medway. Ben confessed to her how miserable he was without his wife, Carola, who was working for the OSS in Washington. It was a condition with which she could well sympathize. At the OSS, she worked and was close friends with Lester Armour, a member of the wealthy Chicago meat-packing family. Other American friends she saw frequently included Raymond Guest, who was chief of the OSS maritime unit in Europe. David Bruce described Guest as an ebullient man, "as if he contained in his own person enough vitamins to supply a nation of people with vitality." (No wonder Gertie liked him!) A champion polo player, he was renting a big house in the country outside London and frequently invited Gertie out for weekends. Anthony and Margaret Biddle were also close friends. Tony, known for his natty bespoke suits, had been the ambassador to Poland when the Nazis rolled into the country in 1939, and came to London with the State Department in 1941, serving as ambassador to the governments-in-exile, or as Bruce described him, "the only ambassador in the history of diplomacy to five nations at one time." By the end of 1943, Biddle had the thankless job of serving as ambassador to seven.   Margaret was in charge of a Red Cross Club for American soldiers, where Gertie volunteered one night a week. Because of her Red Cross duty, Gertie missed a party where she was to have been introduced to the writer Ernest Hemingway — or "Earnest Hemmingway," as she misspelled the name in a letter to Sidney. After this particular party, Hemingway was seriously injured in a drunken-driving accident that landed him in the hospital and forced him to miss his assignment as a war correspondent — covering the D-Day landing.

At the beginning of her stay abroad, Gertie reveled in being in the thick of war activity. Everyone seemed to be in the uniform of one Allied nation or another, including those of countries such as Poland, Holland, Norway and Czechoslovakia that had set up exile governments in London. (Because her suitcases didn't arrive until the end of September, she was in a sort of uniform herself. "I shall be known as 'the Lady of the Purple Suit,'" she wrote Sidney.) Total blackouts during the foggy nights made negotiating the streets fearsome. When she couldn't find a taxi, she went about holding a small hooded flashlight, with a black-jack in her pocket in case of trouble. "You can sit in the Ritz and eat a big lunch and hear the planes going over to bomb the hell out of the continent," she wrote to Sidney. "It kind of makes you feel queer that you can be sitting warm and cozy and well fed when so many of the young pilots probably won't come back."

Worse was to come, something from which no amount of wealth or privilege could shield her.

In January, the Luftwaffe resumed bombing London in what became known as the "Little Blitz" or the "Baby Blitz." "Overnight Hyde Park was bristling with anti-aircraft guns," Gertie recalled. Far from being terrified by the barrages, Gertie drew back the curtains of her blacked-out bedroom at night to watch the incredible displays, comparing them to Japanese lanterns hanging over the city. "Returning to my bed, I often saw the curtain of flame from incendiary bombs rain past my window, as if the fiery tail of a comet was passing," she wrote. She hated the bomb shelters and refused to use them. "I preferred, if I must, to die in bed, tucked in my blankets," she wrote. "The thought of being trapped in a gloomy cellar was by far the grimmest worry."

By spring, the invasion of France seemed a certainty. "May seemed like the logical month," Gertie wrote in her autobiography, "but day after day we waited and nothing happened. D-Day was the best kept secret of the war." On June 4, she was dining at Raymond Guest's home outside London, along with OSS friends Lester Armour and Stu McClintic. One of the other dinner guests was the singer Bing Crosby, who had been entertaining soldiers that day. "The night was clear and quiet," Gertie continued. "We sat on the terrace in the dark and asked Bing to sing our favorite songs. His voice was tired, but he agreed to whisper the songs in the moonlight. I was so enthralled by the evening that I suddenly blurted out, 'Oh, what a wonderful night for an invasion!' It was what everyone was thinking. Lester Armour and Stu McClintic were sitting right there and knew everything, but of course didn't say a word."

The D-Day invasion had been set for the next morning, but bad weather delayed it twenty-four hours. As Gertie walked across Hyde Park the morning of June 6, she saw planes overhead flying in close formation, but she didn't realize anything was different until she got to Grosvenor Square. She dashed home in a taxi and grabbed her radio, then returned to the office and kept it on her desk so she could keep up with the breaking news. In her diary that night, she recorded her thoughts in pencil in a ledger. "The office was electrified with excitement and emotion — One felt like cheering, crying — praying — One felt so upset for the men making that initial landing — their bravery … By lunchtime I was beside myself with excitement." She headed to a restaurant with Lester Armour and two other men. "We each ordered a double martini and drank a toast to success!"

A week later, the excitement having died down a bit, Gertie was writing to Sidney about a house she had rented at 27 Grosvenor Crescent Mews in Knightsbridge. Almost immediately, the Germans began attacking London with their new pilotless V-1 missile, nicknamed "buzz-bombs" and "doodle-bugs" because of the whining sound they made before detonating. The first bombs were launched on June 13, one week after the Normandy landings, and within a day they were raining down on London from launch sites in northern France. One landed half a block from Gertie's house, which was situated in a neighborhood that earned the sobriquet "Buzz Bomb Alley," blowing out her windows, buckling the floor and leaving yard-long cracks in the plaster walls. The V-1 missiles and the V-2 that followed — a forerunner of the modern cruise missile — would kill and injure more than 20,000 British people in the last year of the war and leave many more homeless.

Even so, people were feeling optimistic that the war in Europe was drawing to a close. In letters to Sidney, Gertie suggested the Germans might surrender by November, and she was "very roused and cheered" by the July 20 assassination attempt on Hitler by members of the German high command, even though it was unsuccessful. Along that same vein, she wrote, "Now that the Enemy has started to fight among themselves it sounds awfully good to me."

What better excuse for a party? On August 23, Gertie was the hostess at a memorable gathering, organized by Harvard professor Bruce C. Hopper of the OSS and paid for by the army, called the "Retread Reunion." The twenty-eight guests of honor were men who had been flyers in World War I and were now back in uniform or serving in some other capacity in London. Besides Hopper, they included U.S. Ambassador to England John Winant, Gen. "Tooey" Spaatz, and Gen. Donovan. Gertie, one of three women present, had a U-shaped table set up in the walled garden behind her house, with candles in glass cups along the edges to mimic landing flares of an airfield. The table decorations included models of Mustangs and Hurricanes, as well as a miniature buzz bomb. During the evening, a newcomer to London said he had not yet heard a buzz bomb. Hardly had the words left his mouth when they heard the "faint putt-putt of a deadly doodlebug approaching." It flew past Gertie's house and she gave a sigh of relief. "To think that one buzz bomb could have destroyed most of the American high command!" she recalled.

The menu was enough to make a ration-restricted Londoner commit mayhem and murder. Fresh melon. Lobster. Filet mignon. Ice cream and cake. Dinner was followed by the showing of a propaganda film, *When I*

Next See Paris — especially appropriate because the French capital was on the verge of being liberated. They sang "Lili Marlene"— Gertie's favorite, popularized by the vehemently anti-Nazi German actress Marlene Dietrich — gave speeches and raised toasts, many of them poignant. Gertie's toast was to her friend Tommy Hitchcock, who had been killed in April while testing the Mustang fighter plane. The party was the highpoint of Gertie's time in London, and her OSS album is filled with pictures and mementoes of that night. Wearing a short-sleeved floral dress, her face animated, she was obviously having the time of her life. An admiring gentleman wrote in her album, "For Gertie — Lend/Lease's greatest gift to London S.W.!"

One of the people who was not present for the party was her boss, David Bruce. He had gone over to France to participate in the liberation of Paris where he ran into Ernest Hemingway. Ostensibly a war correspondent, Hemingway had poached his credentials off his wife Martha Gellhorn, much to her fury. He had gotten himself appointed head of a rag-tag band of French resistance fighters and was happily "liberating" wine cellars and brandishing weapons. (Correspondents were expressly forbidden from engaging in combat or carrying arms.) On August 25, Hemingway and Bruce and their companions followed Free French Gen. Jacques LeClerc's division into Paris, where gun battles continued. There they visited a few favorite bars and then liberated the Hotel Ritz. Asked by the suave manager what he could give them, Bruce replied, "Fifty martini cocktails."

London slowly emptied out as duties and offices were transferred to Paris, and Gertie felt discriminated against as a civilian and a female. She wrote Sidney that she wished she could have witnessed the "scenes of jubilation: The flowers and wine being showered upon the troops, and all the French dressed in their best to receive the advancing army."

Her time to depart London was coming. On September 8, Gertie wrote an excited letter to Sidney telling him she would soon be leaving for Paris. All the civilians in the OSS were going into uniform, and she would have the "assimilated rank" of first lieutenant. (The same practice was used with war correspondents.) In all the excitement of packing up and getting vaccinations, though, she was broken-hearted over the loss of a gold pin Sidney had given her, shaped like three fishes. She wore it every day pinned to her lapel or hat and considered it her "heavenly good luck piece of jewelry."

Bad luck was indeed coming her way. Her letter crossed one from Sidney in the mail, telling her that he had at long last been granted some time off. He would be in New York for a month in early October to undergo special training and would have another month of leave after that. "It really seems too good to be true," Sidney wrote. "My only fear is that you will not be able to come back and these wonderful two months will be wasted. Please try everything you can to return, it will be such heaven to pick up our lives again and do all the things that we have loved doing together." She received the letter in Paris on September 23 and responded, "Of course I can return and <u>will.</u> I am going to get cracking on it immediately."

She posted the letter right before leaving on a joy ride with Bob Jennings, a navy flyer who, like her, was spending his war service at an OSS desk. The jaunt would have dire consequences for them and for two others.

11

Bagged

———— • ————

In the plane approaching Paris on September 12, 1944, the pilot took a scenic swing around the city to show Gertie and the other passengers its famous landmarks, like so many charms on a souvenir bracelet: the Eiffel Tower, the Arc di Triomphe, the giant Egyptian obelisk in the Place de la Concorde. She was billeted at a hotel near the OSS headquarters at 80 Champs Élysées, which Col. Bruce deemed unready for staff. That gave Gertie some time to explore the city.

Unlike bomb-ravaged London, Paris had been an occupied city for the past four years and even during the recent battle when the Allies recaptured it, damage had been minimal. "The Place de la Concorde was resuming its former stately charm," Gertie wrote in *Sands*. "Protective scaffoldings were being removed from around the marble figures and fountains, in preparation for the Victory Parade all of France was sure would not be far off. The only damage apparent was that to the morale of the people, who seemed exhausted and worn once the happy smiles of welcome left their faces. Still, there was a great gaiety of spirit, despite the shortages — food, heat and electricity." The Parisians didn't look as shabby as their London counterparts, and she was charmed by the effort at chic exhibited by some of the young women: they had painted the wooden heels of their shoes to match their lipstick.

Gertie connected with Marian Hall, a friend with the American Red Cross, who offered to share her apartment. She also visited the wife of French Gen. Pierre-Marie Koenig, who was organizing a social club for Allied soldiers under the auspices of the Supreme Headquarters, Allied Expeditionary Force, or SHAEF. Back in London, Margaret Biddle had asked Gertie to represent her in this endeavor in Paris, working with Madame Koenig and Mrs. Anthony Eden, wife of one of Winston Churchill's chief lieutenants (and a future prime minister himself). Here, too, she found the club was a work in progress, so she returned to her sight-seeing and connected with a dressmaker to get her new uniform tailored.

Finally, Col. Bruce gave the OSS personnel a formal five-day leave. "I was thoroughly pleased," Gertie recalled. "My first actual freedom in twelve months." The afternoon before her leave began, she drifted into the small bar "on the Cambon side" of the Ritz, a favorite hub of war correspondents. Since liberating the Ritz in August, Ernest Hemingway had moved in and made it his headquarters, often holding court for hours in the bar. (The Ritz re-christened it the Bar Hemingway in his honor in 1979.) Gertie doesn't mention meeting "Earnest Hemmingway" that afternoon, but she was soon conversing with bona fide war correspondents. They were headed to Luxembourg, which was the headquarters for Gen. Patton's Third Army. She was green with envy.

"My precious leave was already beginning to lose its flavor… I wanted so desperately to see troops on the move, to actually feel the urgency of war and to know more of what it really meant," she wrote in *Sands*. About that time, a man she had known in London walked into the bar. He was Robert E. "Bob" Jennings, a lieutenant commander and navy pilot who was attached to the OSS. He joined Gertie at her small table. They talked as much shop as they could — even among themselves, OSS personnel were careful about what they said — and spoke of their desire to get closer to the action. When Jennings remarked that he could get his hands on an old Peugeot the Germans had left behind that could probably handle the trip, Gertie was all in.

He called for her the next morning, September 23, at Marian Hall's flat on Rue Francois Premier. She had just received Sidney's letter about joining him in New York and had shot off an excited, affirmative reply. "I have done my job and the place can get on without me," she declared. Her sudden decision to leave Europe added impetus to her foray to the front with Jennings.

The trip was snake-bit from the start. Rain threatened as they left Paris, and by noon it was a deluge. The Peugeot was a convertible with a rotted canvas top, and despite Gertie's best efforts to patch the leaks with Band-aids, both she and Jennings were soon soaked. A tire blew out in Compiègne, which delayed their arrival in Saint-Quentin until dark. There they found shelter for the night in a pension and breakfasted on Nescafé and K-rations.

Soon they saw signs of battle in the form of bridge-less rivers that military vehicles crossed on "hastily improvised ferries." Bombs had left huge craters in the road, forcing them to take innumerable detours. In a village on the Belgian border, the car ground to a halt, its water pump broken. They spent the night with a farm family who shared fresh milk, cheese and a ham they had hidden from scavenging Germans. The farmer's six-year-old daughter told Gertie she had named her pigs Hitler and Mussolini. Gertie recalled, "At first she thought they were quite proper names for pigs, but now she was in a predicament: she had learned to love them."

They got a tow from a U.S. military truck to the Belgian town of Arlon, which had been liberated by the Americans on September 10. It was night time when they arrived; Gertie may have passed a monument to King Leopold II, her maternal grandfather's benefactor and betrayer, on the main road into town. They abandoned their car on the cobblestone square and trudged through a cold, hard rain, finally finding two spare rooms in a small hotel. The next morning the Belgian commander, eager to return any favor to an American, enlisted his son to tow the Peugeot to Luxembourg, which had a garage with the parts they required. On the way, they passed a stuffed effigy of Hitler hanging from a noose that so amused Gertie she took its picture.

In Luxembourg the Peugeot mechanic informed them it would take until the next afternoon to repair the car. She and Jennings checked into the Brasseur Hotel and walked around the city, which was awash with soldiers and convoys on the move being cheered by crowds of civilians. The next morning, September 26, found them eating a late breakfast at the hotel, brain-storming ways to get to Patton's Third Army Headquarters, seventy-five miles away. With three days of their leave gone, they could see no way to get there and back to Paris in time to report for duty. There seemed no option but to drive back to Paris that afternoon once their car was repaired. They were glumly lingering over their coffee cups when Jennings sat up smartly in his seat and began to smile.

Two army officers had just entered the dining room, and Jennings knew one of them. He was Maj. Maxwell J. Papurt of Cleveland, an infantry officer who had seen duty in North Africa and Italy. Gertie didn't know it at the time, but he was also a member of the OSS, working in counterintelligence. Thus, he was privy to the most secret of secrets, such as the one about the Allies breaking the code to Germany's Enigma machine. The fiendishly complex electro-mechanical rotor cipher machines were used to code military messages.

When the two shared their reason for being in Luxembourg — "so the lady could hear some gunfire" — Papurt readily volunteered to take them to the action. He had a jeep and driver outside and could get them to Wallendorf, about twenty-five miles away. Located just over the Belgian border — the Sauer River divided Wallendorf from the Belgian village of Wallendorf-Pont — it had been the first town captured in Germany by the Allies. He promised he could carry them there and back in time to claim their car from the mechanic and return to Paris that afternoon.

That was all it took for Gertie. Carrying only her shoulder bag, she climbed into the jeep, driven by a young private first class whose only name she ever knew was Dick. (His full name was Doyle E. Dickson.) First, they stopped at Papurt's office so he could check the situation maps and make certain Wallendorf was still in Allied hands. He emerged making the "OK" sign and they were off, Dickson pressing his foot to the floor and the jeep flying along the winding, hilly roads, scattering ducks and geese that found themselves in front of its wheels.

They stopped and asked directions of a farmer, who told them they were just over a mile from Wallendorf. "It seemed incredible that there on that peaceful lane, in the midst of so much pastoral beauty, we could be so close to the angry breath of battle," Gertie recalled. She could hear no gunfire, see no convoys of trucks and men. Before long, though, signs of warfare became evident. Wallendorf was on a slight elevation to their left. To the right was a large green pasture with a small stream flowing through it. The bloated carcass of a cow lay in the field. As they drew nearer to the village, she realized none of the houses had roofs: "War had indeed come to Wallendorf and had not dealt with it lightly."

As they neared a signpost, Gertie chirped, "Well, here's Wallendorf, according to that sign! But I still don't hear any…" Her words were interrupted by a bullet crashing into the front fender of the jeep. Dickson slammed on the brakes and Papurt sprang into action crying, "Sniper! He's mine!" He grabbed his rifle and ran into the bushes as the others waited in the jeep. When there were no more shots, he returned to the jeep, saying he couldn't see anyone and ordered Dickson to drive on.

They had moved no more than ten yards when machine-gun fire burst out of a wooded rise. All four Americans abandoned the jeep to take cover, Gertie

Bob Jennings changed a tire on the Peugeot he and Gertie took on their ill-fated trip to the front.

throwing herself behind the jeep and drawing herself up "into a cowering bundle... I did not dare lift my head and contracted my body into the small-est possible target. I found myself wondering what the sensation of being hit by one of those flesh-rending bullets was like — would it be scorching and a tearing, with a shock of numbness and then excruciating pain? Or would there be no feeling at all — only oblivion?"

Papurt could have told her. He had jumped out on the opposite side of the jeep from the others and crawled into the roadside hedge. "They got me through the legs," he said quietly. She peeked around the front tire to look at him and almost lost her nose as more gunfire burst out. Jennings's hand found hers and pressed a pistol into it. Still in charge, Papurt ordered Dickson back into the driver's seat to turn the jeep around and get them out of there. The young private obeyed but couldn't start the engine. In seconds, he had been shot in both legs and a hand.

Jennings pulled Dickson from the jeep and dragged Papurt across the road, so they were all in a place of relative safety shielded by the vehicle. The young driver's wounds were pouring blood and his lips were turning blue. The jeep was riddled with bullet holes, and the oil from its crankcase mixed with the blood and mud on the ground. They were outgunned and trapped; surrender was their only option. Jennings pulled a white handkerchief from his pocket, planning to tie it to his rifle and wave it at the enemy. "Quick!" Gertie said. "We're OSS. We've got to think fast! Get out your passes. We'll burn them." As regular military personnel, they would become prisoners of war and sent to a camp; as spies, they could be tortured and summarily executed. Gertie's hands trembled as she applied her cigarette lighter to the incriminating documents. She ground the ashes into the mud under her shoes.

As a pair of German soldiers approached, the four concocted their cover stories. Gertie would say she was a file clerk at the American Embassy in London, on loan as an interpreter. Papurt would claim to be an ordnance officer, a field he knew well. Jennings would say he was a naval observer headed to the front for further orders. As for Dickson, he said, "Just a… just a GI, I reckon. Nothing to hide." Gertie lit a cigarette and put it between the boy's lips, then stood beside Jennings at the rear of the jeep.

When the two German soldiers arrived, they allowed Gertie to administer first aid to the wounded men. Using her Red Cross training she fashioned a tourniquet for Dickson's arm, then sprinkled sulfa powder on his and Papurt's wounds and wrapped them in bandages. The Germans found a box spring in one of the ruined houses and used it as a litter to carry the wounded men to a building in the village. It turned out that the Germans had reclaimed Wallendorf that very day; the intelligence at Papurt's office was out of date.

Even though their situation seemed hopeless, Gertie had thoughts of escape. Sitting outside the building, she played out a fantastic scenario in her head about using her compact mirror as a signal to attract the attention of the Allied planes overhead:

> *A pinpoint of light from a bombed and deserted German village below.*
> *An American woman in distress!*
> *Pilot-to-Navigator: "We're going down, lower the rope ladder."*
> *Pilot-to-Nose-Gunner: "Strafe the German devils, but don't hit the lady and her friends."*
> *Zooooooooom. Ratta-ta-tat-tat-tat!*
> *"There swings the lady and her friends. Hold on, we*

are going to pull you up. Heave ho, boys."
Ah, the Secret Life of Gertrude Legendre.

More prosaically, she thought of making a run for it, but when she took a few steps, one of the German soldiers stopped her and pantomimed the dire outcome if she tried to escape. Later, Jennings explained that if one of them escaped, the Germans would make it much harder on the other three. She controlled her impulses and set about finding food, putting together a dinner of pancakes with the help of the German soldiers. Shelling began and continued through the afternoon; Gertie was getting a full taste of what she had sought, but under circumstances she had not imagined.

About six that evening, a scrawny horse pulling a farm wagon arrived and the wounded men were loaded into it. Gertie and Jennings walked alongside as the party of soldiers and prisoners hiked up a mountain to a small bunker. The moon was up by the time they arrived, and the German officer in charge began questioning Gertie in French. His first question was one she would hear many times in the coming months: "How long will the war last?" She answered, "Not long." He told her it was likely the prisoners would be exchanged soon, and he poured drinks for her, Jennings and himself from a bottle of Jamaican rum.

After about half an hour, Gertie asked the officer to bring the wounded men inside; they had been left in the wagon in the cold. She and Jennings helped carry Papurt, groaning and almost delirious, and Dickson, whose face was colorless, into a nearby farm stable where German soldiers were sleeping in the hay. Soon, a German officer with a monocle in his eye arrived and claimed Gertie and Jennings, assuring her an ambulance would come in the morning and take the wounded men to a hospital. When she and Jennings protested, another officer threatened them with his Mauser pistol; in her mind, Gertie compared him to a character in a B movie.

Papurt, in a hoarse whisper, urged them to go and said he would look after his driver. Gertie begged two cigarettes from the monocle-wearing officer — she had given her last one to Dickson hours ago — and handed them to the wounded men. She had developed a strong bond with the younger man, who became for her the quintessential American GI: "boyish, uninhibited, courageous, resourceful, non-whimpering and with spirit unbroken." They never saw Papurt or Dickson again; both perished in the notorious Stalag

12A POW camp near Limburg. Papurt, Gertie learned, died on December 23 when Allied bombs meant for the train station in Diez hit the camp instead. She never learned Dickson's fate.

The Germans loaded Gertie and Jennings into an open troop car with springless seats and set off on what she described as "our mad ride through the Siegfried line… We bounced like popcorn on an open griddle as we flew over the winding, muddy country roads." They arrived in the town of Trier at about midnight where she and Jennings were separated for questioning. Gertie's interrogator was an officer she nicknamed "Weasel Eyes," because they were "like the eyes of a small predatory animal, whose mission of death is accomplished by stealth." A lieutenant translated his questions into French, beginning with, "How long will the war last?" Gertie shrugged and said, "A shorter time than it takes to tell it."

For the first time, she told her cover story, that she was simply a low-level clerk at the American Embassy and had been loaned out as a translator. Under further questioning, she said she had business in Luxembourg for the SHAEF Club — the one she had promised to help set up in Paris. He seemed satisfied with her responses, then asked, "Do you believe the stories you hear about German atrocities?" Gertie shot back, "Are there atrocities?" Weasel Eyes reddened, then asked if she was frightened. "No," Gertie replied. "Of course I'm not frightened. Why should I be? I suppose the Germans treat their prisoners as we do ours."

After her questioning ended, Gertie was reunited with Jennings and their journey continued through the night, ending shortly after dawn in the town of Wittlich. Gertie's greatest wish at this point was for a toothbrush. "I made a mental note for Landine and Bokara: Guess what your mother wanted most when she was stuck in Germany? They'd never get that one." All of her toiletries, additional clothes and other necessities were in her hotel room in Luxembourg. For the next six months, Gertie would find few opportunities for the cleanliness she considered a necessity of life. After all, this was a woman who had braved crocodiles in an African river in order to wash her hair.

In Wittlich they were taken to a large stone barracks, locked in an office and told by the commandant that they would be sent to a prison camp that afternoon. Late in the morning — when they had been awake for more than twenty-four hours — a soldier brought them some food, which they wolfed down. Gertie then acted out her desire for a bath and a cigarette to the young soldier. The soldier appreciated her thespian efforts and escorted her out of the building. "With the lure of a bath I would have walked into any trap that horrible morning," Gertie wrote.

Gertie's shower proved to be a comedy of errors. The plumbing apparatus looked like "a control station for the Coulee Dam," she wrote, and once the soldier got the water flowing and left the room, she was almost scalded when the temperature escalated, and she couldn't figure out how to turn it down. She returned to the office with soap in her hair and her clothing sodden with steam. Jennings laughed at the sorry sight she made and said he planned to take a cold shower.

They moved on later that day. At one point, Gertie was separated from Jennings and rode in a truck with a captured American GI and a German soldier driver. To pass the time, they sang "Lili Marlene" together. "They had good voices and in the communion of song I felt relief from the burdens of a tired mind and an even more tired body," she remembered. Later, the driver stood her a beer at a pub in Flammersheim, where their second round was interrupted by the arrival of a Nazi captain, "typically Prussian, pompous and overbearing." She was hustled up the cobblestone streets to the command post, where, for the first time, she was searched, and the contents of her shoulder bag examined. Her camera, film, Red Cross first-aid card and army identification card citing her as a civilian with assimilated rank of first lieutenant, were confiscated, and Gertie underwent a barrage of questions from the self-important captain. She held her ground, repeating the same answers she had given the other interrogators.

When the captain had exhausted his questions, guards escorted Gertie up the street to a small prison and locked her in a dark cell. The room held three wooden bunks, with straw-stuffed gunnysacks for mattresses. Revolting odors from the courtyard latrine drifted through the tiny window. To her dismay, Gertie found she needed to use it before she could get to sleep. Afterwards, despite the miserable conditions, she was completely exhausted, having had no sleep in forty-four hours. Fully dressed and with her shoulder bag for a pillow, she lay down on one of the bunks and fell into a dreamless sleep.

She awoke the morning of September 28 to learn she had attracted company during the night: her body was covered with red welts from flea bites and they itched something fierce. (The cell in which she slept had previously been occupied by Russian prisoners and they had left the vermin behind.)

The smell of the latrine was even worse than it had been the night before. Breakfast was a cup of lukewarm "ersatz" coffee, "black as soot and tasting like it," and five pieces of coarse bread, her ration for the day. She was relieved when, looking out the window, she spotted Bob Jennings walking by with his guards, but their conversation was cut short. He indicated with movements of his head that he was being held in a cell above hers.

Gertie and Jennings spent the next eleven days in Stalag VI, a transit station for captured American officers. On the fourth day, they were again questioned separately. Apparently, the Germans were confused by Gertie's identity card, which had the word "civilian" in parentheses following her rank. They had not encountered this before. Likewise, they were suspicious of why Jennings, who claimed to be a naval observer, would be so far inland. Their interrogator, an officer who spoke flawless English with an Oxford accent, questioned the two separately and told them incriminating papers had been found on Maj. Papurt. She felt sure this was a ruse to make her break down and confess, so she stuck to her story, as did Jennings.

Gradually, she was given more freedom, being permitted to spend the day-time hours with the imprisoned officers in a common room. Men were constantly arriving and departing for more permanent quarters, and they questioned each other for news about how the war was going. Many were depressed and angry about being captured; one had witnessed the death of several of his buddies, picked off as they descended in parachutes from a disabled plane. Ever the hostess, she tried to cheer them up as best she could, and it is obvious from her account in *The Sands Ceased to Run* that she enjoyed being "The Woman" among all those men. When an officer arrived with a razor, she held her compact mirror as each man took his turn to shave. They wiled away the time before and after their only meal of the day — potato soup — by playing checkers with French and English coins as game pieces and by sharing pictures of their loved ones. Looking at the faces beaming up from the men's photographs, Gertie bitterly regretted she had left her framed pictures of Sidney and the children behind in her hotel room in Luxembourg.

One of the German guards was a talented artist, who responded to Gertie's flattery by drawing her portrait. It would be her favorite souvenir of her time in Germany; she framed it and hung it on a wall at Medway, and she also used it as the author photo on the back cover of *Sands* in 1947. Another

A German guard drew Gertie's portrait. It was her favorite souvenir from her captivity.

guard presented the group with a single new toothbrush. "Chivalry was still an attribute among the men and I was the lucky recipient," she wrote.

Eventually an American captain arrived who made such a stink about the living conditions and rations at the prison camp that both improved, and Gertie was lodged with a reluctant host family up the street, an elderly man and his daughter. Though clearly unhappy to have her in their home, the daughter one morning gave Gertie an *apfelstrudel* and a pie she had baked. Gertie hid them in her helmet and shared them with the delighted American officers at breakfast that day.

On the morning of October 6, Gertie and Jennings were unceremoniously loaded into a large camouflaged limousine and driven to Limburg, where the car entered the gates of Stalag 12A. Gertie got plenty of time to observe the appalling conditions at the camp, which was home to 3,000 men. Among them, though she didn't know it at the time, were Maj. Papurt and Doyle Dickson. Gertie liked being the center of attention in a gathering of men, but the prospect of being the only woman prisoner at Stalag 12A filled her with apprehension. To her relief, she and Jennings were taken by car out of the prison a few miles up the road to the village of Diez on the Lahn River.

Their destination was Diez Castle, a forbidding thirteenth century pile of stone towers and turrets looming over the little town. Gertie thought it looked like the lair of an ogre and "conjured up pictures of dungeons and thumbscrews." She and Jennings stayed at the castle for the next twenty-three days, in separate solitary confinement cells, and were interrogated for hours by a German lieutenant. Meanwhile, her desperately worried family and friends finally found out what had happened to her.

The news broke on October 20 when German propaganda radio announced that Lt. Gertrude Legendre had been taken prisoner near Trier. A telegram from the provost marshal's office in Washington — which oversaw prisoner of war matters — confirming the report was delivered to the Legendres' apartment in New York, where Sidney was staying. By October 24, the story had spread to the newspapers and news magazines. Headlines included "Nazis Seize N.Y. Socialite," and "First U.S. Woman Seized by Nazis on Western Front."

Newsweek ran a brief article with an unflattering file photo of Gertie, looking furious, that described her as "the big-game hunting, 42-year-old sister of polo star Laddie Sanford." The caption under the picture said, "The Nazis bagged Mrs. Legendre."

12

Gertie's War

———— • ————

American spymaster Gen. "Wild Bill" Donovan had a ferocious temper. According to his biographer, Douglas Waller, he once threw a jar of pencils at his long-suffering female secretary. When he took umbrage at an American army intelligence officer who he felt had insulted him during a meeting in London, he swore that unless the man "withdraws this slur on me and apologizes I shall tear him to pieces and throw what is left of him through the windows into Grosvenor Square." We can only imagine his rage when he discovered Gertie and her companions had been captured while tooling around German territory without permission.

When Maj. Papurt's jeep did not return to Luxembourg on schedule, a search team went out looking for it but came up empty-handed. Donovan learned what had happened to Gertie the same way everyone else did, through the German broadcast on October 20. The broadcast identified Gertie as a Red Cross worker — the cover story she had devised while pinned down in Wallendorf — but Donovan was not convinced she could maintain the story under interrogation. He had more faith in Jennings and Papurt; after all, they were men. Donovan made sure his agency did not claim her or the others, and made no effort to negotiate their release, fearing that would jeopardize OSS agents in the field. In a memo to the War Department, he warned that if the Germans got wind of the "tremendous fund of information" she had, it would have "grave consequences not only for her personally but also for the organization," wrote author and editor Christopher Dickey in an account in *The Daily Beast* seventy-two years later. Neither did the German government confirm to the U.S. military or the Red Cross that she was a prisoner, as Sidney learned in late November in response to a letter he wrote to the provost marshal's office in Washington.

Donovan's biographer, Douglas Waller, writes that when the general learned the nature of the trip — essentially a joy ride in enemy territory — he was anxious to keep that detail secret not only from the Nazis but from the public because it made his organization look reckless and unprofessional. For this, he could only blame his own leadership. When it came to Gertie and her joy ride, Donovan hardly had room to talk.

Donovan "never saw a hare-brained scheme he did not like," wrote David Bruce's biographer Nelson D. Lankford. It was one of the qualities that endeared him to President Roosevelt, who loved cloak-and-dagger escapades. Nor did he recognize any other authority than the president himself. Gertie was no doubt aware that Donovan had willfully disobeyed orders from Gen. George Marshall, Gen. Dwight Eisenhower and Secretary of the Navy James Forrestal forbidding him to take part in the Normandy invasion because they could not risk his being captured. Instead, Donovan had managed to get passage for himself and Col. Bruce on a destroyer headed to Belfast, then boat-hopped onto the USS *Tuscaloosa*. Once ashore on June 7, they spent the day more or less as sight-seers, commandeering vehicles and making nuisances of themselves. A dangerous moment came when they were pinned down by German gunfire in a French agricultural field and realized they had left their poison pills at home. Donovan told Bruce that if worse came to worse and capture appeared inevitable, he would shoot him in the head and then shoot himself. It did not come to that, fortunately, and the two made it safely back to London. Donovan's detractors derided his joy ride, but President Roosevelt was thrilled by the first-hand account his spymaster gave him when he returned to Washington later in June.

The furor over their capture broke while Gertie and Jennings were prisoners at Diez Castle, which had room for about thirty prisoners who the Germans felt needed detailed interrogation. It was a bright, sunny day when they arrived, and the two leaned apprehensively against the battlement wall of the ancient castle. A few minutes later, a tall, trim German officer emerged from the castle and addressed them in precise, American-accented English. "Follow me, please. You are my prisoners now." The man was Lt. William Gosewisch, and he would become Gertie's guardian angel.

Conducting them into the grim castle, he paused at cell door No. 38 in the hall and told Gertie it would be hers. He then led her and Jennings up a flight of stairs to his office, got them seated and, turning on a smile, said

Lt. William Gosewisch was initially Gertie's interrogator, later her guardian angel.

"Please call me Bill." He offered them a package of Camel cigarettes. Both accepted gratefully, and as Gertie smoked, she sized up Gosewisch: "I judged him to be in his early forties. He was a man of education, with apparent refinements. His brown hair was thinning out above the temples. The features were good, finely tuned and yet somewhat rugged. He acted and spoke with assurance, as if authority came to him easily. There was nothing about him to suggest deceit or subversive intent, still I was on guard. My intuition told me, 'This German is all right,' but I was determined to take no chances."

Over the next three weeks, Gertie spent many hours with the German *Wehrmacht* lieutenant, usually late in the evening. The early interrogations sessions were severe, though Gosewisch never raised his voice. He gave Gertie a variation on the line, used in a thousand war movies, "We have ways of making you talk." Gertie stuck to her cover story, even embroidering it a

Castle Dietz on the River Lahn -

175/189

The grim 13th century castle where Gertie was kept in solitary confinement reminded her of an ogre's lair.

bit to invent two female co-workers she said worked with her at the State Department in Washington. The next evening, Gosewisch handed her a sheet of paper with the words "SCI Agents" at the top and a list of thirty names. As she well knew, the SCI was the Special Counter Intelligence, and she recognized several of the field agents' names. Again, she played dumb, saying she couldn't keep up with all those alphabet agencies the government had created.

She slipped up, though, when Gosewisch asked her if she knew members of the high command. She admitted to having met Patton and Spaatz socially, thinking it would impress him. Later, she concluded the admission resulted in her being kept in Germany much longer than she might have been had the Germans dismissed her as a lowly file clerk. "I had a feeling, later on, it was entirely possible that I was being kept in reserve as a means of contact, or as a courier, should certain negotiations be in order at a time of imminent collapse," she wrote in *Sands*.

After that evening, Gosewisch lightened up in his questioning, and the meetings "became rather sociable," Gertie wrote, sometimes accompanied by glasses of French wine and cups of Nescafé. She learned that he had attended Columbia University in New York, where he studied psychology, and that he and his American-born wife had run a lunch counter there. His American accent was the product of eighteen years in New York, his German army conscription the result of an ill-timed return to his native country with his wife and two children. He finally confided in a low voice that Germany had been subjected to "an unbelievable reign of terror. Only the American army can kill this evil thing!" That opened the door to broad discussions of the war, politics and what a post-war Germany would look like.

Gosewisch later told Gertie that the SS counterintelligence branch, the SD, wanted to get its hands on her, but he was trying to have her case cleared up as soon as possible through *Wehrmacht* channels. He even promised to try to pass her over the Swiss border. Unfortunately, the next day he had to report for three weeks of combat duty. His departing gift to Gertie was a much-coveted roll of toilet paper.

Diez Castle was the only place Gertie spent time in solitary confinement. For a creature as sociable as she was, it could have been a nerve-wracking trial. Yet she managed to fill her time by sleeping — she admitted to exhaustion to the core of her being — day-dreaming about Sidney, Medway and her daughters, reading the only English books in the castle (one was Zane Grey's *Sunset Pass*), and a short exercise period in the courtyard each day. She wasn't allowed baths, but she sometimes was provided with a pitcher of hot water for washing her hair. She also wrote two letters to Marian Hall, the friend she was staying with in Paris. One reached Marian in December, the only letter from Gertie to leave Germany. She never received mail from the outside during her imprisonment.

"You see how my innocent little trip to Luxembourg ended up!" she began in the October 12 letter. "I am behind a double row of iron bars in a 13 C. prison, eating black bread and potato soup, with plenty of time to catch up on my sleep. No alcohol or fattening foods to spoil the health regime, and I shall come out a new woman (some day)." She gave Marian a run-down of her capture and the places she had been interned and joked that she was "quite flattered to be considered smart enough to play the part of an International Spy." Gertie also mentioned that an army nurse had been captured shortly after she had, taking away her "rather dubious distinction of being the only American woman in captivity." (The nurse was Reba Z. Whittle, whose evacuation aircraft was shot down over Belgium the day after Gertie's capture. She returned to the U.S. in January 1945.) She signed the letter, "So long, lots of love to you from your caged lion, Gertie."

Gertie had not been a spy before she was captured, but she conscientiously gathered intelligence while she was a POW, in effect becoming a spy behind enemy lines. Through visual observation and lengthy conversation with her German captors, she ferreted out details about life in Nazi Germany and the opinions of the German people about Hitler and the war that were usually hidden by a veil of Nazi propaganda. She gauged their reactions to the bombing of their cities and how that would make it difficult for the Allies to build a new government after the war. She observed the state of their clothing and food supplies and the condition of their roads and railroads. What she lacked was a handler or a network to get her intelligence back to the OSS, but she felt sure her release or exchange was imminent and what she learned would be valuable to her organization.

What Gertie yearned for most during her time in isolation was news of the progress of the war. The air raid siren for the village was perched on the castle's roof, and it screeched warnings constantly, though no bombs fell on Diez during Gertie's stay there. She did not know that the Allies had been stalled in their progress by supply chain issues — most notably a shortage of gasoline — or that the Germans had a counterattack in preparation that would be launched December 16: the Allies would dub it the Battle of the Bulge.

On October 22, Bob Jennings came to her cell to say good-bye. They got a few moments of privacy, during which they whispered their impressions about Bill Gosewisch and whether their stories had gone over. Unlike Gertie, Jennings had been allowed to mingle with the male prisoners, and he shared some of their experiences with her. When his guards returned for him, they shook hands and wished each other luck. He was headed to an air corps officers' POW camp and Gertie would not see him until the following spring, after the war in Europe was over.

Gertie had neared the end of her endurance when Col. Kostner, Bill Gosewisch's superior, came to her cell on November 3 and told her she was to leave immediately for Frankfurt, then Berlin, where she would be going to a neutral country, Sweden perhaps, and then home. She and Kostner shared a couple of friendly glasses of cognac in his office before three men in civilian garb arrived and took her into custody. They turned out to be members of the dreaded Gestapo. She just missed being intercepted by friends of Lt. Gosewisch who were planning to take her to Switzerland.

The car that Gertie rode in to Frankfurt was fueled by wood, an indicator of how desperate the German gasoline shortage had become. Her heart singing with thoughts of going home, she drank in the sight of farmers working their fields, everything imbued with the golden light of late autumn. It was not until they reached Frankfurt and entered the only building standing for blocks and she saw the letters "SD" — short for *Sicherheitsdienst* or Security Service — that she realized she was in the hands of the Gestapo. At about midnight, her captors drove her through the ruins of the city to the depot and put her on a cross-country train to Berlin.

She arrived the next afternoon in what she described as a "truly dead city. Only a few buildings had escaped at least partial demolition. There was no wheeled traffic, and pedestrians moved about slowly wearing masks of defeat and apathy." She walked through the desolate streets with her escorts, clutching her few pitiful possessions in a used Red Cross POW box, and entered the dreaded Gestapo headquarters at 8 Prinz Albrecht Strasse. Some 15,000 prisoners spent time in solitary confinement in this building between 1933 and 1945, many subjected to the so-called "intensified interrogation" of the SD. Much to Gertie's relief, she was on her way a few hours later to another destination, a large mansion in the Wannsee suburb of Berlin.

On January 20, 1942, fifteen German leaders met at a mansion in this suburb, which was used as a Nazi guest house. The notorious Wannsee Conference was convened and led by Gen. Reinhard Heydrich, the much-feared chief of Reich security and second-in-command to Heinrich Himmler in the SS. They spent the day eating rich food and cold-bloodedly discussing the "final solution of the Jewish question," including "the expulsion of the Jews from every sphere of life of the German people" and "the expulsion of the Jews from the living space of the German people." The meticulous notes kept at the conference were used as evidence at the Nuremberg war crime trials after the war; the house itself is now a holocaust museum.

The mansion where the Gestapo took Gertie, located at 16 Am Kleinen, was also a Nazi guest house. Her companions in the car were two police women, a young one with some basic English, and an older one Gertie immediately disliked: "The forced smiles appeared foreign to a face which reflected meanness." A "fat and aggressive housekeeper" who did not bother to hide her feelings of hate and suspicion opened the door. Walking into the house, Gertie observed its comfortable modern furnishings and vases of attractively arranged flowers. At first glance, the second-floor room where she was taken seemed to be a pleasant improvement over her cell at Diez Castle, with two beds, a sofa and an adjoining bathroom. Then she learned she would be sharing it with the two police women. When she asked about going to Sweden, the older woman answered her with a mocking laugh as they turned in for the night. She began to feel uneasy, and for good reason: Gertie spent the next two months at the mansion, with the jailers as her constant companions.

The young police woman's name was Ursula Sebastian, and she eventually warmed toward Gertie and did her many favors. The older one, Frau Krautheim, was a Nazi to the core, and Gertie's original dislike turned to loathing. Frau Heizer, the housekeeper, stole her rations and gave her hot water for a bath only on Christmas. During the dreary days of November and December, Gertie was either locked up in her overheated room, eating meals with her captors in a small office across the hall with a bust of Adolf Hitler glowering at her, hiding in the bomb shelter during air raids or taking endless 210-step turns around the small garden. Occasionally she saw high-ranking Nazi officials in the house or the bomb shelter, including Gen. Ernst Kaltenbrunner, who had become head of Reich security after Reinhard Heydrich's assassination in June 1942. They ignored her.

One day a man from the Ministry of Propaganda arrived with his English-speaking wife. In the course of the conversation, Gertie again admitted that she knew Gen. Patton, and the man asked if she would like to write a note to him. On a scrap of paper Gertie wrote, "Dear General Patton: I am waiting like Lili Marlene at the barracks gate for Old Blood and Guts to come and get me. Gertrude Legendre." When her captors offered Gertie a chance to interview Adolf Hitler, she declined, though she later had some regrets, "for it might have been interesting to have a close look at the tyrant who had brought so much evil down on the whole world."

Because of the limited English of the police women and the need for a translator during the inevitable SS interrogations, a young English-speaking woman was added to the mix. Gertie found Ursula Zeichang a sympathetic companion and during long conversations persuaded her that most of the Jews in Germany had been murdered in concentration camps. Like many Germans at the time, Zeichang simply believed they had been deported to countries outside Germany. Gertie was fully aware of the truth due to her access to top secret cables, as well as reports in the mainstream press. The Soviet army had liberated the concentration camp in Majdanek, Poland in July, and a chilling eye-witness report about the camp atrocities by correspondent William H. Lawrence appeared in the *New York Times* on August 30. About the time of Gertie's conversations with Zeichang, millions of Americans were reading a Reader's Digest condensation of Lawrence's story under the headline "Nazi Murder Factory." Allied liberations of the camps at Auschwitz, Dachau, Ravensbrück, Buchenwald and Bergen-Belsen took place in the months to come and the full horror of the holocaust was revealed to the world.

Ursula Zeichang, who was just nineteen, confided that some of her friends, under pressure from the Nazi government, had had babies with members of the SS elite, the children raised in government nurseries and schools to become "potential soldiers for the Reich." Gertie was appalled, and particularly hated a painting on the wall of the room where she ate her meals that showed a "young girl in an advanced state of pregnancy. It was meant to portray the ideal state of womanhood in Germany." With her young interpreter's help, Gertie was sometimes able to tune into BBC broadcasts on the radio and catch a bit of war news. Zeichang put herself at considerable risk by doing this. Listening to the BBC in Germany and its occupied countries was a crime punishable by death. Most of the time, though, Gertie had to content herself with Zeichang's interpretation of the propaganda-filled German newspapers and radio broadcasts.

Once the Ardennes Offensive, or Battle of the Bulge, began, Frau Krautheim was delighted to share war news with Gertie. "When the Germans attacked Bastogne [Belgium, shortly before Christmas], Krautheim suggested that I pay closer attention to the map of France than that of Germany, as she was certain her countrymen would soon be back in Paris," Gertie recalled.

Even so, Gertie managed to summon up some cheer. During an early Christmas celebration on December 23, she put together a Santa Claus costume, making a beard of cotton balls and stuffing a pillow under her raincoat. The gardener contributed a little Christmas tree, which they decorated with candles and silver bells. Gertie had nothing to give to her captors except poems she had written, but the two Ursulas delved into their meager earnings to buy her a few luxuries: cold cream, a handkerchief, a flask of vodka and a box of Kotex. On Christmas day, she was allowed her first hot bath since her scalding shower at the Wittlich *stalag* in September. She and the two young women took a long walk across frozen Lake Wannsee "through the pine forests, which seemed to glisten like a fairyland of spun sugar frosting." That resulted in a furious dressing down from Frau Krautheim.

The next morning, about the time Patton's army came to the rescue of the besieged troops in Bastogne, orders arrived for Gertie to leave Berlin for an internment camp in Czechoslovakia. Fortunately, the orders were changed, and on December 28, Gertie, accompanied by Ursula Sebastian, headed off for her strangest POW experience of all. They returned to the Gestapo headquarters at 8 Prinz Albrecht Strasse, where they were held for a few hours. Gertie had another "Secret Life of Gertrude Legendre" fantasy there, "with me standing in the center of the room with a ticking grenade clutched in an upraised hand. Nazis of the Secret Police cowered or scuttled for safety as I scooped up important data and made for the door, tossing the explosive into their midst before vanishing." Instead, she endured another harrowing cross-country journey in bone-cracking cold by rail, military truck, car and foot that took them east to Bonn. The city, which had been the target of incendiary bombing that day, was a veritable Dante's inferno, tongues of fire licking out of windows, buildings falling, residents running madly through the streets.

At 2 a.m. on December 30, they reached their destination, the Rheinhotel Dreesen, a favorite vacation spot for bourgeois families — and Hitler — prior to the war. It was where he held some of his fateful meetings with British Prime Minister Neville Chamberlain in 1938 that led to the agreement signed in Munich handing over the Sudentenland and Chamberlain's fatuous declaration of "peace for our time." Though it was still being run by the Dreesen family, the hotel was guarded by German soldiers, and a high wooden fence surrounded the building and grounds with armed sentries posted at regular intervals. Gertie was transferred from her Gestapo minder

Rheinhotel Dreesen-Bad Godesberg
Orig. Fliegeraufnahme

Prison here two months with the French.

A favorite hotel of Hitler's, the Rheinhotel Dreesen served as a high-level internment camp.

to an SD officer and relieved of the 22,000 French francs in her shoulder bag. She said good-bye to Ursula Sebastian, who immediately had to make the perilous return trip to Wannsee. Guards took Gertie to a small room on the second floor where she found a comfortable bed and a good night's sleep.

Walking downstairs the next morning, she was astonished to hear French voices emanating from a large salon to the right of the front desk. The room, with crystal chandeliers dripping from the ceilings and a fine view of the Rhine, was occupied by more than a hundred men and one woman. To her further astonishment, an older gentleman with a "fine and kindly face" approached her and in cultured, Parisian-accented French introduced himself as Gen. Maxime Germain. "Allow me to introduce my compatriots," he said, as if she had just arrived at an embassy reception.

Gen. Germain's 130 compatriots were mostly retired and inactive military leaders from the first World War who had been swept up by the Germans following the D-Day invasion for fear they would be called into service or join the Resistance. There were forty-nine generals, seventy-five colonels and six civilians, including the lone woman. She was Madame Alfred Caillau, an elder sister of Gen. Charles de Gaulle. She had been in German custody for two years; her husband was being held in a concentration camp. Germain introduced these *Internés d'Honneur* one-by-one, and then they besieged Gertie with questions about France, continuing until the bell rang for luncheon. She was delighted to learn that the food was a marked improvement over what she had been given at Wannsee, and she began to replenish the fifteen pounds she had lost.

As the ranking officer, Germain presided over the internees with skill and grace, navigating among the cliques that had inevitably formed. Formal protocols reigned; Gertie was amused that each morning and evening everyone shook hands. She also learned that rather than simply languishing about the hotel, the internees had developed a range of activities to keep themselves occupied. There were language classes, a library of about a hundred books, board games, walking in the bedraggled garden when the weather was good and lectures on various subjects. She soon agreed to teach an English language course using the humorous Jerome K. Jerome novel *Three Men in a Boat* as her textbook. Doubtless she was able to embellish the course with descriptions of some of her own adventures as they discussed Jerome's account of a trio of disaster-prone Edwardian gentlemen and their dog taking a camping trip down the River Thames.

Because most of the internees had left their homes with little but the clothes on their backs, there was a constant need for repair work of one kind or another. Gertrude had always depended on her loyal servant Rose to handle mending for her, but she willingly took up a needle and thread and set to work on a mound of socks. One of the men had taken on the duties of village cobbler, repairing shoes with bits of carpeting and nails filched from the floors. Another was a bookbinder, reinforcing the fragile paperbacks in the library with cardboard from cigarette cartons. The internees furtively snitched the mats from chair seats and pulled threads from the curtains when they ran short of supplies. One man repaired watches, another one cut hair.

Once a month, the German colonel-in-charge went shopping for the internees, returning with items that ranged from the much-valued cigarettes — their ration was seven a day — to toothbrushes, soap, shampoo, buttons and other necessities as well as a grab bag of luxuries. All were distributed by lottery, with furious trading sessions afterward. As in prisons everywhere, there was a barter system based on tobacco. Gertie noted that one of the heaviest smokers "had traded off nearly everything but his dressing gown."

For Gertie, who reveled in being greatly outnumbered by men, the Rheinhotel Dreesen was something of a treat. Her favored companion was Comte Jean Couiteas de Faucamberge, a good-looking and wealthy Frenchman who had been active in the Resistance. He had flown with the French air force early in the war, was a gifted poet, and had played on the French Davis Cup tennis team. "Brilliant and fluent, he combined wit with intelligence to keep me amused and increasingly informed by the hour," Gertie wrote in *Sands*. "There were days when Jean wrote poetry in French or in English, depending on his mood. Other times he would say, 'Well, what shall we talk about today?' It became a fascinating game as I tried to introduce a subject on which he had not some authority." She never succeeded. He also taught her card tricks and Gertie spent many unsuccessful hours trying to beat him at deck tennis. She did much better with the geriatric generals, who resented being beaten by a woman.

While the companionship at the Rheinhotel Dreesen was a welcome change from the situation in Wannsee, the inmates exhibited all the eccentricities of characters in an Agatha Christie novel. The ancient, creaky generals were thin-blooded and insisted on keeping the salon suffocating hot. There was a trio at Gertie's regular dinner table who hoarded bread. Madame Caillau was never satisfied with the food and complained constantly, while suspecting (correctly) that her "*frére* Charles" was regarded with suspicion and dislike by many of the old generals and colonels. There were not enough chairs for everyone in the salon, and the elderly officers jealously laid claim to certain seats, sometimes requiring the diplomatic intervention of Gen. Germain.

One evening Gertie managed to get everyone out of their ruts by proposing a party game she had played as a youngster. She bet Jean she could lie on the floor, balance a glass of water on her forehead and get to her feet without spilling the water or using her hands to rise. It was an amazing feat, and at forty-two she was thrilled to have the "control and equilibrium" to perform it. Several of the men were inspired to try, spilling water all over themselves in the process. For her next trick, Gertie perched on the back of a chair and removed a cigarette in the back corner of the chair seat without touching her feet to the floor. "More chairs containing generals crashed to the floor that evening than during the entire history of the French army," she wrote. "The room rocked with mirth and wild applause greeted each successful performer." The next day, it was as if nothing had happened, as "the old serious calm returned to the group, to stay."

Gertie had one very welcome visitor during her time at the hotel: Lt. Gosewisch. He said he had decided to drop in and check on her. She eagerly asked for news of the men who had been captured with her. Bob Jennings was all right, Gosewisch said, but Papurt had been killed in an Allied bombing raid in December. Their reunion was interrupted by the German colonel in charge of the hotel, who spoke harshly to Gosewisch and sent him packing. Gertie went upstairs, totally disheartened, realizing that Gosewisch had little power to intervene in her case.

By the conclusion of the Battle of the Bulge on January 16, the net was closing in on the German army. There were constant air raids, when Gertie and the other internees were herded into the dank basement under the hotel. She hated being underground, and sometimes evaded the guards and hid upstairs during the raids. Occasionally she lucked out and found a bathtub full of hot water that had been drawn for someone expecting his once-monthly bath. She thought nothing of disrobing and enjoying the luxury herself, and never 'fessed up when the deprived prisoner discovered his bath water had been sullied. Even more important than staying clean, however, was the progress of the war from the Allied point of view. By February 27, Gertie wrote in her diary — a tiny datebook with a blue leatherette jacket — that the front was now just a dozen miles from the hotel. The long faces of the Germans at the hotel were met by wide smiles from the French.

The next day, the internees learned they would be evacuated on March 1. Their dinner was a gala occasion, fortified with Rhine wine from the cellar, presented by Herr Dreesen himself. "With the wine we drank toast after toast to victory and liberation," Gertie wrote. In the morning, the Germans divided them into two groups, the "young people" who were capable of walking, and the elderly who would have to be bused. They crossed the

Rhine by ferry and headed to the Petersberg Hotel, located at the top of a thousand-foot rise overlooking the river. As one of the youngest prisoners, Gertie was thrilled to be stretching her legs, and had to be called back when she got too far ahead of the heavily guarded line.

Unlike the Rheinhotel Dreesen, the "very swell and elegant" Petersberg Hotel had been closed for years and was unprepared for guests. There was neither running water nor electricity, and very little food. The daily ration was two plates of soup, a few slices of bread and half a glass of cider. Gertie brushed her teeth with the remnants of Herr Dreesen's Rhine wine. In a few days even the bread was gone, and the prisoners ate ginger snaps instead.

Madame Caillau's husband joined the group at some point — Gertie's contemporary journal says at the Petersberg, her *Sands* memoir says the Dreesen — and everyone was shocked by his condition. His wife did not at first recognize him because he had lost so much weight in the Buchenwald concentration camp; even his voice had changed. He shared the horrors of camp life, unable to think or talk of anything else: the daily collection of four hundred dead prisoners, the burning of their bodies in open pits, the clubbing to death of inmates who were too weak to stand. With the Nazis in a corner, Gertie and her companions wondered if even special prisoners like themselves might be subject to this savagery.

For Gertie, the crude amenities of the Petersberg were more than offset by the panoramic view she had of the battle that began March 7. From the window of a second-floor suite where Prime Minister Chamberlain had stayed during his negotiations with Hitler at the Dreesen, Gertie and a gaggle of generals watched the bombardment of Bonn and Siegberg. "I was in the midst of a caucus of experts on the use of artillery, of which the French army has long been a leading exponent," Gertie wrote in *Sands*. "The generals, as observers, were in their element and I was amazed at their ability to name shell calibers and judge distances between gun positions and targets merely by the sound of firing. It was a wildly exciting experience, and I was thrilled as I had never been before."

Finally, she had the front-row seat to a battle and gunfire that she had risked her life to claim.

Gertie and the generals stayed up until dawn and then retired to their rooms. A few hours later, she awoke to the sounds of pounding on her door and shouts of "*Fünf Minuten!*" from a guard. They were being evacuated.

Hurrying downstairs, she gulped a cup of bitter ersatz coffee and grabbed some gingersnaps. This time, there was no dividing the able-bodied from the elderly. They all marched down the mountain, where they joined a bedraggled column of hundreds of refugees. As a cold sleet fell on them, Gertie worried about the elderly men and Madame Caillau. Noticing she had no hat, one of the generals gave her an extra wool beret, which she gratefully accepted. The internees stopped at the train station in the little village of Ober-Pleis, about three kilometers from the hotel, where their guards herded them onto empty train cars.

Early in the afternoon, three men entered Gertie's car, stopped in front of her seat, and commanded, "*Komm!*" Filled with dread, she bade good-bye to her fellow *Internes d'Honneur*, hating to be separated from them. She had no way of knowing that they would barely escape death themselves. They were taken to the town of Essenberg in Bohemia, where the Gestapo planned to kill them. In the final, chaotic days of the war, the German guards deserted them, and, with the aid of the Red Cross, they arrived in Paris on May 13. Gertrude corresponded with several of her fellow internees for years after the war. In her one true act of spy craft, she carried a tiny piece of paper upon which one of the men had written the internees' names and addresses in almost microscopic script. She sewed it into the lining of her coat.

After Gertie sat down in an open car, the stern German colonel who had been so hard on Lt. Gosewisch came out to say good-bye. She saw him smile for the first time since she met him and found the expression on his saber-marked face a little unsettling. "You understand where you are going, do you not?" he asked. Gertie said she had no idea. "You will be sent to your people, then you will return to us again!" What did it mean? Once again, Gertie wondered if the Germans might use her as a go-between to negotiate a truce.

Late that day, the car pulled up outside a house in a wooded area near Kronberg, about thirty kilometers from the flattened city of Limburg. One of the men in the car entered the house and returned a few minutes later with an attractive young woman. She turned out to be Nena Grieme, who lived in the house with her husband, Hans. (Gertie refers to him as Dr. Grieme, but he appears to have been a Ph.D rather than a physician.) Although the house was full of company — mostly friends who were evacuees from Frankfurt — she had agreed to house Gertie. Smiling hospitably, she asked Gertie if she would like a bath. "More than anything in the world!" Gertie responded.

For the next two weeks, Gertie was treated as a house guest rather than a prisoner, socializing with the Griemes and their other guests. At Dr. Grieme's insistence, the guard the Gestapo had posted at the door went away; Grieme would not allow his home to be treated like a prison camp. Air raids went on the entire time, one of them destroying Dr. Grieme's machine tool plant in Frankfurt. When the skies were clear, Gertie walked outside, often chatting amiably with the Griemes and their friends. Several times she joined them on social outings. One afternoon Dr. Grieme even allowed her to sit in his garden with a .22 rifle over her knees to try to shoot a hawk that had absconded with some of his chickens.

This treatment emboldened Gertie to suggest that Dr. Grieme try to reach Lt. Gosewisch, who was likely still stationed at nearby Diez Castle. She told him she was due a Red Cross box, which would add to the badly stretched household provisions; her secret hope was that Gosewisch could get the wheels turning again for her release.

A couple of days later, Gosewisch and his commanding officer, Col. Konstanz, arrived with welcome gifts: three Red Cross boxes, a bouquet of hand-picked violets and a pair of silk stockings. They sat in the Griemes's living room, sipping cognac and talking over the war. It became obvious to Gertie that Gosewisch hoped she could bring some influence to bear on the American side to negotiate a truce rather than the unconditional surrender that President Roosevelt had demanded. "I did not have the heart to tell him that our conversation, on a personal level, would have no more importance than the chirping of sparrows to warring eagles," she wrote in *Sands*, "and besides we wanted to bring the war to their country this time." However, Gertie assured the men she would do her best to convey the message, hoping it would lead to a speedier release for her.

By March 21 bombs dropped almost constantly and planes strafed the nearest road. As she had in England and at the Rheinhotel Dreesen, Gertie eschewed the dank cellar for the open garden, figuring if her number was up, so be it. That night, Dr. Grieme opened bottles of his best Moet & Chandon champagne and he and Gertie stayed up late, talking and drinking. He told her to be prepared for a major development the next day, which she took to mean she was going to be exchanged or set free. About dusk on March 22, a small Opel car arrived at the Griemes's house bearing a man named Mr. Gay, who was secretary at the SS office in Frankfurt, a driver and a teen-age girl, whose presence in the car was a mystery never solved. Gertie exchanged warm farewells with her hosts and left behind a letter for the invading army attesting to her kind treatment and asking for "full consideration and a minimum of trouble" for them. Mr. Grieme asked a small favor. When she got to Paris, would she look for a replacement part for his electric razor?

What followed was another wild, dangerous and heart-breaking trip through war-torn Germany. The only building she saw standing in Frankfurt was the I.G. Farben office building, which would soon be seized by the Allies and become the home of the Supreme Allied Command. They narrowly avoided being bombed when their exhausted driver stopped near some railroad tracks to get a little sleep. Traveling at a snail's pace on a road clogged with refugees on foot, they saw desperate people who begged for help by beating on the doors and windows of the car. Gertie tried to close her eyes to their misery, realizing she had no way to help them. It was an image that lingered in her mind long after the war ended and inspired her to reach out to the destitute people of Europe. Outside Ulm, they stopped at the remnants of what had been a nice stone house. Gay quietly informed them that the house was his. He left the car and returned a few minutes later, vastly relieved; his wife and mother had hidden in the cellar during the bombing and were unhurt. He got back in the car and they drove on.

It was early afternoon on March 23 when the Opel boarded a ferry on Lake Konstanz. The lakefront was German on one side, Swiss on the other, and it was Gertie's passage to freedom. Konstanz, on the German side, was totally undamaged, and Gertie waited in the warm spring sunshine as Gay went into the customs house to arrange her transfer. He emerged an hour later, his face gloomy with defeat. He explained to her that the written orders for her release had not come through and his word was not acceptable to the border authorities. Miserable, Gertie went with him to a small guest house and collapsed on a chair in the sitting room. Then, while furtively looking over his shoulder, Gay whispered to her that he had made an unbreakable promise — to whom he did not say — to get her over the border. He quickly outlined the steps she would have to take on her own and then, much to her surprise, gave her an envelope holding the 22,000 French francs that the Gestapo had taken from her at the Rheinhotel Dreesen. This indicated to her that he indeed had the Gestapo stamp of approval, and she readily agreed to his plan.

He instructed her to hide on the last train leaving Konstanz and ride it over the Swiss border to where it was to be cleaned in the railyard at Kreuzlingen, just a few minutes away. At eight o'clock that night, Gertie and Gay arrived at the Konstanz railroad station and walked to the end of the platform. There a mysterious stranger in a light overcoat joined them and spoke rapidly to Gay in German. After listening to him, Gay emphasized to Gertie that she must adopt a cover story with the Swiss authorities that she had escaped from the German interior with the help of French land workers — prisoners the Germans had pressed into service as agricultural laborers. Under no circumstances was she to mention the assistance given her by any Germans. She promised.

When the train stopped and the passengers disembarked, Gertie insinuated herself into the crowd, acting as if she had just left the train herself. Then she pretended to have forgotten something and entered a car. She crouched between two seats, her coat buttoned to the neck to hide her American uniform, the French general's beret on her head. She felt burdened by her leather shoulder bag and a simple rucksack her friend Jean had made for her at the Rheinhotel Dreesen. "I was breathing heavily with excitement," she wrote in *Sands*. "I began to perspire, not from exertion but from nameless fear. My rucksack felt cumbersome and the leather bag slipped from my shoulder. Would the train never start?"

Then, to her consternation, she spotted a train watchman approaching, swinging a lantern and peering between the seats. She scuttled to a nearby door, which turned out to lead to the toilet. Heart pounding, she slipped inside and locked the door. The steps came closer and closer, and finally they stopped outside the door. The knob turned. Gertie waited, her heart in her mouth, expecting to hear a jangle of keys. But nothing happened. The footsteps receded, and when all had been quiet for a few minutes, she cautiously cracked the door. The car was deserted again. She heard a whistle blow and the train began to slowly move. She left the toilet and again crouched on the floor between two seats.

The nineteenth-century Konstanz *bahnhof* where Gertie caught the train is still in use today, but the sleek bullet-shaped Swiss train with its colorfully upholstered seats that travels to Kreuzlingen every few minutes bears no resemblance to the train carriage on which she hid that night in 1945. A passenger today reaches the border in about three minutes. Gertie recalls her trip seemed to take "a lifetime," but estimated it lasted about fifteen minutes, the train inching along the track. Finally, the train jerked to a halt; she looked at her watch, illuminated by the full moon. It was eight-forty-five.

She silently made her way to the car door, which opened with a loud groan. "My mouth felt dry. My knees were weak. I think for the first time in my life I was genuinely scared… terrified," she remembered in *Sands*. Ever the hunter, she was now the prey, just as she had been when the Germans ambushed her jeep at Wallendorf. When Gertie poked her head out the car door and looked up the line of cars, she realized the train had stopped about a hundred and fifty yards short of the border.

"I was in a tough spot, and I knew it," she wrote in *Sands*. "… I forced myself to walk slowly into the shadows of a line of empty freight cars standing parallel to my train. Smoothly I edged along the box cars until I neared the last one. There were still more than a hundred yards between me and freedom, and I knew that distance contained certain peril."

The coast seemed clear. Just as she was preparing to make a dash for the border, she realized the tall German in the overcoat who had been standing on the platform with her in Konstanz was again beside her. He must have ridden the train. He put a finger to his lips, then took her arm and shoved her forward so hard she almost fell. Though she did not understand the German words he muttered, the message was clear: Run for it!

Gertie began running, her legs feeling like slabs of concrete, her coat flapping and her rucksack banging against her back. She was fully exposed, bathed in light from both the moon and floodlights illuminating the border. Suddenly she heard a shrill whistle and a shout, "Halt!" from a German soldier. Her account of what happened next varied in different tellings. Her earliest version, including what she scribbled in her POW diary and an account in a letter to Sidney, was that the soldier shoved a gun into her back. In *Sands*, published in 1947, she admitted that could have been her imagination. By the time she wrote *The Time of My Life,* more than forty years later, she didn't mention a gun at all. But what happened next was pretty much the same in all her accounts. The Swiss border guard shouted, *"Identité?"* and Gertie, forgetting every word of French she knew, screamed, "American passport!" He lifted the barrier and she was on Swiss soil, the German guard "yelling and gesticulating with rage" but unable to harm her.

She was free.

13

The Damages of War

———— • ————

Gertie spent that night in the Kreuzlingen city jail, and subsequently became the houseguest of the police chief, Otto Raggenbass, and his wife while the American authorities were notified of her escape. On March 24, she had her first day of freedom in more than six months, when Mrs. Raggenbass casually gave her the address of a doctor who would conduct a required physical check-up and told her she could find it herself. The experience of walking about in the spring sunshine without a guard, Gertie wrote, "was like walking on air."

The American Embassy in Bern, Switzerland fronted her a loan of Swiss francs and Gertie went on a shopping spree, snapping up a new toothbrush, underwear, stockings and cigarettes. She had been wearing a heavy pair of boots someone gave her along the way, utilitarian and warm but two sizes too large, and she happily chucked them for a new pair of square-toed oxfords. At a restaurant on Lake Konstanz, she stuffed herself with fish, reveling in satisfying her hunger with dishes she chose herself.

Within the State Department and the OSS, the wheels turned quickly to get her back in American hands, but she was warned repeatedly not to talk about her experience or give any interviews. After four days, she and Mrs. Raggenbass boarded a train for Bern, where Allen Welsh Dulles served as OSS chief. Dulles welcomed her to his apartment, exclaiming, "Surely this can't be our Gertrude Legendre, returned from the beyond!" During her debriefing, Gertie learned for the first time that no efforts had been made to retrieve her by either the OSS or the State Department. "You were 'too hot,'" Dulles confided, explaining any acknowledgement of her would have jeopardized the lives of agents in the field. She shared her experiences as a POW with Dulles, a statement that was transcribed and sent to Washington,

The Son.   Mr.   Mrs. Raggenbass.

Safe in Switzerland and wearing new shoes, a freed Gertie posed
with Chief Raggenbass's son and wife.

then asked how soon she could get to Paris. Dulles promised to get her there
as soon as possible, once again cautioning her to keep a low profile and give
no interviews.

During her debriefing, Gertie created a dramatic moment. She pulled out
her pocketknife and used it to slit the sleeve lining of her raincoat, where she
had hidden the names of the internees at the Rheinhotel Dreesen. Trium-
phantly, she handed the list to Dulles, who quickly scanned it. Then, eyes
twinkling, he handed it back to Gertie, asking, "Have you read this?" It was a
message in German, written by Chief Raggenbass. Dulles translated it for her:

For the attention of Mrs. Legendre:

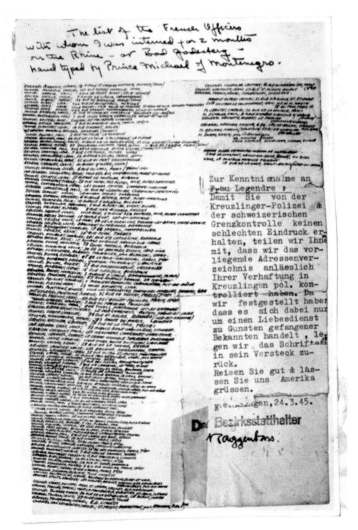

In her one true act of spy craft, Gertie hid a list of the French POWs in the lining of her raincoat.

In order that you will not have a light opinion of the police force of Kreuzlingen and of the Swiss Border Control, we inform you herewith that we have politically examined the enclosed list of names while you were in the custody of the Kreuzlingen police. Since we realize that it is only an act of charity in behalf of imprisoned acquaintances, we are herewith replacing the manuscript in its original hiding place. Travel well and our greetings to America.

O. Raggenbass

Dulles dispatched a bottle of champagne to Chief Raggenbass and flowers to his wife, with his thanks.

The news of Gertie's escape quickly spread to Sidney and her family. "I cannot wait to hear the story of what happened," Sidney wrote on March 27. "It must be absolutely amazing and will read like a Phillips Oppenheim tale. You have seen a side that not many men and practically no women have experienced and must be as full of adventure as a pot full of water… I certainly admire you, sweetheart, and hope that you have come out of this affair without any harm." While she was in Switzerland, Reuters reported her escape, still using the cover story she had given the Germans as the reason for her being in enemy territory.

On the morning of March 29, Gertie arrived by train in Paris and ran up the four flights of stairs to Marian Hall's apartment on Rue Francois Premier. She caught Marian outside her flat in her Red Cross uniform, headed to work. "Yes, it's me and today is my birthday!" Gertrude cried. She was forty-three. That night a few friends gathered at Marian's flat, including Gen. Tooey Spaatz, for champagne and celebration. From there, she flew home on a military transport plane, sharing the ride with returning soldiers, and spent a few days in Washington at the home of David Bruce and his new bride, Evangeline Bell Bruce. Although she had spoken to Sidney by phone, they would not reunite until July.

During her time in Washington, Gertie had an interview with Gen. Donovan that she does not describe in any of her writings. Donovan's biographer, Douglas Waller, said he sternly ordered her to maintain the cover she had used with the Germans, and impounded her diary. On May 5, he wrote her a curt letter, addressing her as "Dear Mrs. Le Gendre," thanking her for a memorandum she had written about her experiences and requesting a memorandum on "DeGaulle and his government." He signed it simply, "Donovan."

Three days later, on May 8, 1945, the Germans surrendered, and New York was engulfed by a VE Day celebration. That same day Bob Jennings called to say he was in town. Over a long lunch at the River Club, they compared notes. Jennings had regained the fifty pounds he lost; he had dwindled to 105 pounds from starvation and typhus by the time his camp was liberated on March 28. "I guess we both got away awfully lucky particularly in view of the atrocities lately uncovered in all those Concentration Camps," Gertie wrote to Sidney. However, Jennings's punishment had not ended in Europe:

Donovan had come down on him like a ton of bricks. "Not only did he kick Jennings out of his agency, he ordered him drummed out of the navy," Douglas Waller wrote.

The OSS itself was soon drummed out of government. Donovan's great friend and protector, President Roosevelt, died of a cerebral hemorrhage on April 12, and was succeeded by Harry S. Truman, who was not a fan of Wild Bill or his cloak-and-dagger agency. With the war winding down, Donovan's many enemies closed in, Congress slashed his budget and Truman moved to parcel intelligence duties to the State Department and branches of the military. By early September, the OSS was history, and Donovan was given a stilted thank-you letter from President Truman acknowledging his "capable leadership."

Donovan's final letter to Gertie was much kinder. Dated June 18, it greeted her as "My dear Gertrude" and was signed simply, "Bill." He wrote, "You have made a real contribution to this organization and I will always remember the enthusiastic interest and intelligent effort you gave to all the duties you were called upon to perform. Most of all, I am glad your understanding is so clear of what could have been a very tragic experience." She got her diary back.

Donovan's vision of a post-war intelligence agency was realized in 1947 when Truman asked Congress to authorize the Central Intelligence Agency. According to Waller, Donovan lobbied for the job of director but was not appointed.

Like Donovan, Gertie was not ready to throw in the towel on derring-do. She reunited with her children in New York — Bokara later claimed not to know who this "strange woman with dark hair and small dark eyes" was — while Gertie admitted to finding it very difficult to adjust to life in America after living on the edge for so long. "N.Y.C. is a terrific comedown. Everyone fat, bored, overfed, sodden with liquor and stupid," she complained to Sidney in a letter that gave a brief overview of her POW experience, which she described as "terrifically exciting and stimulating." The only drawback, she said, was that she had not been able to let him know she was safe.

She was thrilled to receive carbon copies of all the letters Sidney had written to her during her imprisonment, the originals of which were still in the hands of the Red Cross. In between lunching with friends and taking the children to an ice carnival, she began pulling strings to join him in Hawaii. Sidney had fallen in love with the place and was again entreating Gertie to make it their home. He had opened a women's ready-to-wear shop with a woman partner, and while Gertie loved the bathing suits he sent her, she needled him about his partner and tried to involve herself in the buying end of the shop. Musing over how the three years apart had changed them, Gertie wrote that only having him to love and share her life made anything worthwhile. "The children don't fill my gap, never have and never will," she wrote, frankly and rather brutally. "They are awfully sweet, but I can't be satisfied with that."

Despite her promise to Donovan to be utterly silent, Gertie was telling her story to anyone who would listen. She also dictated to a secretary an account that she hoped to sell to a magazine. She sent the manuscript to Col. Bruce for approval, and in early June a two-page memo arrived ordering removal of all references to the OSS, changing the names of her companions in the ill-fated trip to the front, and otherwise keeping to her old cover story of simply being an interpreter loaned by the U.S. Embassy. Soon she was submitting the sanitized manuscript to major magazines, including *Life* and *Collier's*.

On June 30, she got a letter from International News Service, a newspaper syndicate based in New York, that was interested in developing her story as a serial feature. She apparently submitted the manuscript with strings attached: She wanted to be dispatched to the Pacific theatre as an INS war correspondent. General manager Seymour Berkson wrote her that Guam was a possibility, and if that didn't work out, "we can then consider China, which I think is going to be very exciting during the days ahead."

In late July, Sidney came to New York to take a short-term course for his navy work and they stayed in a suite at the Carlyle Hotel. Their reunion was joyous and passionate. In a short, typed letter on August 8, the day after he left, Gertie wrote, "Do you still ache in every joint, or did you sleep on the plane without chuckling?" However, their reunion was not without its arguments. She wrote a second letter to him that night, apologizing for her "lousy jealousy streak that crops up and eats my heart out."

Nevertheless, she taunted him a bit once he got back to Hawaii and she was spending two weeks in a beach town on Long Island. Describing a party shortly before the Japanese surrender on August 14, she wrote, "I was blitzed by that Buzz bomb — Piggy Weeks who is a wild man and found myself waltzing in the hall at 3 a.m. to the accordion player." Sidney didn't take the bait, simply replying that he had met Carnes Weeks in Hawaii with Admiral Bill Halsey, whom he served as personal physician. (In a letter the previous

June, he had written to her of meeting Weeks, who was friends with Ben and Carola Kittredge and had once gone duck hunting with Laddie.) A few weeks later, she brought him up again, saying he had been a "blitzkrieg at every party and has given me a whirl," but added, "As a matter of fact this fellow is a good guy, very much like a Legendre, and a lot of fun. He has a perfectly good wife and four children which he is crazy about, so you see my beau is very harmless." Although he was not tall and slim like Sidney, Weeks did share some of his features, including dark eyes and thick, curly dark hair that he parted slightly off center.

All three would have been very surprised to know that Weeks would become Gertie's second husband in 1951.

Family members tell stories of infidelity on both sides during the three-year separation, a very long time for two healthy, relatively young people to remain celibate, especially in the sexually charged atmosphere of war zones. In a letter to Morris written in November, after he got out of the navy and permanently reunited with his jealous wife, Sidney wrote that Gertie had given him the "low down on the gossip our 'friends' had brought back from Honolulu about us, a lot of poppy cock about our having girls and all that sort of thing. People will say anything just to be able to talk." Gertie's jealousy was evident not only when it came to Sidney's attraction to other women, but to his developing business interests that weren't her idea, such as the dress shop.

With the Japanese surrender, Gertie's hopes of becoming a correspondent ended. She lamented to Sidney that no magazine wanted the story of her experience, not even *Harper's Bazaar*. She apparently took the advice of a literary agent to flesh the article out with detail into a full-length book and aim for publication in 1947, when the public would not be quite so war-weary. She did, but the reception for the resulting memoir *The Sands Ceased to Run* was still underwhelming. A publication run of a thousand copies was released in 1947. As of March 1949, only 388 copies had been sold.

By December, the Legendres were back at Medway, repairing the damages of neglect and war. Sidney wrote a jocular letter to his brother Armant in New Orleans, saying the plantation required three times the work as the navy. "It seems that I have never taken off my overalls and have killed all the guests that have come down," he wrote. "The last was very frank and wrote in the guest book 'too damn much work for me.'" He joked that he made his guests "string electric lights from hot fuse boxes" and "go into tractors until their elbows are deep in dirty oil."

The most serious problem was their home reserve lake, which Gertie described as "nothing but a muddy bog." The navy had condemned some of their property and used it for storing missiles, draining some of the land and piping the water into the lake. This blew out the banks. Although this had happened early in the war, Gertie and Sidney had decided to wait until peace came to bring suit. Their suit was successful. The government paid $33,300 in damages in 1946, and they put the lake to rights.

Sidney had begun to have a change of heart about selling the plantation — though he still did not want to make it their anchor home — due to correspondence he had begun with a consulting forester in the last year of the war. He and Gertie were pleasantly surprised to learn they could harvest selected pine timber and generate a steady income, something that had begun to worry them. Eventually, the Medway Timber Company, under Gertie's first professional land manager, Bill Baldwin, would provide some of the income they needed to maintain Medway.

They had a big Christmas, inviting Laddie and Mary and Morris and Nancy to join them, and allowing Landine to bring guests as well. By this time, Landine was enrolled in Foxcroft and Bokara in day school in Aiken; Landine with her "mademoiselle" and Bo with her nanny Mamie in attendance. Photos in Gertie's album show a typical winter at Medway, with guests coming in to hunt quail and ducks. Bokara was presented a western pony, dubbed Wyoming. Although there are many pictures in Gertie's photo albums of the girls astride mounts, both professed to hate horseback riding. The following summer, Gertie and Sidney decamped for Hawaii for two months, leaving their daughters stateside. Gertie's Hawaii album is loaded with pictures of beautiful scenery, fishing, parties, lei-making and hula-dancing. In her two-piece bathing suits, she looks tanned and trim. But for some reason — it's not clear why — they scuttled their plans to buy a home and live there. Perhaps there wasn't enough challenge for Gertie in paradise.

While they were in Hawaii, news came that Janie's husband, the Italian diplomat Mario Pansa, had died. The Pansas had coasted through the war unscathed, Mario continuing to play polo, Janie getting her hair done every week and wearing expensive clothes as usual. Apparently, his life of ease had continued after the war, for the July 10 report in the *New York Times* said Pansa had been with "a party of Romans" at a beach near Rome. He had gone for a swim while they were eating lunch, and never returned. At the time, Janie was living with Laddie and Mary on Long Island and expecting her husband to join her. She never remarried but lived in comfort and luxury to the end of her life, leaving her considerable estate to Gertie's daughters.

Even as Gertie eased back into the life of social activities and entertaining that she had so enjoyed before the war, she could not forget the desperate refugees she had seen — and been unable to help — on the roads of Germany and the people who had helped her survive her imprisonment. She corresponded regularly with the two Ursulas and Bill Gosewisch, sending them packages through the Cooperative for American Remittances for Europe, or CARE. The packages were filled with staple goods such as bacon, coffee, powdered milk, sugar and flour, as well as small luxuries such as chocolate. "Like Santa Claus in person did the postman look to us last night, when he brought a parcel sent by a Mrs. S. Legendre," Bill Gosewisch wrote in December 1946. "Gertie, Gertie, what we couldn't do to you! It's a good thing the ocean is between us otherwise, I am afraid, we all would have squeezed you to death. For a while we imagined ourselves in fairy land going through the dainty contents." Even more important, Gertie was eventually able to help Gosewisch and his family emigrate to the United States, where he worked for Morris Legendre. He was a regular visitor to Medway and sent Gertie red roses every Christmas.

She wanted to do more. Working with a Charleston friend, William Montgomery Bennett, Gertie and Sidney devised the Medway Plan, an effort to link communities in America to those in devastated Europe. They began with the city of Flers de l'Orne in Normandy, collecting over 120 tons of relief goods. The people of Flers were so grateful that they named one of their squares Place du Charleston and continue to fly the American flag beside the French one to this day. Charleston officials entertained a delegation from Flers in 2017 and installed a plaque commemorating the Medway Plan at the city's Waterfront Park.

The Medway Plan effort snowballed, eventually linking sixty-four European communities with the same number of sponsoring communities in America. "By 1951, through this process, nearly 23,000 American adults had adopted a like number of French, German, English and Austrian adults and 28,000 children in those countries as brothers and sisters," wrote Sanford family biographer Alex M. Robb. "There was no guesswork about the gifts. If little Pierre or Gretchen needed shoes, they got shoes. If Farmer Rojek needed seeds, he got seeds. There were no salaries and no fancy offices." The work continued for years after the war ended. In 1951, Gertie teamed up with her glamorous sister-in-law Mary Sanford to throw a benefit party at New York's River Club for the Medway Plan, auctioning off performances by actresses Judy Garland and Celeste Holm. Garland fetched $500 for performing a dance and another $500 for singing a song. Holm, probably best known for her part as the Bette Davis character's best friend in the Oscar-winning movie *All About Eve*, performed the Charleston. In her book *Medway*, Virginia Beach gives the Medway Plan credit for linking 304 foreign and American towns as well as settling nearly 4,000 refugees. It was a monumental philanthropic effort that Gertie didn't even mention in her autobiography. Perhaps she thought it bad form to brag about her charitable work.

The absence of danger in her everyday life made Gertie hunger for a new adventure. When the opportunity came to join an expedition to India, she jumped at it. The expedition, mounted by Yale University and the Smithsonian Institution, was led by S. Dillon Ripley, an ornithologist and at that time the associate curator of zoology of Yale's Peabody Museum. A decade younger than Gertie and Sidney, Ripley shared a common background of wealth and privilege, as well as a zest for life and curiosity about the world that would be fully realized during his twenty years as head of the Smithsonian. (Beginning in 1964, he oversaw the construction of eight new museums, a tripling of visitors and the creation of *Smithsonian* magazine.) He and his wife, Mary, had both served in the OSS during the war in Southeast Asia.

Ripley's leadership relieved Sidney and Gertie of the burden of planning the expedition and dealing with the inevitable problems. "Dillon had an extraordinary memory for history, a wealth of information on all subjects and wit and humor to boot," Gertie wrote. The final two qualities were most important when they were traveling for months "in all sorts of conditions and with all sorts of delays, disappointments and unexpected problems to contend with." Besides Ripley and the Legendres, the party numbered eighteen, including Ripley's ornithological assistant, Ed Migdalski, and native porters, skinners and bearers.

The Yale-Smithsonian Expedition to India began in December 1946 and started in Assam, a region in the northeast corner of the country that is famous for its tea. Assam had been occupied by the Allies during the war, and they had left huge amounts of surplus equipment behind. Arriving at an air base in Chabua, they discovered an abandoned military hospital and seven square miles of supplies, everything from jeeps to cases of Barbasol shaving cream. They bought a jeep and other equipment from the mountain of leftovers.

Gertie reveled in the beauty of the Himalayas and the fascinating customs and dress of the native people, as well as the opportunity to be out in the wild with her husband again. On the last night of 1946, she welcomed the new year curled up against Sidney at the base of a fallen tree trunk. She wrote in her autobiography, "Instead of popping corks, we watched the orange moon float above the silent jungle." Her autobiography bursts with details as she describes the Naga tribesmen with their Mongolian features, blue homespun tunics and ears pierced with "chunks of bone, soapstone or ivory." Head-hunting had been a tribal manhood ritual as recently as 1937, and the expedition wisely avoided areas of the jungle where it was said to continue. The other major tribe she encountered were the Mishmi, who were said to be fond of opium.

While Ripley and an ornithologist from the Bombay Museum who joined the party focused on collecting birds, Sidney and Gertie hunted for larger specimens, including a yak-like creature called a takin, sambar deer, tiger and buffalo. During part of the hunt they rode a large and fussy elephant named Alfred but there was plenty of hoofing it, and Gertie prided herself on being able to keep up. After a number of fruitless days of hunting, Sidney shot a sambar deer and he and Gertie simultaneously shot a tiger, which disappeared into the jungle. "The first lesson of big game hunting is never follow a wounded animal into thick bush," Gertie observed. That night, the tiger tracked them back to camp — they later found his paw prints overlapping their shoe prints — but something spooked him and he retreated into the jungle.

Gertie did nab one big cat on this trip, but it was, she admitted "an inglorious prize." At the end of the journey, they accepted an invitation in Calcutta to visit the palace of a young maharaja known for his carefully staged leopard hunts. Each of the nineteen guests sat on an elephant while beaters on elephants flushed animals out of the jungle. She shot a beautiful leopard, but admitted, "The whole thing was very unsporting." Her views on hunting were evolving, and she would become less and less enamored with killing as time went on, though she continued to enjoy shooting birds at Medway.

That spring, Gertie's friend Toni Frissell, a celebrated professional photographer, came to Medway and shot a spread for *Harper's Bazaar*. Bo and Frissell's daughter, Sidney, dressed in old-fashioned clothing reminiscent of Alice in Wonderland, while Landine, a leggy teen, modeled contemporary styles with a friend of her parents from Hawaii, Ruth Ackerman. Frissell took many pictures of the Legendres and their guests on quail shoots. Among the guests was Piggy Weeks, who had begun coming to Medway in late 1946 with his wife, Margaret.

The following summer, the Legendre brothers rented a house in Southampton and for the first time the two families spent a long vacation together. (Morris's wife, Nancy, had given birth to a daughter, Jeanette, during the war.) Sidney jokingly wrote to his brother Armant in New Orleans that "if the roof does not come off with two sets of nurses, two wives, two sets of children and two men looking for women, it never will." Pictures from Gertie's photo album feature Bo, winsome and adorable in a frilled bathing suit, playing with one of the dogs. "We played a great deal of tennis that summer, with Sidney winning the club singles, Morris and Sidney winning the men's doubles, and Sidney and I winning the mixed doubles," Gertie wrote.

They were back at Medway in the fall and winter, inviting friends to visit for shooting and picnicking, though Sidney and Morris made stag trips to New Orleans to see Armant in October and again for Mardis Gras in February. There the brothers rode the float of the Mystic Krewe of Comus and attended the ball. Armant, who always seemed to struggle for money, had formed a coffee importing business with a partner after the war and Sidney had made him a $25,000 loan. He also paid for Armant's daughter Katherine to attend Newcomb College, assuring Armant that once he got the coffee business on its feet, he wouldn't need any help.

Sidney's frustrated desire to go into business was finally being satisfied. In addition to the investment in Armant's coffee firm and the theater chain, he and Morris had bought the franchise for both Carolinas of a beverage-dispensing company called Drink-O-Mat. He wrote to Armant of inspecting the machines in use in Charlotte, bragging that he watched one machine "ring up 598 drinks. There was a long line of people there waiting to drop the nickels in." He was also becoming more and more immersed in the timber business and making plans to plant more pastures at Medway for

Toni Frissell photographed Gertie with, far left, Piggy Weeks, and her sister Janie preparing for a quail hunt. Landine and Bokara are in the wagon.

cattle grazing.

In a humorous letter to Armant that winter of 1948, he told of being invited to speak at a forestry association meeting in Valdosta, Georgia, and convincing Gertie to go with him. Once they made the three hundred-mile drive, though, no one in Valdosta seemed to know anything about the meeting. He finally produced the letter of invitation and discovered that while the organization was indeed headquartered in Valdosta, the meeting was being held in Jackson, Mississippi, five hundred miles away. "When I read that Gertrude let out such a shout that you could have heard it back at Medway," Sidney wrote. "She roared with laughter for at least half an hour... Now whenever I say anything, Gertrude just says, 'Remember Valdosta.'"

In a letter dated March 1, 1948, Sidney detailed a long and exhausting business trip that had taken him from Charleston to Charlotte to New York, where he had raised Cain at the Drink-O-Mat corporation about delayed delivery of machines and done some buying for the dress shop he still owned in Hawaii. Then he had taken the night train to Boston to the Drink-O-Mat factory to be sure the machines were being prepared as promised. From there he returned to Charlotte for a day inspecting vending machines, arriving home at midnight to tumble into bed.

He was hoping for another visit to New Orleans with Morris in the spring. "We are all breaking up so quickly that I want to grasp every possible moment together, because those are the times I enjoy the most," he wrote Armant. As usual, he signed the letter, "Love, Sidney."

14

Widow, Bride, Divorcée

———— • ————

At Foxcroft School, Headmistress Charlotte Noland put all her students in uniforms and had them drill with wooden guns. They also marched to their meals. Fourteen-year-old Landine Legendre was marching to breakfast the morning of March 8, 1948 when she suddenly said aloud, "My father just died." Her premonition was correct. Half an hour later she was called to Miss Charlotte's office and given the sad news that Sidney Legendre had suffered a fatal heart attack at Medway. He was forty-seven years old.

"Memories push time together," Gertie wrote in *The Time of My Life*. "It seemed that I had only been back a moment with Sidney when, suddenly, he was gone forever. One morning in March 1948, with no particular warning other than his complaining about feeling a little out of sorts, he died." A heart attack had already claimed the life of Hennen Legendre at forty-six years of age, and was most likely the cause of the sudden death of their mother at forty-five.

Bokara, then seven, was living in Aiken with her nanny, Mamie, when she got the word. Mamie gently told her that her father had died, and Bokara remembered feeling nothing. "To me, my father was practically a stranger," she wrote in her autobiography *Not What I Expected*. Both girls were brought home for the funeral, attended by members of the Sanford and Legendre families and dozens of friends. Everyone made a fuss over Bokara, passing her from lap to lap, and, to her surprise, her mother allowed her dog Timmie into the living room and even patted his head. (In Bokara's telling, Timmie was the only dog Gertie ever met that she didn't like.)

The next morning, she walked between Gertie and her Uncle Morris to an open grave on the plantation grounds. Standing there, she was astonished to realize she was being stared at by dozens of people. "As the coffin was lowered into the grave, I had to struggle to keep from grinning over the fact that, at last, I was a part of my family," she wrote.

Neither Landine nor Bokara remember their mother crying over her husband's death, but it was a devastating blow that she addressed with simple eloquence in her autobiography. "After Sidney's death, I lost track of time for a while, but I knew that Sidney wouldn't want me to give up Medway and wouldn't want me to stop living as we had lived," she wrote. "Still, it was nearly a year before I traveled again." She apparently made little effort to comfort her children or create a home for them. As she had written to Sidney during the war, she needed a partner, and children did not fill the gap.

After the service, which included the singing of spirituals led by the plantation's black staff and concluded with Gertie firing a shotgun, Bokara learned she would be returning to Aiken that afternoon. She and Mamie stopped on the way home at a lunch counter for grilled cheese sandwiches and chocolate milk shakes. "I wasn't part of the family after all," she concluded. Landine returned to Foxcroft, the first place she remembered being happy and making friends. She adored headmistress Charlotte Noland, as her mother had, calling her "a fabulous woman." Trying to be adventurous like her mother, she once ran away from school but got only as far as Washington, D.C. She placed a collect call to Foxcroft, where Miss Charlotte instructed her to take a taxi back to school, where she would be waiting. They had hot cocoa together and talked about places they hoped to travel. She was surprised to learn the headmistress wanted to take a ride in a rocket ship.

Within five years, Landine had escaped into marriage with another unhappy young person from an upper-class family. Bokara would spend the rest of her life bidding for her mother's attention and trying to find a home, a suitable man, a calling and spiritual fulfillment.

Gertie filled the first few weeks of Sidney's absence with ambitious projects. She gave a benefit for a medical relief fund at Medway, featuring "the serving of tea and the presentation of songs by the plantation negroes." In a letter written on March 29, her forty-sixth birthday, she thanked Sidney's brother Armant and his wife Olive for the big box of fruit and candy that arrived at Medway for Easter. She had thrown the traditional egg hunt among the azalea bushes for the children and the day had been beautiful. "Morris and I have chosen a very nice, simple, gray-blue marble slab for Sidney's grave and have dug up over 2,000 old bricks on the plantation to build a low wall around it," she wrote. "I have received hundreds and hundreds of letters from Sidney and my friends, and they pay wonderful tribute to Sidney." Morris was coming to Medway every weekend to help her sort through affairs of the plantation that Sidney had managed. "I am going to stay on here through April and carry out Sidney's plans for planted pastures for the cattle and hope it will turn out the way he wanted it to be," she wrote.

Toward the end of the letter, Gertie said she also planned to edit Sidney's plantation diary and have bound copies made for everyone in the family. It had to be a heart-breaking experience, especially when she came to passages like this one from December 1940:

How insignificant our lives are beside the sands, the granite, the virgin forests, the vast swamps of the earth. How we hurry towards our humble destiny filled with the belief that our passing is fraught with significance. But then it is to us. Our dreams, our passions, our existence are far more real to us than those sands and forests. Our tiny world encompassed by the walls of our house is more impervious than the globe on whose surface we live. For the marvel of a house is not that it shelters or warms a man, nor that its walls belong to him. It is that to him it embodies all that is worthwhile in the world. It is his castle to which he may return at night raising the drawbridge behind him against the failures of the day. Within its warm clasp lies the woman that he loves. She is the key that unlocks all the pleasures of the earth, her arms about him draw out the pains and disappointments. The laughter in her eyes, the softness of her lips, the bewitching curves of her body are the beginning and end of all his emotions. Show me a man who says that his pleasures are intellectual, and I will show you a gelding.

As a young widow, Gertie joined legions of American women who had lost their men during the war. Closer to home, she also had sister Janie as an example, and soon her good friend Ellen Barry would be a widow, when her playwright husband Philip died of a heart attack at age fifty-three. It wasn't much solace.

When Gertie accepted an invitation from Dillon Ripley to join an expedition to Nepal in early 1949, she was acutely aware that she was traveling alone for the first time. "It was to be a trip of firsts," she wrote in her autobiography, "my first without Sidney and my first prolonged transatlantic flight." Shortly before her departure in January, she contacted her Charleston attorney, George Buist, to revise her will, specifically to appoint guardians for her children "in case anything happens to me." Two of the guardians she chose were not surprising — her brother-in-law Morris and Charlotte Noland. The third was: Dr. Carnes "Piggy" Weeks. Although Weeks was married, his relationship with Gertie had apparently evolved to the point that she felt comfortable entrusting the future of not only her children but her home to him. He had been at Medway in January shortly before she departed for Nepal. Gertie took pictures of him grilling steaks outdoors and giving Landine tips on shooting, his arms around her to position the gun. The provisional will Buist drafted stipulated the three guardians would "determine what should be done with the plantation" until both girls had reached age twenty-one and could decide about Medway for themselves.

With the legalities covered, Gertie began a long and unpleasant trip on the Pan Am Clipper out of New York. She was vastly irritated by a loud-mouthed fellow traveler who boarded in New York, cold fish and overcooked meat in Brussels and a delay necessitated by a broken cockpit window that led to her spending the night in a hotel whose bathroom lacked towels, toilet paper and hot water. It was raining everywhere they landed. "All of the delays and stopovers in the past had been endurable with Sidney," she wrote. "Now I was disinclined to go out and see the local sights or visit the local night spot and see Fatima wiggle her fat hips to tinny Arab music."

Things perked up considerably in Calcutta, where she made her rendezvous with Kurt Wentzel, a young photographer with *National Geographic* who was also joining the expedition. He had been sitting in the hotel lobby all day, checking out every woman who came in the doors. "It was like having a blind date," she wrote. "He was a bright-eyed, thirty-three-year-old with a good sense of humor. I was relieved." Things got even better when they reached the camp near the village of Jagbani, where they found Ripley and his assistant Ed Migdalski, who she knew from the 1947 expedition to Assam. Once again, Gertie was the only woman in the company of interesting men. They included Howie Weaver and Dick Mack, both recent graduates of Yale, and Francis Leeson, an Englishman who had been stationed with the British Army in Pakistan after the war.

Gertie seemed quite taken with Dick Mack. "Dick had done the kinds of things that I might have done, had I been a man. He was only twenty-three, but he'd driven trucks for a hauling company from California to Mexico and had guided fishing parties on the MacKenzie River [in Canada]," she wrote. "Then he was a cow-hand on his father's ranch before going to Yale and graduating with a degree in psychology." She didn't mention it in her autobiography, but Mack was a member of the secretive student club Skull and Bones at Yale, in the same class year with a future president of the United States, George H.W. Bush. She also didn't mention that more than twenty years after they met, he became her son-in-law. Bokara was Mack's fourth wife, described the marriage as "a terrible mistake" and later came to believe her mother had slept with Mack during her widowhood.

In addition to the expedition team, they had a small army of servants, including sixty-two porters, each of whom was expected to carry sixty pounds on his back. Their first day's trek was eight miles on foot, up and down steep grades. The pattern continued, accompanied by colder and worsening weather. One night, Wentzel's tent collapsed during a hailstorm and the next days they trekked through ice and slush. The westerners at least had warm clothes and rubber-soled boots. "The coolies shivered in their thin, white clothes and bare feet," Gertie wrote. "I slept in a cashmere undershirt, flannel pajamas and several layers of sweaters in my sleeping bag on top of my fur coat." She helped doctor the porters' feet and kept the liquor flowing for the westerners.

On the rare occasions when the clouds parted, and they got a glimpse of Mount Everest, everyone grabbed their cameras and took pictures. "Dillon informed me that I was the first white woman to see the south face of Everest," Gertie wrote proudly. "Wherever we went, scores of natives came and stood on the edge of camp to inspect us." After a six-and-a-half-inch snowfall, the porters mutinied. The specimen hunting had been poor; they said the goddess Blendini didn't want them hunting in her preserve. The party descended 6,000 feet into the heart of Nepal, where Ripley said they were the first white people other than a geologist to visit. "Dillon was full of that kind of information and thrilled us with it," Gertie wrote.

During this leg of the trip, Gertie experienced the only serious injury of any of her expeditions, and she blamed herself entirely. She and Kurt Wentzel climbed to a village that was "bleak and covered in a chilling fog." They accepted an invitation from a Nepalese woman to come into her hut and warm up with rice wine. Many drinks later, they emerged into the dusk, and decided to "skip, hand-in-hand, downhill. We didn't see the edge of the steep terrace

The Nepal expedition team, middle row from left, was Francis Leeson, Kurt Wentzel, Gertie with her dog Boolie, S. Dillon Ripley, Ed Migdalski, Howie Weaver and Dick Mack.

of the rice paddy until we were tumbling through the air." Gertie broke her collarbone and Wentzel cracked three ribs. Rather than being sympathetic, Dillon Ripley was furious and cut them no slack as the expedition moved on. They had to grin and bear it.

In Dharan, Gertie visited in the tent of a Nepalese princess and her ladies, where she apologized for her wrinkled khakis and complimented them on their glowing silk brocade saris. They responded by giving the saris to her as a gift. She responded with the only appropriate item she had, a bottle of Elizabeth Arden nail polish. Gertie, who never seemed to meet a dog she didn't like — except Bokara's Timmie — took up with a Nepalese terrier and insisted on bringing him along with her. "Boolie" caused all sorts of problems in camp — he particularly hated the cook — and the only way she was allowed to get the dog on the plane for home was by threatening to wire Pan Am president Juan Trippe, a good friend. Boolie flew home sitting in the captain's lap.

As the expedition ended, Gertie made a side-trip with Dick Mack, visiting the remote city of Kathmandu. Getting there required a long train trip, followed by a dusty ride in a station wagon and a final ascent on the backs of ponies. They stayed as guests of the maharaja and were given an audience with King Mahendra. "I wore a hat, gloves and my best dress and Dick wore his grey flannel suit," Gertie wrote. The king received them in a "French living room crammed with overstuffed gold chairs," wearing a "knee-length blue overcoat, white jodhpurs and yellow shoes." The charming king sent her away with lovely gifts and fond memories of his beautiful country, but she never kept her promise to return to Kathmandu. She reflected, "Even then, the corrugated tin roofs were beginning to replace the ancient tiles. It's a mistake to return to paradise. I've never found it looking back. It's always just ahead."

Gertie parted from Dick Mack, and she and Boolie made one last excursion before flying home. She visited a coffee plantation in Mysore, India, owned by a friend of a friend, located in excellent game country. She spent many afternoons and evenings hunting with her British host, Ralph Morris, and her trophies included a large bison. But even as Gertie posed for a photograph with the downed bull, she was feeling uneasy about what she was doing. She missed two shots at a tiger and wrote that she was "relieved." She reflected, "When you come to the final moment, when the hunt is over and the prize is within reach, the truth dawns on you that you don't really want what you thought you wanted at all. What matters is the pursuit of it." Gertie wasn't quite ready to put down her big guns, but she was close. More and more, she chose to shoot with a camera.

She returned to Medway from her safari in good health other than the collar bone that mended improperly and made her wince every time she swung a golf club for the rest of her life. In November, she received a postcard from Piggy Weeks that was casual in tone: "Hi, Pal. I miss you. Mag [his wife, Margaret] is in Pittsburgh as her mother is worse again. Had a big snow, but it's all gone. Shooting has been good. How are things down there — swell I believe. Must be plenty of ducks by now." He closed by disclosing plans to arrive by train on New Year's Day 1950, signing it, "Lots of love. Pig. Write!"

By June 1950, there was no pretense about Gertie being just a "pal." A brief letter Weeks wrote to her c/o the Morgan & Cie bank at Place Vendome in Paris is addressed to "Darling." He began, "Just a line to tell you I love you." He was facing surgery the next day, what he hoped would be a "final operation on my belly. This is the big one so keep your fingers crossed. As long as it stops the frightful pain I've had and the draining of bile I don't care what else happens." He thanked her for the carnations she had sent, and continued, "Oh Gertie, I hope the future has something in store for us. All my love Pig." A postscript scrawled up the side of the letter says, ""Tomorrow's op is no picnic, I know I'll come through fine but if I don't. You know I've loved you since the day I met you."

The nature of Weeks's health problems is a little fuzzy. In her autobiography, Gertie said he developed hypertension during the war and that he had undergone spinal surgery in London that made him "jittery." Neither seems to be related to the condition he is describing in this 1950 letter. However, whether it was nerves or pain, the result was that Weeks heavily self-medicated with both alcohol and morphine. He eventually became his own best patient. "The doses increased and increased and, soon, there never seemed to be enough," Gertie wrote.

Gertie's tone when writing about Piggy Weeks is regretful. She describes him as "a brilliant New York surgeon" whose life "was meant to be exceptional." Born in Cedarhurst, Long Island in 1901, he had graduated from the exclusive St. Paul's School and Yale, earning his medical degree at Columbia University in 1923. From there he interned at Bellevue Hospital and Presbyterian Hospital in New York and taught at Columbia. He and his wife, the former Margaret Shoemaker, had four children, including a son, Carnes Weeks Jr., who also became a physician. They had a home in New York and a farm in Woodbury, Connecticut.

When World War II began, Weeks enlisted in the navy and received the rank of lieutenant commander in the medical corps. (Sidney Legendre met him in Honolulu in 1944 when he came to dinner with another officer at the apartment Sidney shared with Morris.) In late 1943, Weeks met Admiral William "Bull" Halsey at a cocktail party on the island and apparently impressed him so much that he made him his personal physician as well as the medical officer for the Third Fleet he commanded. As personal physician, Weeks's duties went far beyond taking the admiral's blood pressure and prescribing aspirin for his hangovers.

"Wisecracking and determinedly, if somewhat maniacally, upbeat, Weeks functioned as a kind of all-purpose morale officer for the staff," wrote Evan Thomas in his book *Sea of Thunder*. "He wrote funny, ribald diagnoses of their various ailments, which usually seemed to center around sexual deprivation." Although alcohol had been banned from navy ships since Josephus Daniels was secretary of the navy in the Wilson administration — his insistence on serving nothing stronger than coffee was the genesis of the drink's nickname "cup of Joe" — Halsey's flag ship was well-stocked with scotch and bourbon. Even in times of combat, Weeks helped the admiral sleep at night by dosing him with whiskey, reasoning that he could awaken more quickly from an alcohol-induced sleep than one promulgated by sleeping pills.

Weeks was aboard the USS *New Jersey* on October 23, 1944 when an exhausted and ill Halsey made the fatal decision to chase glory and Japanese aircraft carriers north of the Philippines rather than use his ships to guard the San Bernardino Strait during the Battle of Leyte Gulf. "Medicated" by Weeks, he sought a few hours of uninterrupted sleep, and his staff was unwilling to wake him even when it became evident the carriers were a Japanese decoy and the Third Fleet was greatly needed elsewhere. The second-string fleet headed by Admiral Thomas Kinkaid was pummeled by the Japanese navy, with many of the men on one sunken ship left in the water to be devoured by sharks. Although the battle was a clear American victory, Halsey's blunder dogged him for the rest of his life.

Weeks's other duty as "morale officer" was to see that Halsey had female company. The admiral's nicknames "Bull" and "Big Bill" came not only from his reputation as a hell-for-leather commander but for his prowess as a sailor with a girl in every port. After Leyte Gulf, hoping to cheer up the morose admiral, Weeks organized a party. He wrote his wife that he was "getting some nurses from a hospital ship — God help them, the nurses I mean!" The party was described in detail by one attendee, who witnessed a burning cigarette setting off a fire in a trash can. An officer put out the fire with the aid of a CO_2 bottle. "Then he pushed the nozzle up the dress of one of the nurses and squirted her between the legs. She let out a scream as the dry ice burned. Other snockered officers grabbed CO2 bottles and started chasing nurses around the wardroom." Weeks's account of the party to his wife was rather more general. "The nurses were grand, good sports — they had been working very hard with the wounded and were just as ready for a break as we were."

Weeks's son, Carnes Weeks, Jr., a marine corporal, was also pressed into service to minister to Halsey's libido. Invited to have drinks with the admiral during shore leave in San Francisco, the younger Weeks was ordered to guard Halsey's door after the cocktail party ended. In an interview with Evan Thomas, he recalled, "Inside I could hear him down on all fours barking like a dog with this nice lady who was his friend for the evening."

By the time Gertie met Piggy on Long Island in August 1945, he was no longer serving with Halsey — his old boss was still in the Pacific and witnessed the Japanese surrender in Tokyo Bay on September 2 — but had reopened his surgical practice in New York. He closed it prior to marrying Gertie on March 29, 1951 in a small ceremony at Medway, having obtained a divorce from Margaret in Las Vegas the previous December. Black and white photographs capture a happy occasion: Gertie wearing a cocktail dress with full skirt and sawtooth neckline, Piggy a three-piece pinstripe suit. In one photo they both raised their hemlines to show they are wearing garters. In another, they cut the cake in the dining room under the watchful eye of Sidney's portrait in his hunting clothes. It gives a new meaning to the words "shotgun wedding."

Morris Legendre gave away the bride, and Landine and Bokara served as attendants. By then Bokara was attending day school in Charleston, living in a small cottage downtown with her nanny, next door to Ben and Carola Kittredge's daughter, also named Carola, and *her* nanny. At Charleston Day School, Bokara told classmates she was adopted; her true identity was that of a Russian princess. Landine, a freshman at Bryn Mawr, was violently opposed to the marriage. "He was horrible," she said of Weeks, who she was convinced was after Gertie's money. Her mother, she said, could be very naïve about men. Gertie took Weeks's name but within a very short time she realized she had made a serious mistake. An unspecified health problem cut short their honeymoon in Norway so that Weeks could seek treatment at the Mayo Clinic. Bokara recalled that he came down with chicken pox.

At their Medway wedding, Gertie and Piggy, with Bokara, left, and Landine, were all smiles. It didn't turn out so well.

In the first year of their marriage, they built a rustic log cabin overlooking the home reserve lake, within view of the main house. Though the cabin was indeed made of logs, it was hardly humble: the main room was forty by sixty feet, making it ideal for large parties, as well as an appropriate display place for her collection of animal trophies, including many mounted heads, elephant tusks and a tiger skin. There was a broad terrace for al fresco drinking and dining, a covered grill area, and two detached bedrooms and a bathroom. The log cabin became Gertie's primary entertainment venue, the location of her annual New Year's Eve costume party, dinner parties, charity benefits, family reunions and weddings, birthday gatherings and barbecues for her grandchildren and their friends.

While married to Sidney, Gertie spent the summer months away from Medway traveling and visiting friends and family, the itinerary different each year. Seeking a summer anchor after her second marriage, Gertie bought a home on Fishers Island, an isolated, WASP-y enclave on Long Island Sound, reachable, then and now, only by private plane or ferry from New London, Connecticut. The island, known for its relaxed atmosphere, natural beauty and world-class golf course, had a year-round population of about five hundred that more than doubled in the summer months, including Piggy's old commander, Admiral Halsey. Gertie bought a mid-century modern beach-front house on Chocomount Beach on the southern underbelly of the island and added a wing to accommodate Piggy. The wide, white sand beach is edged with large, smooth rocks and pebbles and strewn with driftwood, slipper shells and mermaid's purses. Gertie loved to sit on her patio and inhale the sweet scent of white and pink wild roses and honeysuckle and hear the birdsong. She spent summers at Fishers Island for the rest of her life, swimming every morning in the ice-cold water.

Her daughters were regular visitors to Fishers Island — Landine ultimately settled in a nearby town in Connecticut — but they much preferred spending time in Palm Beach with their Uncle Laddie and Aunt Mary at their Los Incas estate. Laddie and Mary did not have children of their own but doted on their nieces. Landine said she learned many of her social graces from Mary, things her mother never had the time or inclination to teach her, like not running up the long-distance phone bill when you are a guest in someone's home. Mary also instructed her to pay attention and be charming to Laddie, to sing for her supper, so to speak. "Laddie was spoiled rotten," Landine said. "Aunt Mary handled him fabulously… Laddie would act badly, which he would do all the time, with other women, and she would get jewelry each time. So the amount of jewelry she had was staggering." Mary loaned huge diamonds to Landine to wear to polo matches. "I just thought I was the cat's meow, but I must have looked like a total idiot," Landine said with a rueful grin. Mary's advice to Bokara was, "Collect jewels; they never lose their value." Laddie was still playing polo in the early 1950s, but eventually injuries and his own excesses landed him in a wheelchair, partly paralyzed, for at least the last fifteen years of his life. He still managed to hunt, fish and have affairs, a bon vivant until his death in 1977.

The charms of Medway and Fishers Island weren't enough to keep Gertie from seeking adventure and thrills. Shortly after their wedding, the Weekses began making plans for a trip to Africa, signing up for an eight-week expedition jointly sponsored by the American Museum of Natural History — home of her beloved mountain nyala group — and the National Geographic Society. In her autobiography, Gertie described this as an attempt to save their marriage. "I had tried everything else," she wrote. The trip reunited her with an old friend, Donald Carter, who had traveled with her and Sidney to Africa and French Indochina, as well as Kurt Wentzel, the *National Geographic* photographer who shared broken bones with her in Nepal. As one of the objectives of the trip was to fill in some of the gaps in the museum's ornithology collection, a bird artist, Walt Weber, was also on board. Gertie's duties included recording bird calls, so she got some training prior to departure from two famous ornithologists from Cornell University. As she explained, "I've always believed in going to experts for advice." For the first time, she was also to document the lives of what one newspaper account described as "human inhabitants of the area" through photography and recordings of native dialect and music. She brought along one of the new Polaroid Land cameras, which could produce prints about a minute after they were taken.

Gertie and Piggy, Donald Carter and Walt Weber departed New York on April 20, 1952 for what was then called French Equatorial Africa. That long-gone colony encompassed the present-day countries Chad, the Central African Republic, Cameroon, the Republic of the Congo and Gabon. They landed in Leopoldville, Gertie reflecting on her grandfather Henry Sanford's role in colonizing the Belgian Congo seventy years before. Their next leg took them to Fort Archambault — Sarh in present-day Chad — where they were met by two jeeps, a truck and a group of naked native men, their bodies smeared with red clay, their faces covered in masks. They became the first human inhabitants the expedition documented.

Over the next few weeks, Gertie and Kurt Wentzel took pictures of Ubangi women with their huge lips distended by balsa wood plates, a wild tribal dance and music spectacle she called a *tamtam* and mostly naked natives fishing with woven baskets and nets. The pictures in her album document the proud and noble faces of her African subjects, as well as plenty of bare breasts. (This was the buttoned-up fifties, after all, when many an adolescent boy employed *National Geographic* to fuel his sexual fantasies.) Gertie's account of the trip, "Into the Heart of Africa," appeared in the magazine in August 1956, and she gave a talk as part of the National Geographic's 65th Annual Lecture Course in 1952.

As a seasoned explorer, Gertie was prepared for hot weather, but her husband was not. The oppressive heat bothered everyone, but Piggy worst of all. Gertie wrote, "A poor sleeper, exhausted by the tracking, he was often irritated and on edge. The trip was clearly no fun for him or for anyone else with him, so he finally decided to fly back to Europe… He preferred to go and I, to stay. Perhaps I knew then that our marriage was over."

The safari continued, with two especially memorable events. A rogue bull elephant was causing problems for villagers and Gertie was asked to shoot it. She brought him down with one shot and the dead elephant was soon covered by natives "fighting for the choice fillets." A picture in her album shows a line of men walking away with baskets of meat on their heads. One man balances an elephant foot on his. "Kurt filmed the entire bloody spectacle, but his magazine evidently decided that it was too gory for public consumption because they never ran the pictures," Gertie wrote. She never shot another elephant.

The second memorable event was traveling to Rei Bouba, a mysterious French-administered territory about the size of Belgium ruled in medieval splendor by a Muslim sultan. Emissaries dressed in red plush dressing gowns and matching fezes welcomed them to his kingdom. Next came horses for them to ride into the mountains along with mounted escorts dressed in colorful padded coats and chain mail, like members of the Crusades. The sultan himself greeted them from a golden palanquin, a golden parasol held over his head and a translator groveling at his feet. He was six-feet-six-inches tall and draped in white cloth "like an Arab."

Over the following days, the members of the expedition were treated to feasting and another *tamtam*. They also exchanged gifts. Gertie's present of a cigarette lighter was the sultan's favorite, and he invited her into his hut to photograph his wives — a tremendous privilege. She took Polaroid pictures of each woman, which amused the king. The pictures never left the hut; the women were for his eyes alone. Gertie recorded the harem chanting, and playing back the tape, she was "reminded of this enchanted kingdom with its medieval costumes and its giant, benevolent king propped up on his brass bed among the languid harem like a painting by Delacroix."

The official expedition concluded with the visit to Rei Bouba, but Gertie was not ready to go home. She and Kurt Wentzel decided to extend their trip by visiting Lambaréné in Gabon and the hospital of Dr. Albert Schweitzer, a revered but controversial figure, both then and now. The Alsatian-born medical missionary first came to Africa in 1913 and had been there continuously since 1924, funding his work with donations, book royalties and speaking fees. Gertie had supported his hospital for some time, including donating for the treatment of lepers. A polymath, Schweitzer was a physician, preacher, philosopher and gifted organist. In 1953, the year after Gertie met him, he was awarded the Nobel Peace Prize. Gertie counted him among the great men of her time, along with Winston Churchill and Gen. George C. Marshall. "He was imperious, authoritative and a determined dreamer," she wrote. At their initial meeting, she couldn't believe the stooped, weary-looking man with the thick moustache and the white pith helmet could possibly be the celebrated Dr. Schweitzer.

During her stay, Gertie observed surgeries in the primitive operating room, including the removal of a tumor the size of a coconut. "Dr. Percy [a Hungarian staff surgeon] simply popped it out like a cork from a bottle," she remembered. "Miraculously, I remained on my feet." She joined the staff for their highly regimented meals and listened to complaints from one of the young doctors about Schweitzer's shortcomings. This American doctor said Schweitzer refused to modernize — he pedaled a stationary bicycle to generate electricity in the operating room — and patronized the natives his hospital served, declaring they were ignorant and incapable of change. Schweitzer told her much the same thing about the natives himself. Gertie appreciated the criticism but found Schweitzer and his endlessly churning mind fascinating. They had wide-ranging conversations at night about subjects that included Einstein's Theory of Relativity. "When he tried to explain it to me, I tried not to look totally blank," she admitted.

Schweitzer's reverence for all life — human and animal — was evident in the compound at Lamberéné, where Gertie was told to lock her door at night to avoid a close encounter with a pet gorilla. "Animals were everywhere underfoot," she wrote, observing goats and cats, a bush buck, a white marabou stork, chickens and several dogs. She did not say if Schweitzer's philosophy influenced her own decision to stop hunting, but the trip to Africa was the last where she killed game other than birds. From that point on, her focus steadily veered toward preserving life rather than preserving animal heads.

Gertie had a second encounter with Schweitzer at his home in Gunsbach, France the following year that fed her music-lover's soul. He invited her to join him in the chapel on his property where, sharing the wooden organ bench, he played music by J.S. Bach for her; on top of everything else, he was one of the foremost modern interpreters of the works of the German composer. "Now that is a memory unequalled in my life," she wrote.

She needed good memories to sustain her, for life with Piggy went from bad to worse. Desperate to make a home away from her stepfather, Landine, who was just nineteen, accepted a proposal of marriage from her boyfriend, Peter Wood, planning the January 24, 1953 ceremony with her governess. Not only was Gertie not involved in planning the wedding, Landine wasn't even sure her mother would attend the ceremony at St. James' Church, the same church where she had married Sidney in 1929. Gertie arrived at the last minute. Her Uncle Morris gave her away and Bokara served as her maid of honor. Landine presented Gertie with her first grandchild, Peter Harrison Sanford Wood — known as Sandy — in March 1954, followed by a granddaughter, Wendeney Legendre Wood — or Wendy — in October 1955.

The nature of life with Piggy Weeks is summarized in a letter from his New York physician to Gertie early in 1955 and with a memory Landine shared. Dr. George Eaton Daniels wrote in response to a letter from Gertie, "I was greatly encouraged on the whole with your report and would agree with you that Dr. Weeks's inability to handle anything which he considers may be criticism is due to his not being entirely himself yet. For the time being, therefore, it would be important to keep such questions to the minimum and to those that are most essential. However, if he continues to hold his own and further improve, it will be important that he develop more ability for give and take." Dr. Daniels was pleased that Weeks had gotten involved in the Medway timber operation and hoped he could continue to "keep himself occupied with some constructive activity." To imagine Gertie holding her tongue when she felt someone else was wrong is to know how hopeless the prognosis was. Landine recalled visiting Medway with her husband and Weeks blaming the liquor bottles left behind in a duck blind on Peter Wood. They were his, of course.

The marriage went out with a bang rather than a whimper, less than five years after it began. The family tells of a wild night when Weeks had become so irrational that he had to be locked outside the Medway gates. Bokara said he tried to poison her mother. Morris, always Gertie's rock during a crisis, had died in a plane crash just a few weeks after Landine's wedding, so she turned to another man — Landine believes it was a highly placed government official in Washington — to get him off her land. Weeks was awarded alimony in the divorce. He eventually remarried and died in 1968. His physician son, Carnes Weeks Jr., who remained on friendly terms with Gertie, became a specialist in addictions treatment. He was a founder of the McCall Center for Behavioral Health in Torrington, Connecticut; its inpatient treatment facility is named the Carnes Weeks Center.

In 1964, when 27-year-old Doris Walters became Gertie's secretary, she was instructed to purge the office files of any mention of Weeks. Walters wanted to know what she was throwing away, so, with Gertie's permission, she read the correspondence, including "fatherly" letters to Landine and Bokara. Despite the stories she had heard, she said to Gertie, "I think I would have liked him." Her employer's response surprised her: She would have, Gertie said; it was the addiction that ruined him.

Doris gathered something else from conversations with long-time planta-tion employees that made her sympathize with Weeks. He had given up his career to come to Medway and Gertie would not allow him to change or do anything; Medway was her show.

After the divorce, Gertie took back her Legendre surname and never embarked on another serious romantic relationship, although she enjoyed the company of men to the end of her life. In her autobiography, written when she was eighty-five, she confessed how much she still missed Sidney. "Every evening, I sit at one end of the dining room table facing his portrait. He stands there in his shooting jacket with a gun over his shoulder, looking cool and detached at the portrait behind me — that of a young, confident woman looking less like me than I remember. Sidney is exactly as he was. I have no memory of his aging. In my mind, I shall always be married to a young and vital man who sees only the youth in me."

When Gertie was in her nineties and recovering from a bout of pneumonia at Medway, her adult grandson Sandy Wood knocked on her bedroom door to check on her. He heard her say, "Is that you, Sidney?"

15

Second Act

———— • ————

When Gertie published *The Time of My Life* in 1987, she concluded with her 1952 meeting with Albert Schweitzer, dealing with the subsequent thirty-five years of her life in a two-page epilogue and a few references earlier in the book. She lived a dozen years after her autobiography's publication. However, she hardly considered herself in decline or irrelevant after 1952. Indeed, she spent the remainder of her life at center stage in three arenas: grandmother to four adoring grandchildren, grande dame of Charleston society, and a respected leader of the conservation movement on the South Carolina coast. Her accomplishments, besides publishing her autobiography at age eighty-five, included mounting her first one-woman art show at age eighty-two and spearheading an acclaimed Charleston production of *Porgy and Bess* at age eighty-three. Her greatest regret, expressed very seldom, was her often fraught relationship with her daughters and the family turmoil that ensued when she decided to leave Medway in the hands of Bokara.

Gertie clearly favored her youngest daughter from an early age. In letters to Sidney during the war, she criticized and complained about Landine while sharing cute anecdotes about little Bo. Bokara resembled her physically and had her "zest for life," Gertie wrote in her autobiography. "When she wants something from me, she knows exactly how to get it. I guess that she is more like me than I care to admit." As Bokara grew into adulthood, friends often commented on their similarities, from their appearance and throaty voices to their love of the spotlight; when they were together, they competed to be the center of attention. However, Bokara's account of her relationship with "Mummy" told in her autobiography *Not What I Expected* is mostly an angry screed about being ignored, manipulated and bullied. Her lifelong friend Carola Kittredge Lott, who had similarly distant parents, sighed when asked why Bokara so resented her mother. "Shrinks do damage," she said. "I always thought that [when she got into analysis] it put a bee in her bonnet." Lott adored Gertie, saying, without any irony, that Gertie treated her "like a daughter." When Gertie was in her early nineties, Lott wrote a glowing article about her for *Town & Country* magazine titled "Charleston's Grandest Dame."

Gertie's insistence that Bokara attend Foxcroft School led to the most miserable chapter of her life. She entered the school in 1954, minus her nanny, Mamie, and her dog, Timmie, who went to Medway to live. She hated the paramilitary regimentation at Foxcroft, thought headmistress Charlotte Noland was a kook, made few friends and consoled herself with food, sometimes stuffing stale tea sandwiches into her mouth while hiding in a supply closet. She barely graduated in 1957 and because of her poor academic record there was no thought of college. Instead, she dabbled in theater and journalism, never sticking with one career for long. Depending on how you look at it, she lived a life of searching, or a life of dilettantism.

About the time Bokara graduated from Foxcroft, Landine's first marriage ended. In 1959 she married Peter Manigault, the publisher of Charleston's family-owned newspaper, *The Post and Courier.* She gave birth to a daughter, Gabrielle Hamilton Manigault, known as Gay, in 1960, and a son, named simply Pierre, in 1962. The children of her first marriage, Sandy and Wendy, were shuffled around between their father in the northeast and their mother in Charleston and, much like Landine and Bokara, were cared for by English and French nannies and attended boarding schools.

In 1963, Gertie took twenty-three-year-old Bokara on a round-the-world trip, flying first-class on Pan Am. In her autobiography, Bokara complained that the two-month trip doomed a serious romance she was having and that her mother probably just "wanted a companion she could order about." But she conceded, "Mummy was at her best *en voyage*, unfazed by delays, inedible food and bathroom showers that drenched our beds in Afghanistan." During stops in Bali, Cambodia, Thailand and India, Bokara had eye-opening experiences touring temples, lunching with the legendary silk entrepreneur Jim Thompson (an old OSS friend of Gertie's who mysteriously disappeared in 1967), visiting an Indian maharaja, and riding camels to view the pyramids of Egypt. She said she was grateful she got to visit these places "BT," shorthand Gertie used that stood for "before tourists." At the pyramids, she wrote, "There were so few tourists at the time, we saw nothing but sand and one lone Egyptian visitor astride a lonely camel." Their travels took them to Ethiopia, where Gertie had been so enthralled with Emperor Haile Selassie as a young woman, and to Venice, where she rented a house with her friend Ellen Barry, and Bokara made friends among the rising new jet set.

Gertie's diaries and photo albums over the next three decades cover a dizzying portion of the globe. (During one of her trips in the early 1960s, she threw her cigarettes overboard a ship and went cold turkey. Nevertheless, cigarettes had done their damage. Her voice was "gravelly," and a cancer appeared on her lip decades later.) She traveled with friends and family to Europe, Africa, South America, Japan, the Galapagos Islands, Morocco, New Guinea and Indonesia. In 1987, when she was eighty-five, she traveled to Thailand for a reunion of seventy OSS personnel.

In 1972 she went on her first purposeful expedition in twenty years. Taking along Bokara and her then-husband Dick Mack, she traveled to the Indonesian island of Siberut on behalf of the International Union for Conservation of Nature. Their mission was to observe the effect of logging on the habitat of an endangered species, the pygmy gibbon. The highlights of Bokara's account were that a pig on the island ate half her bikini when it was left to dry on a clothesline and that when the lynch pin fell out of the motor of the boat they were riding in "[m]y intrepid mother held it together for the rest of the trip with her Swiss army knife." Gertie was fascinated with the island natives who, she wrote, with "their sleek tan bodies, beaded headbands with eagle feathers, red and blue loincloths and artistic tattoos looked handsome and dignified." Her recollection was that both Bokara's bikini top and the red bandana tied to her hat were probably taken by one of the natives: "They love red." It turned out the pygmy gibbons were threatened not only by logging but by the natives, who found them good eating.

Bokara remembered that it was on this trip that she asked her mother the question, "When I was a little girl and later growing up, was there some reason you didn't — well —include me in your life?"

Gertie's reply was both simple and accurate: "I was never around."

Gertie recognized her shortcomings as a mother and apparently tried to make up for them with her grandchildren. She wrote in her autobiography, "Being a grandmother is so much easier than being a mother!" Medway, and to a lesser extent Fishers Island, became a haven and an anchor for the grandchildren, especially after Landine divorced for a second time and moved to New York. Sandy, Wendy, Gay and Pierre have tremendous nostalgia for the childhood days spent at Medway with the woman they called GG, short for Grandma Gertie.

"From the moment I had a conscious memory of Medway, it became my home," Sandy said. "It was where I wanted to be, where I longed to be, where I needed to be." His earliest memories of Medway are of pulling carrots from the garden, fishing for bream with a bamboo pole using balls of Wonder Bread as bait, and building forts and slides in the hay barn. (Walter Gourdine, who managed the stables, finally dissuaded Sandy and his siblings from playing in the hay — and therefore ruining it as feed — by hiding a dead rattlesnake under a bale.) Later, Sandy learned to drive Medway's antique horse carriages and shoot clay pigeons, leading up to shooting quail, woodcock, doves and ducks. Wendy also learned to shoot at Medway and loved to go fishing with her grandmother. "I'd go out with GG in the early evening, paddling a canoe, and we'd cast our poppers for bass," she said.

Gay and Pierre, the youngest grandchildren, spent most weekends from November to May, when Gertie was in residence, at Medway, as well as Easter, Thanksgiving and Christmas. Gertie had strict rules requiring children to eat separately from adults until they were sixteen — the old adage of little children being seen but not heard — but Gay recalls going canoeing and fishing with GG when she was small and a very memorable walk with the spaniels when Gertie "blew away a copperhead snake" with the gun she carried. Gay's father, Peter Manigault, first led her around on a pony at Medway when she was two and she learned to ride from Walter Gourdine. She began to show horses competitively in middle school. Both she and Sandy remember the creepiness of sleeping in the log cabin full of animal trophies, with all the eyes "watching" them in the dark. Sandy summoned the courage to sleep there alone. Gay and a bunch of scared-silly friends had a slumber party. Gay sums up the Medway experience for all of them: "We loved Medway because we could run wild." That lasted into their teen and young adult years, when GG welcomed them to invite their friends to big parties — Gay estimated several hundred people attended — at the log cabin. "All the food and booze were on Grandma," Gay said. Sandy and Gay said the only time Gertie got mad at them was when their antics caused extra work for the staff or damaged Medway property.

Once they were promoted to the grown-up table, Gertie's grandchildren benefited from conversation with her fascinating guests. "Here we would be, these young teenagers having meals and real conversations with amazing, incredibly accomplished, sometimes famous people from all over the place," Pierre said. "My siblings and I feel that we became friends in our own right with many of them despite a fifty- or sixty-year age difference and would make a point of trying to time our visits with those of our favorites of GG's friends. Seeing her interest in and acceptance of people was a wonderful influence and example for us all."

They also have fond memories of travels with GG. Gertie took Wendy, Sandy and Landine to a dude ranch in Montana when the grandchildren were in their teens. Wendy remembers going fishing with her, as Gertie "pulled in one trout after another while I was left empty-handed. She just laughed and laughed." On a trip to the island of Nevis in the Caribbean, Wendy played golf with GG on a nine-hole course "that looked like it had been cleared and mowed by hand." In her early twenties, Gay and Gertie flew to California to visit Bokara at her home on Big Sur. "Grandma was very proud because it was the first time in her life that she had ever unpacked her own suitcase," Gay recalled. On another trip, Gay got a flat tire in the middle of an Indian reservation and had no spare. A passing cowboy offered to drive her to a gas station, and Gertie said she would be perfectly happy waiting with the car until they returned. She explained that she always came prepared with a book to read because of the many mechanical breakdowns and delays she had experienced on expeditions.

When Pierre was in his late teens, Gertie took him on a ten-day pack trip in a wilderness area in western Montana with three other family members. They went fly-fishing and while sitting around the campfire at night she told stories of her expeditions with Sidney. "She was close to eighty by then, but she rode all day, fished, slept on the ground and loved every moment of it," Pierre remembered. As an adult, Sandy often accompanied his grandmother and her friends to Provence, where she rented a large house. "We spent the time driving to small towns for market day, restaurants for lunch and dinner, or antique shops for browsing and buying," he recalled. Even when she was in her mid-nineties and confined to a wheelchair, she was game for travel, such as a trip she took with Sandy to Barbados. Her last international journey, at age ninety-six, was to Morocco. On that visit, though, she declined to ride a camel.

The grandchildren also remember Gertie listening to them, something she seldom seemed to have done for Landine or Bokara. "I have many memories of us in a canoe or walking in Grandmother's Garden [at Medway] or sitting on her bed at Fishers Island or riding in a golf cart, and I would have some problem or another and she would listen," Wendy said. "Sometimes she offered advice, sometimes not, but she never took my problem lightly and to me that meant respect."

After graduating from college in 1985, Pierre spent six months working as a member of the deck crew of the Sea Cloud, the world's largest private sailing yacht. When his contract ended, he was in Rome where he received a letter from Gertie telling him she was wiring him $10,000 to finance further travels. "I had been making $125 a month on the ship, so this was a fortune!" he said. Pierre spent four and a half months in Africa, India and Nepal, and returned home bursting to talk about his experiences. No one wanted to listen, except GG. "She listened to me for hours as I rambled on, asking questions and sharing her own memories and stories of the places I'd been," Pierre said. "In a real sense, coming home and reliving my travels with her was as exciting and memorable as the trip itself."

And then another generation came along. Sandy named his daughter Sidney for the grandfather he never knew. The next great-grandchild was Gay's son Miles Brewton Boley, whose name reflects his Manigault family ties. Pierre has two daughters, one named India, the other Gertrude, known in the family as Gigi. "When my oldest daughter, India, was born, two years before she died, GG became a doting great-grandmother and loved just sitting with India on her lap," Pierre said. "I think she got a lot out of a small child for the first time in her life."

All four grandchildren reflect some aspect of Gertie in the life paths they chose. Sandy has been a caterer and restaurant owner, a contractor specializing in restoring and renovating historic homes and the proprietor of a fine art and antiques gallery. Gay lives on a 40,000-acre ranch in Wyoming with five thousand head of cattle, a herd of horses and other assorted animals; Gertie urged her to move there from the east coast and co-signed a loan so she could expand her acreage. Wendy became a golf professional, competing in the U.S., Europe and Asia. She has operated building and renovation businesses in Virginia and Maine.

Pierre joined his father in the family business, Evening Post Industries, as an editorial writer, executive and, upon Peter Manigault's death in 2004, chairman of the board. "Along with my father, she instilled in me a deep wildlife-and-land conservation ethic," he said of his grandmother. He has served on local, national and international conservation boards, including the Coastal Conservation League, of which Gertie was a founding director. Pierre took over as steward of the Sanford horse racing legacy as, among other things, a jockey and thoroughbred owner. With his daughters, he continues to present the Sanford Cup at Saratoga each year. In 2007, he co-founded a magazine called *Garden & Gun*, which "celebrates the modern South and features the best in Southern food, style, travel, music, art, literature and sporting culture," according to its website. In 2018, *Garden & Gun* had 400,000 subscribers with an average household income of more than $370,000. Each issue includes a feature called "Good Dog," where a writer tells the story of a beloved canine, usually one that hunts. Surely Gertie would have devoured every issue and submitted a guest column about Clippy.

Gertie's role as Charleston's grandest dame was partly a consequence of her passion for the arts. Her cultured mother diligently exposed her children to the great museums, concert halls and theaters of New York and Europe. While Laddie had focused his attention on horses and polo, the cultural lessons stuck with the girls. Janie was an art collector, specializing in works by the Impressionists. Gertie's interests were more far-flung, reflecting her international travels and fascination with foreign culture of every stripe. In part because of her co-habitation at Medway with the Gourdine family, she developed a sincere, respectful appreciation for the music and African-American, or Gullah, culture of the South Carolina coast. This led her to spear-head the mounting of a production of *Porgy and Bess* in 1985, the fiftieth anniversary of the George Gershwin opera's debut on Broadway. *Porgy and Bess*, based on the writings of Charleston author Du Bose Heyward, was daring in its time because of its all-black cast and its subject matter, the joys and sorrows of the people eking out a living on Charleston's Cabbage Row (called Catfish Row in the opera). Its production history in Charleston was troubled. Gershwin would not allow the opera to be performed for segregated audiences, and Charleston's venues were segregated well into the 1960s. In 1970, the tricentennial of South Carolina's founding, an acclaimed production was finally mounted in Charleston.

Gertie's friend Connie Wyrick worked closely with her on the 1985 revival. The planners formed a nonprofit, Catfish Row Company, to mount the production, and Gertie put up some of the money needed and raised most of the rest. Wyrick recalled that Gertie had at first insisted that all the performers be local to give the production an authentic Lowcountry voice. Eventually she realized the operatic voices required for the leads would have to come from elsewhere, and professional singers from New York were hired. However, a local choir, the Choraliers Music Club, performed the chorus parts and the Charleston Symphony Orchestra played the music. (Both groups performed in the 1970 production.) Catfish Row Company presented thirteen sold-out shows at the Gaillard Auditorium, and when Governor Dick Riley requested a last-minute ticket, they had to squeeze a chair for him in an aisle. Proceeds from the sale of tickets were donated to the Charleston Museum, the South Carolina Historical Society and the Gibbes Museum of Art, as well as a scholarship fund for African-American music students.

Gertie's love of visual art was also wide ranging, from fine portraiture to the paintings, carvings and crafts she encountered on her travels. She first picked up a paintbrush herself during her marriage to Piggy Weeks, when, after a few private lessons, she filled out an application in a magazine for an art correspondence course. The evaluation she got back was fair to good, but she was not daunted. She continued taking lessons and set up art studios at both Medway and Fishers Island, inviting friends who dabbled as well as respected professionals to join her. Both Bokara and Landine also painted, and granddaughter Gay has fond memories of GG dressing her in a tiny smock and letting her have a go at a canvas at the studio on Fishers Island. Gertie's paintings were like the clothing she wore at that stage in her life, primarily florals in bold, bright colors. Often, she used a palette knife to lay the paint on thick. At her first — and only — one-woman show, held at the Nancy Gray Gallery in Charleston in 1986, she presented the fruits of thirty years of work. The proceeds were donated to a campaign to save the snow leopard.

The following year her focus was on literary arts, when *The Time of My Life* was published by Wyrick & Company, the Charleston-based house owned by Pete and Connie Wyrick. In an interview, Pete, who had come to Charleston as director of the Gibbes Museum of Art, diplomatically declined to comment on Gertie's skill as an artist. However, he greatly enjoyed working with her on the autobiography, one of the first books his nascent company released.

Gertie signed copies of her autobiography in 1987 with her publisher and friend, Pete Wyrick.

Friends crowded to her signings, she gave a talk at the Henry Sanford Museum in Sanford, Florida — where the mayor presented her the key to the city — and collected enthusiastic letters from readers ranging from old friends to Barbara Bush, then the wife of the vice president. One fan enthused, "Your book is enchanting. You are the American Beryl Markham." Carnes Weeks Jr. commended her treatment of his father in the book. "I thought you were very fair with him," he wrote in an affectionate note.

Porgy and Bess, her one-woman art show and the publication of her autobiography were high points in Gertie's life, but she met even ordinary days with energy and joy. "Just a simple sunny day could cause her to say, 'Oh, happy happy, aren't we lucky?'" recalled Carola Lott. Grandson Sandy described Gertie's daily routine in her later years, whether she was at Medway, Fishers Island or abroad. She had breakfast in bed and spent part of the morning there alone. Afterward she might take a long walk or a swim or do a bit of painting followed by lunch with guests at one. After lunch, there might be a round of golf or some tennis (she played until she was in her mid-eighties) or quail hunting if she was at Medway, exploring a new place or shopping if she was elsewhere. Tea at five was followed by a bath and dressing for dinner, preceded by cocktails. "After dinner there were parlor games or general conversation until she went to bed at ten or eleven, depending on how much fun she was having," he said. The grandchildren were astounded by the energy she exuded. She told Gay that naps were "an absolute waste of time."

Living on that scale meant having a devoted and highly competent staff. By the early 1960s, many of her staff members had become too old to fulfill their duties or had decided to retire. Gertie's beloved Rose Brind had given up her job as executive housekeeper to Mamie years before. Rose lived on at Medway until her death in 1976, but Mamie went home to England, receiving a life-long pension in reward for her loyal years of service. In 1963, Gertie hired a woman named Alva Johanssen, who had worked for the family of Charles Lindbergh, as her executive housekeeper, and the following year she hired Doris Walters to work in the office and, eventually, to serve as Medway's bookkeeper and her personal secretary. Doris's husband, Ray, oversaw Medway's bird-hunting operation and kennels, and the couple lived with their children at the gatehouse. Both women were crucial members of the Medway staff for decades, part of the team that handled oceans of guests, parties, charity benefits and other social events.

Now retired and living in a town an hour from Medway, Doris Walters has many fond memories of her years as Gertie's secretary, and some not so fond. She said her job was stressful, for Gertie demanded a lot of her employees. At the same time, she was always very fair. She would walk into the office in the morning and give a string of verbal orders, then she was off, and Walters was scrambling to remember all she was supposed to do. Gertie was very particular about details. She didn't nag you, Walters said, but she expected you to get things done and get them done right. The staff always called her "Mrs. Legendre," and Gertie was very formal with them, too. She called her secretary "Mrs. Walters" for the first five or ten years of her employment.

Handling details of entertainment was a major focus of Walters's duties. Gertie had guests virtually every day, some locals from Charleston, some overnight guests from far away. Her entertaining style was formal and structured. Three meals a day were prepared by Alva Johanssen's cooks, and dinner was a formal affair with everyone dressed up for dinner and place cards on the table. "She was always decked out in pink or blue or another bright color. It was very refreshing," said Charleston resident Coy Johnston II, a close friend and frequent guest. He remembered that at the end of every occasion, guests were offered crystalized ginger, which he described as Gertie's "signature." A favorite dessert was Medway Snow, a Charlotte Russe cake with coconut flakes on top served with raspberry sauce or strawberries in syrup with rum sauce on the side. He also chuckled to recall how much Gertie enjoyed the company of men over women — something mentioned repeatedly during interviews for this book.

"She was a stickler about her table being even," Walters said, meaning an even number of women and men. Walters's duties included following up on invited guests who had not sent a response, and one of the most difficult calls she remembers making was to a home where the husband had been invited to dinner and his wife had not — because she would have made the table uneven. The wife was not very happy about it.

Personalities around her table rival the guest list at one of Gatsby's parties. They could include crooner Bing Crosby, who she met in England during the war; portrait artist Charlie Baskerville, whose subjects included Bernard Baruch, the Duchess of Windsor and the King of Nepal; Armant and Olive Legendre's daughter Anne Armstrong, who was the first woman to serve as ambassador to the United Kingdom; New York socialite Glenn "Doogie" Boocock and her daughter Leslie Barclay, whose first husband was an Italian count; Gen. William Westmoreland, former commander of the American forces in Vietnam, who taught Doris Walters to eat with chopsticks; photographer Toni Frissell, famous both for her fashion photography and coverage of wars; financier E.F. Hutton and his third wife, Dorothy; Lil Phipps and her daughter, Lillian McKim Rousseau, better known as fashion designer Lilly Pulitzer (Gertie adored her bright-colored clothing and ordered her golf shirts by the case); *Wild Kingdom* television show host Jim Fowler, who dated Bokara, and Arthur Patterson, a venture capitalist who married her after she divorced Dick Mack; actor Robert Montgomery and his wife Buffy; then-Congressman (and later governor) Mark Sanford (no relation) and his then-wife Jenny; former television heartthrob Jameson Parker of *Simon & Simon* fame; Vietnamese scholar Chi X. Diep; and, of course, her children, grandchildren and their friends. Carola Lott observed that Gertie was unusual in that she had close friends of many ages.

Gertie liked to mix out-of-town guests with Charleston friends. Conversa-

Gertie and daughter Bokara are dressed as a maharaja and his wife at a New Year's Eve party at Medway.

tion was substantial: she wasn't big on chit-chat. Charleston resident Virginia Christian Beach, who, with her husband, Dana, got to know Gertie in the last decade of her life, remembers her being "gracious and generous" as a hostess, but the point of conversation was to get beyond themselves. It was about ideas, not people. "She was helping Charleston broaden its horizons," Mrs. Beach said. "Medway became a hub for philanthropic endeavors and the exchange of ideas… Charleston was fortunate she landed here." This was especially true with causes that mattered to her: the arts, historic preservation, and, above all others, conservation. Her friend Connie Wyrick said Gertie had democratic tastes — with a small "d." The only drawback, she said, was that Gertie couldn't quite comprehend that some people had to work for a living. Connie and her husband Pete lived a forty-minute drive from Medway. "Half the time we had to change clothes in the car," she laughed.

Medway's mistress hosted many events that supported her favorite causes: as Doris Walters said, "Any excuse for a party." However, many of the social events at Medway were just that — social, and outrageously fun. The highlight was her annual New Year's Eve party, held from 1955 until almost the end of her life. That first year, Gertie wore the elaborate costume of the Maharaja of Magador, complete with turban, partnering with a sari-clad Bokara as the maharini. One guest came as the decapitated John the Baptist, accompanied by Salomé. A cave woman wore a mink mini-skirt and bra. "Half of Charleston was invited," Gay remembered. "Grandma's friends, Mom's friends and our friends and rarely did anyone lucky enough to be invited decline." Gertie later instituted a different theme each year, including "Come as Your Favorite Fairytale Character" and "Come as Your Favorite Cocktail," and it was the height of bad taste to come as yourself. Gay said she and Pierre always seemed to be scrounging at the last minute in an outbuilding that was full of costume material: "You could find anything from a sea captain to a mermaid or Turkish prince — curled up shoes, turban and all — or fairy princess, belly dancer, cowboy, whatever."

One year the theme was the circus, and a Camden friend who owned a small circus came with a trailer holding the star of his show, a baby African elephant named Flora. Gertie instructed her plantation manager Robert Hortman and chauffeur/butler Sam Washington to hide the elephant until the guests arrived — they stuck Flora in the pasture with the horses — and then Gertie rode into the log cabin on her back. She handed Flora some of the place cards, which the elephant deftly set on the tables with the "fingers" of her trunk.

Each year after dinner, the band began to play, and the guests drank and danced until a few minutes before midnight. Then Sam Washington appeared with Gertie's 20-gauge shotgun. At exactly twelve, she shot one shell over the lake for the old year and one shell for the new one. The band played "Auld Lang Syne," and the household staff, the women dressed in pink gingham dresses with white aprons and caps, the men in white mess jackets with black tie, rolled out an early breakfast buffet of scrambled eggs, sausage, collard greens and hoppin' john (field peas and rice), with more champagne for good measure.

The other annual celebration missed without fail was Gertie's birthday, March 29, celebrated at Medway. In concluding her autobiography, she wrote, "Tomorrow is my eighty-fifth birthday. There will be a small lunch at the log cabin with dear old friends. Sam will carry the birthday cake, with Lizzie, Elizabeth, Rebecca, Pam, Laverne and Candace parading behind singing 'Happy Birthday.'"

It's significant that the people she named were her employees. At the end, she had out-lived many of her friends and most of her family were at odds or living far away from Medway. She had her staff, and she had the land and the house that she loved beyond anything else. Saving Medway would be the focus of the last years of her life.

16

Saving Medway

———— • ————

On a cold December night in 1989, Virginia Beach and her husband Dana joined Gertie and a dozen guests at Medway. Sam Washington ushered them into a room off the central hall, "encased from floor to ceiling with old cypress paneling and lined with books, guns and exotic souvenirs from distant lands." Gertie greeted them with a bright smile and welcoming words, "It's so nice to see you!" and introduced them to her other guests. It was a heady gathering for the young couple: Russell Train, president of the World Wildlife Fund; Peter Manigault, passionate conservationist and publisher of the Charleston *Post and Courier*; John Henry Dick, nationally known wildlife artist and owner of Dixie Plantation on the Stono River; Bill Baldwin, the state's preeminent wildlife biologist and Gertie's land management advisor; Agnes Baldwin, Bill's wife and a local historian in her own right; and Robert Hortman, Medway's land manager for the previous ten years. Dana Beach had recently founded the Coastal Conservation League, an organization whose mission is to protect the natural landscapes, abundant wildlife and traditional communities of the South Carolina coast. Gertie was a founding board member. Virginia, a writer and editor who specializes in conservation and natural history, later wrote a lavishly illustrated book called *Medway*.

Their purpose that night was to discuss conservation of the land, wildlife habitat and natural resource heritage of the South Carolina coast, which had just taken a horrendous beating at the hands of a fellow named Hugo — as in Hurricane Hugo. The category four storm made landfall north of Charleston on September 22, 1989, bringing with it winds of up to 140 miles per hour. The nation's most destructive hurricane up to that date — a record it still holds in South Carolina — it caused $7 billion in damage in the U.S. and killed twenty-six people in South Carolina, including five young children. All along the South Carolina coast, Hugo snapped pine trees in half as if they were strands of dry spaghetti in the hands of an angry giant.

Gertie, then eighty-seven, was vacationing in France with grandson Sandy when the storm hit. She called Bob Hortman, who told her not to come home for a few more weeks. It took six and a half days just to clear the long driveway into Medway. Three weeks after the storm, Hortman met Gertie and Sandy at the airport, and their conversation stopped once they hit the dirt road leading to the house and she saw the extent of the disaster. The main house was standing virtually undamaged, but the ground was covered with limbs. Trees had crashed into some of the outbuildings, including the greenhouse. And this was the least damaged portion of the Medway land; five thousand acres of pine trees had been destroyed. She looked at him and said, "Well, look what's left." After that, whenever anyone remarked on the devastation at Medway, Gertie always said, "'Oh, not to worry, Bob will clean it up,'" Hortman remembered. "She always had that glass half full." Her experiences in war-torn Europe helped her believe in rising from the ashes, he said. And she kept her sense of humor.

Pictures in Gertie's post-Hugo photo album illustrate his point. There's one showing a sign nailed to a tree that reads "Gone with the Wind Plantation." Another shows a stack of toppled pine logs with a sign reading "Gertie's Toothpick Pile." In another, Gertie and a friend pretend to play tennis on the court, which is covered with debris, using a pine cone in place of a tennis ball. The picture she chose for her Christmas card that year showed her and her staff sitting on the trunk of a huge tree that had fallen through one of the outbuildings, everyone smiling broadly.

It took Hortman, the plantation staff and all the help he could hire three years to clean up Medway. Pine plantation owners all over the Carolinas were doing the same thing, competing for labor and equipment and driving the price of lumber down to a pittance. In the end, crews hauled off 3,657 truckloads of fallen trees, and Medway lost $6 million on its timber.

There were larger repercussions. Gertie was planning to leave Medway outright to the National Audubon Society as a nature preserve, a place, she said, "for the beasts to grow old and die." The world had changed irrevocably since Gertie's youth, when herds of zebras and wildebeest filled the plains of Africa and the skies over South Carolina's old rice plantations were black with

Gertie and her staff posed on a fallen tree for the post-Hugo Christmas card. Grandson Sandy is at far left, with Bob Hortman, Doris Walters and Gertie.

ducks. She evolved with the times, laying down her hunting guns — except for shooting birds — with her last safari in the early 1950s. She was not alone in her conversion; her trajectory, Dana Beach explained, is the story of the conservation movement over the twentieth century. Many hunters exchanged their guns for cameras. Others realized that if they didn't take steps to protect fragile wetlands, there would eventually be no more ducks and waterfowl to hunt. Organizations such as Audubon, The Nature Conservancy and Ducks Unlimited were partnering with landowners, state and local governments and people with a passion for the outdoors to protect delicate habitat.

But to take on Medway, the Audubon Society needed income. Previously, Gertie had sold a portion of her land for $2 million and put that money into a trust. That, along with income from selective timber harvesting, would have satisfied the needs of the Audubon Society. But the destruction of the timber by Hugo made the project untenable, and Audubon walked away. After a couple of years of study, Gertie decided in 1991 to place the property in two conservation easements, which would be enforceable even if Medway changed hands.

Gertie worked closely with Coy Johnston II, a business partner of her original land manager Bill Baldwin, who was also an environmental consultant associated with Ducks Unlimited. Although Gertie initially scoffed that Ducks Unlimited was "all men who wanted to shoot ducks and drink beer," she came to believe it was the best one to oversee most of Medway's acreage. Founded by hunters who were concerned about the sharp drops in American waterfowl, Ducks Unlimited has been working since 1937 to protect their habitat. Today, DU and its Wetlands America Trust arm hold conservation easements on more than 400,000 acres, including most of Medway. However, the central 82.75 acres surrounding the main house and outbuildings at Medway she placed under the purview of the Historic Charleston Foundation, which holds easements on 385 properties, mostly in the historic district downtown.

The conservation easements put strict limits on use of the property, and permission for any change must be obtained in advance. Inspectors from the two organizations visit properties under their control annually to make sure the easement provisions are being followed. As just one example, Medway's owners can't change the color of the paint on the buildings without approval. With conservation easements, it's a matter of getting permission, not asking forgiveness, Johnston said.

Johnston is a legendary figure in the conservation movement on the South Carolina coast, one of the key people involved in the creation of the 217,000-acre ACE Basin formed by the Ashepoo, Combahee and Edisto rivers. After putting Medway into easements, Johnston said, Gertie urged other landowners to do the same. Writes Virginia Beach in her book *Rice and Ducks*, "Under Legendre's stewardship, Medway became a beacon for conservation and philanthropy, the site of countless meetings and fundraisers to benefit the Lowcountry environment. Other Cooper River landowners soon afterward permanently protected plantation lands on both the east and west branches of the river." Beach lists thirteen plantations that were thus protected due at least in part to Gertie's influence.

A great movement gained steam, and South Carolina coastal land was protected from development in various ways, some through easements, some through outright donation to organizations such as The Nature Conservancy, some through purchase for public parks. Federal, state and local governments joined in, and crucial pieces of legislation were signed into law. But essentially it was a grassroots movement, and thanks to the efforts of men and women like Johnston and Gertie and organizations like the Coastal Conservation League, over 1.1 million acres of South Carolina coastal property have been spared from development since 1989, protecting wildlife habitat, bolstering waterfowl populations and enabling more people to enjoy the wonders of nature that Gertie did. Johnston likes to say, "Asphalt is always the last crop." In other words, once pristine land has been broken up and sold for commercial use, it will never be reclaimed for wildlife habitat.

An even earlier leader in South Carolina's coastal conservation movement was Belle W. Baruch, daughter of financier and advisor to presidents Bernard Baruch, who owned a 17,500-acre property in Georgetown County called Hobcaw Barony. Bernard Baruch bought Hobcaw in 1905 as a hunting preserve and entertained many of the great personalities of his day there, including President Franklin Roosevelt and British Prime Minister Winston Churchill. Belle bought the plantation from her father in 1956. At her death in 1964, she left a multi-million-dollar trust that evolved into the Belle W. Baruch Foundation. In accordance with her wishes, Hobcaw Barony is today a nature preserve open to the public for educational tours as well as a giant outdoor laboratory used by South Carolina universities for research and teaching.

Gertie wanted to do something like this with Medway. In 1991 she invited her grandchildren, Sandy and Wendy Wood, to come to Medway to live, giving them land to build homes and paying them salaries to operate the Medway Environmental Trust. Its mission was to use Medway's historic, cultural and environmental resources for educational purposes. They celebrated the creation of the trust with a three-day gala weekend in 1994, including a black-tie dinner in a big tent on the Medway grounds and an auction of wildlife art. Sandy said Hobcaw Barony was one of the models he and Wendy looked at in planning their programs for Medway. They began working with local schools and searched for an architect to build an educational facility, such as the Hobcaw Barony Discovery Center. Pictures in her photo albums of those years show Gertie surrounded by her family, including her first great-grandchild, Sandy's daughter Sidney.

Visitors to Medway at this time continued to marvel at Gertie's energy and ability to get around, even as her frame bent and her fingers — though always beautifully manicured — became gnarled with arthritis. Her mind was sharp too; in an interview over lunch with Virginia Beach in 1996, she talked with great animation about the Republican field for president, bemoaning Colin Powell's decision not to enter the race. She was excited about a project Sandy had proposed to bring visiting archaeologists to Medway. But her age was gaining on her. In her mid-nineties, a bout with pneumonia landed her in the hospital, and a series of strokes put her in a wheelchair. She became impatient and worried about Medway, unsure if Sandy and Wendy could meet its challenges.

The problem was that the cost of operating Medway — easily $750,000 a year — far outdistanced donations to the Medway Environmental Trust and the income from timber. Even Gertie had a hard time living on the income of her family trusts without touching the principal. "[Medway] had a way of requiring every dollar you could scrounge up," said Doris Walters, who kept the plantation books. When she died, the principal of the family trusts that had supported Gertie throughout her life would be inherited by her daughters. With this inheritance, they would have the money to operate Medway as Gertie wished and continue the activities of the Medway Environmental Trust. But would they? Landine had a stormy relationship with her mother, and Bokara professed no interest in Medway.

Eventually, Bokara agreed to take on Medway and underwrite its costs — but only if she was given sole authority for its management. Gertie made the difficult decision to leave Medway to her youngest daughter and force Wendy and Sandy to leave. In 1997 she and her lawyer shared the decision with the grandchildren. The decision caused hard feelings all around. Pierre Manigault thought his grandmother was making a mistake and told her so in a letter. But today he sees things somewhat differently. "I think that GG was tired," he said. "She was old, frail and weak and for the first time in her life I think she was just plain tired. She knew she was close to the end, and I think she wanted peace." Instead, her decision caused a rift in the family that continues today.

Gertie bought the homes Sandy and Wendy had built at Medway and gave them each a year's severance pay. Sandy never returned to Medway and never saw his grandmother again. Wendy visited her late in 1999, a few months before her death, where she found GG in her room slouched in her wheelchair. "She just looked at me with incredibly sad eyes and finally, with some difficulty, said very simply, 'I'm sorry.' I knew what she meant and I was sorry too." It's impossible to know if Gertie was apologizing for her decision to leave Medway to Bokara or for its repercussions. By then, she had realized that Bokara's vision of what Medway should be and her own were decidedly different.

Bokara was an adventurous traveler and, in her own way, as curious as her mother. But her curiosity was more introspective. Since the mid-1980s, she had been living mostly in California where she reveled in the company of others seeking enlightenment through Buddhism, transcendental meditation, imaginary shamanic journeys and other metaphysical avenues. Periodically she would jet off to Asia or South America to meet a new lama, guru, shaman or swami, admitting, "I *had* to rush off and find another teacher in an exotic costume." The Bokara who sought spiritual relief from the "monster of restlessness" in her soul warred with the self she called Society Bobo, who loved gathering interesting guests around her tastefully appointed dinner table and hobnobbing with the beautiful people. Both Bokaras sought ease from psychological and physical pain — she had a debilitating spine condition — with copious amounts of alcohol. Under her leadership, the Medway Environmental Trust morphed into the Medway Institute, whose main activities were sponsoring weekend conferences — the subject of the first was UFOs — and month-long residencies for writers. On a walk through the Medway woods, she admitted she found the Lowcountry unappealing, much preferring the California mountains.

Aside from the occasional conferences, Bokara spent little time at Medway in the last years of her mother's life, preferring California and New York, where she had homes, friends and activities that interested her. (She had divorced her second husband some time before, saying "I told Arthur he should find someone better.") The last time she saw Gertie was in November 1999, just before departing for a long vacation in Uruguay. Their last words were an exchange of "I love yous." She was not there on Gertie's last New Year's Eve, when Sam Washington had to help her hold her shotgun for its ceremonial blast and she was so tired she went to bed at 9 p.m. Pierre still visited often, and occasionally friends would come over. Coy Johnston II remembered getting a call from Doris Walters one night inviting him and his wife to come to Medway. "Mrs. Legendre is all alone tonight," she told him.

Reflecting on her last meeting with her grandmother, Wendy Wood said,

"This amazing, independent, brave woman had been reduced to living alone, with no family, no friends and an apology that came too late." The exception was her grandson Pierre, who lived in Charleston and visited on a regular basis. But Gertie was surrounded by a different kind of family — her staff — who cared deeply about her. When she gave up driving, Sam Washington chauffeured her around town, taking her into Charleston to have dinner with friends such as the Wyricks. In 1989 the movie *Driving Miss Daisy* came out, the story of an elderly white woman and her evolving relationship with her black chauffeur, Hoke. They went to see it together and he began teasingly calling her Miss Daisy. She continued to spend summers on Fishers Island, but Walters or Washington or someone else on her staff always accompanied her. "The people who took care of her were the most important people in her life," Walters said. Gertie didn't tell her staff that she cared about them or loved them, but she demonstrated it in many ways. Walters learned not to mention liking something she saw in a catalog that came in the Medway mail because Gertie would order it as a gift.

At the end, Gertie was unable to even sit in her wheelchair. Lying in bed the afternoon of March 8, 2000, the anniversary of Sidney's death, Sam Washington tending to the fire in her fireplace, she began staring fixedly at him, although she had lost most of her eyesight. "She kept telling me, 'Sam, I love you.' I kept telling her, 'It's going to be alright,'" he remembered. She had never used these words with him before, though, like Doris Walters, he knew she loved him.

Bokara was in New York returning home in a taxi from a film award ceremony. Like Landine when their father had died on the same day more than fifty years before, she had a sudden flash that her mother was gone. She found a message from Walters on her home answering machine. "Mrs. Legendre died at 7:05 tonight in her sleep." Bokara called Landine at her home in Connecticut to share the news and ask her to help plan a funeral. Landine declined to plan it or to attend. Instead, she joined friends for dinner and celebrated. "Mummy's dead!" she exclaimed, and her friends, knowing how she despised Gertie, gave a cheer.

Gertie had died on a Wednesday. Bokara flew to Charleston the next day, packing three black designer outfits in different fabric weights so she would have a choice of apparel at the funeral depending on the weather. With Doris Walters and Bob Hortman, she planned the service for 11 a.m. the follow-

A stroke put Gertie in a wheelchair and added to her anxiety about Medway's future.

ing Sunday, forgetting that every minister in the state would be conducting church services at that time. Though she had been raised and married in the Episcopal faith, Gertie was not a member of a congregation and had not attended church in the forty years Doris Walters had known her. Nonetheless, Bokara tasked Walters with finding a retired minister who would be willing to preside at the funeral. Then she notified the housekeeper to expect twenty houseguests and more than a hundred for the ceremony and lunch at the log cabin, and assigned roles in the service to Wendy, Gay and Pierre. Sandy was out of the country and unable to attend.

Bob Hortman drove to town to pick up Gertie's ashes at the mortuary.

No one had thought about an urn, so he brought a big silver racing trophy. For the return trip, he placed the trophy in the front seat, strapped it in with a seat belt and conducted a one-sided conversation with Gertie all the way home to Medway. At the bridge leading to the house, where Gertie had often fished, he stopped the truck. The ashes came with a small metal identification disk. He stood on the bridge a few moments, thinking about the remarkable woman he had worked for his entire adult life, and then skipped the disk into the water.

That Sunday morning was sunny but cool. Bokara selected her black wool designer suit to wear and plunked one of Gertie's hats, a black felt fedora, on her head; she was having a bad hair day. She had a podium set up beside the graveyard where Sidney was buried, flanked by elephant tusks, the elephant's feet holding palm trees. "Spiritual singers in old-fashioned costumes stood under a nearby oak poised to sing 'Old Time Religion' and 'Swing Low, Sweet Chariot' between the eulogies and poems," she wrote in her autobiography. Pete Wyrick read aloud from Gertie's book *The Time of My Life*. (He still chokes up when he remembers it.)

Bokara gave the main eulogy "about my adventurous and original mother. Oddly, despite a history of problems, I was also friends with her — and rather good, if I say so myself, at writing little speeches." (Bokara soon began performing bitingly humorous monologues for audiences in New York, beginning with "Mummy Was a Wild Game Hunter.") After the service, Wendy, Gay and Pierre helped her empty most of the ashes into a hole beside Sidney's grave. She saved the remainder for fertilizing the azalea bushes in Grandmother's Garden. As they walked to the log cabin for lunch, the choir sang "I Got Plenty of Nothing" from *Porgy and Bess*. "Many people said, 'You look and sound just like your mother,' or 'It was like listening to Gertie,'" Bokara wrote. "All the old retainers said, 'You are jes' like your mother,' which they all meant as a compliment."

That night, Bokara went to bed feeling anxious and overwhelmed. "Medway is like owning a shark, I thought. Anything I have, it will take. Why is the Valium in New York, the Vioxx in California? The trouble was, I lived in too many places and now I lived in one more." The next morning, she began exorcising Gertie's presence from the house. She ordered the men on the staff to switch the living room furnishings with the dining room. Over the next few months, she did away with the green and brown color scheme that Gertie had thought befitted Medway's colonial heritage. She had the living room painted pink and put turquoise curtains and a turquoise rug in the dining room. She turned the gun room into a library, mounting on the wall a huge Tibetan *thangka,* or mandala, "to push the evil spirits out."

"Finally, I attacked the inner sanctum," she wrote: Gertie's bedroom with its priceless antique cypress paneling and Aubusson carpet. She had the paneling painted white with pale blue trim and replaced the Aubusson. On her first night in the newly decorated room, she decided to build a fire and almost burned down the house. Instead of asking Sam Washington for help, she set the fire herself, neglecting to open the flue. The room filled with black smoke. When Washington rushed in to put the fire out, he saw a vision of Gertie in the smoke wearing her familiar blue robe. She asked, "Are you alright?" and Sam replied, "I'm perfectly alright."

Her changes made, Bokara took off for the Amazon and a new shaman who used purges, perfume and a psychedelic tea made from the ayahuasca plant in his healing rituals. Before she left, she met with the staff of twenty-two and told them she couldn't afford to have so many people on the payroll. She didn't want to be waited on hand-and-foot like Gertie had, and she would not be spending nearly as much time as Medway. She dismissed all but seven employees.

Through the Medway Institute, Bokara continued to host conferences on different subjects, some environmental, some spiritual. At an early gathering in the log cabin, she took in the stony faces of her "New Age friends" and realized "there was a big hippo over my head." She looked around the room with their eyes, taking in all the mounted heads, animal skins and elephant feet. "Even the sofas were covered with animal skins, and I thought, I've just got to get rid of this stuff." She spoke to a woman at the American Museum of Natural History in New York and "reminded her that over the years Mummy had killed all these animals and had been so helpful to the museum," offering 150 heads for the collection. "And she said, I'm sorry, we only take the whole animal." She then contacted the Ralph Lauren Corporation, famous for its Polo brand, and offered the collection of an "authentic WASP polo-playing family." They were interested, but explained it was illegal to ship exotic species over state lines, even if it was only the heads. One collector said he would take some of the heads, but Bo declared, "I want a full animal deal." She was convinced the animal heads represented her late mother's power "and I can't really take over the plantation while they are here."

Finally, she decided to build a huge bonfire to burn the heads and invite friends to drum, sing and dance while the spirits of the animals went up in the smoke. "We'd be absolved of the whole problem… and I thought afterwards I'll have an oyster roast and I'll hire a band." When she approached Bob Hortman, telling him, "I want to do something you won't like," he was appalled, thinking, "Mrs. Legendre would absolutely come back and haunt all of us." He told Bokara that the formaldehyde preservative released by the fire would probably poison the guests. She didn't really believe him, but they found a compromise. She burned photographs of the animal heads, with a shaman presiding over the ceremony, and Pierre and Gay bought the heads from the Medway Institute. Everyone was satisfied. Gay placed the head of an elk bull, Gertie's first big kill in Wyoming, over her ranch fireplace. Pierre kept some of the heads at his home, some at the *Garden & Gun* office and stored a lot more in a Charleston warehouse. Bokara had a hilarious conclusion for her comic monologue "Mummy Was a Wild Game Hunter," which she delivered to an appreciative audience at the American Museum of Natural History. Bob kept a lion head at the plantation office, gave one to each of his sons and didn't have to worry about further stirring up Gertie's ghost.

Bokara eventually reconciled and reached a state of friendship with her nephew Pierre and his family, becoming especially fond of his two daughters. Pierre came to believe Bokara had undergone a spiritual transformation that "was startling and genuine" in the years after Gertie's death. They made peace over what he still calls "the Medway debacle" and co-hosted a conference on conservation at Medway. But she decided after a while that arranging the conferences and residencies was more work than she wanted. In 2004 she put Medway on the market for $25 million and bought a house outside Mill Valley, California for $5.9 million. In 2006 she was pleased when Hortman notified her there was a buyer for Medway. The sale fell through and though she professed to be glad, she still found fewer reasons to visit the plantation. In 2009, she deepened her roots in New York by buying a Fifth Avenue apartment on the upper east side for $8.1 million. In addition to buying real estate and traveling, Bokara contributed generously to numerous environmental, animal protection and human rights charities. In the years after Gertie's death, her name appeared as a major donor in the glossy annual reports of the Rainforest Action Network, the Fund for Global Human Rights, the Wolf

Conservation Center and the Rhino Resource Center, among many others.

The stock market crash and financial meltdown in 2008 hurt her investments, and two years later her financial advisor sat her down for a serious conversation about her spending. Bokara wrote a light-hearted poem about it that began:

The money master came to lunch;
It's always fun we laughed a bunch
He said it's time to make a choice,
I heard a slight catch in his voice —
"In seven years you will be
Dead or in penury."

His prediction turned out to be amazingly prescient: In 2017, seven years after their conversation, Bokara died of thyroid cancer at age seventy-seven. She was still rich.

In 2011 Bokara put Medway on the market again and that December she accepted an offer of $11 million from Tradeland Investors Inc., a company owned by Greek shipping magnate Gregory Callimanopulos and his family. The sale closed the following spring. The new owner shares Gertie's love for the outdoors as well as fishing and quail hunting. Like Gertie, he lives at Medway only a few months of the year, but has pumped money into the house and grounds, maintaining Bob Hortman as his land manager and most of the staff who served Gertie, including her beloved chauffeur and butler, Sam Washington. (Doris Walters had retired some years before.) He restored the interior to its pre-Bokara appearance, stripping the paint off the antique cypress paneling and toning down the color scheme. However, he is a very private person and Medway's time as a center of social activity and the sharing of ideas and furthering of causes has passed.

The sale of Medway triggered a great sweeping out of the house. Although Gregory Callimanopulos purchased considerable contents — including the remaining animal skins and a large collection of china — Bokara and the Medway staff, particularly Oneathea Rogers and Wanda McFann, had their hands full as they sorted through decades of possessions, papers and the personal effects of Gertie and her ancestors. "Packing up Medway was not only breathlessly exhausting, calling on every grain of self-discipline I had, but it was also a walk through time — flipping through generations at the click of a trunk lock or a clothes bag zipper," Bokara wrote. She donated the family papers, including Gertie's journals and diaries, correspondence dating back to her grandparents, photographs, slides and photo albums to the Addlestone Library at the College of Charleston.

The proceeds from the Medway sale went into two trusts, one controlled by Bokara, the other, the Medway Charitable Trust, controlled by Sandy and Wendy Wood. Since Bokara's donation to the library came without any money to organize, preserve or digitize the papers for public use, the Wood siblings decided to make their first grant to the library for that purpose. "After all, GSL had made it possible for us to enjoy Medway and create memories as children and adults," Sandy said. "It was only right that we preserve those memories." The Gertrude Sanford Legendre Papers, all 171 linear feet of the collection, are encased in 22 cartons, 114 document boxes, 49 slim document boxes, 97 flat storage boxes, a roll storage box, 26 negative boxes, 10 oversize folders, 28 audiocassettes and a videocassette. It was a goldmine for the writing of this book, and this author barely scratched the surface.

Dipping into the files about Gertie's fabulous life in the hush of the Addlestone Library's research room was to be reminded again and again what it means when someone is willing to say "yes." Yes to adventure, yes to danger, yes to travel, yes to learning, yes to friendship, yes even to love, with all its heartbreak. The only instance where saying yes had not turned out well for Gertie was in saying yes to bearing children, and she was hardly alone in being a poor parent. "Half the battle is opportunity," she wrote in *The Time of My Life*. "The other half is the willingness to say 'yes.' For me, 'yes' was always easy."

It's a message we can all remember as we go through our daily lives: You don't have to be an heiress or an explorer, a socialite or a spy, to learn to say "yes."

Epilogue

A Visit to Medway

I t was the last week in October but fall and its cool weather had just arrived in the Lowcountry when I drove to Mount Holly — known by my GPS as Goose Creek — to visit Gertie's plantation and meet Robert Hortman and Sam Washington. A long-sleeved sweater felt good. Rain was threatening but the clouds had not yet released their drops as I turned off busy Goose Creek Boulevard, flanked by factories and gravel plants, onto Medway Road, driving past a heavy equipment leasing company. As my car bumped over the railroad tracks, I thought fleetingly of a young and besotted Sidney, delivering Gertie to the Mount Holly train depot and being embarrassed that her departure brought him to tears. For the first mile or so, I passed new subdivisions that had popped up on the right-hand side of the narrow road, the almost identical houses sitting shoulder-to-shoulder on tiny lawns. Once I rolled over the narrow bridge to Medway property, with its sign warning against trespassing, it was a different world. As I slowly drove up the long sand-and-gravel drive through pine and hardwood forest, the ground studded with the fans of saw palmetto, an occasional bird flew in my path, too quick to identify. *Was that a dove?*

At the gate, I punched in the code Bob had given me that rang his cell phone, and he gave further instructions. The gate swung inward, and I passed a picturesque log gate house, which I knew had been the home of Gertie's secretary Doris Walters for most of her life. She moved away to live in the same town as one of her sons when she retired; another staff member lives there now. Three more miles of sandy road until I reached the house.

And then there it was, looking just like the photographs. Two stories of brick painted a soft salmon pink, accented with seafoam green shutters, the walls partially covered by clinging vines. It stood at the end of an expanse of green lawn, framed by an allée of ancient oak trees, their twisted limbs trailing Spanish moss. It is not a grand house, but it has tremendous grace and

Well-maintained under its new owner, Medway still dreams on the banks of the Back River.

dignity — and serenity. Immediately I knew why Gertie and Sidney loved it.

There were other, more ordinary buildings close by, among them a multi-car garage, stables and the office. Most of them are painted white with the same seafoam paint as trim. A mustached African-American man in a baseball cap and a windbreaker told me where to park; he would soon be introduced to me as Sam Washington. In later years, when she was confined to a wheelchair and needed more assistance in order to gad about, he was the Hoke to her Miss Daisy. Standing outside the office was a tall, trim man with a full head of curly, snowy white hair, brushed straight back from his forehead: Bob Hortman, Medway's manager for forty years.

Bob grew up in Summerville, going to movies at the Jungle Theater where Gertie and Sidney's trophy heads were mounted on the walls. He earned a degree in biology at Presbyterian College and afterward became acquainted with Coy Johnston II. He told Johnston that if he ever heard of a job opening for a plantation land manager to let him know about it. That led to his meeting with Gertie and Bill Baldwin, who was ready to pass the torch at

Medway to a younger man. Bob recalls Gertie saying to him, "I just want to give you an opportunity to change your life." Knowing how all-consuming the job would be, Gertie insisted he bring his wife Janet with him to the interview so she would be fully aware of the commitment her husband was making. Bob trained for a year with Baldwin and then was on his own.

Sam's story is somewhat different. He is a member of the Gourdine family, which had lived on Medway Plantation from its earliest days. His father worked for Gertie and he and his nine siblings grew up in a house on Medway land. When Gertie's chauffeur was getting ready to retire, Alva Johanssen, then the housekeeper, asked young Sam if he would be interested in the job. He came and talked to Gertie and they decided to give it a try. He passed muster and, like Bob, spent his adult life as an employee of Medway. He is the last member of the Gourdine family working there.

Bob and Sam ushered me into the office, where the first thing I noticed was a large lion's head mounted on the wall and wearing a couple of hats. It is one of the few trophy heads from Gertie's expeditions that remain at Medway, Bob said, and the hats belonged to his mother and Mrs. Legendre. Like Doris, he and Sam still refer to her as Mrs. Legendre, though occasionally they will slip and call her Gertie. They never did that when she was alive, Bob said. It would have been disrespectful.

For the next two hours, Bob and Sam regaled me with stories of their employer, each topping the other, laughing all the while:

The time Mrs. Legendre caught a soldier, from the nearby military weapons station, dressed in camouflage and armed with an M-16 rifle, who had strayed onto her land. She hustled him into her car, drove him to the highway and told him never to trespass at Medway again.

The time the dog trainer, a rather simple soul, called Bob on his walkie-talkie — this was prior to cell phone days — and said tragically, "We lost the madam." Thinking Gertie had suddenly died, Bob hastened out and learned to his relief that the trainer had last seen her in a wooded area nearby. He soon found Gertie, who was not the least bit lost.

The time Bob had to summon EMS when a guest at the famous New Year's Eve party fell while dancing on a table and broke a hip. The party girl was ninety-three.

The time Mrs. Legendre found a strange car on one of the plantation roads and, suspecting it belonged to a poacher, let all the air out of the tires.

It turned out to belong to one of her employees.

The time Mrs. Legendre was sitting outside, and a tiny bird repeatedly visited her, pulling out stands of her hair to weave into its nest. She loved it.

The time Mrs. Legendre borrowed a friend's private jet to fly from Fishers Island to Medway when a hurricane was threatening because she wanted to "do a hurricane." She was in her nineties then, and Bob told her it was impossible, that she had to get out of town. Doris Walters drove her to the North Carolina mountains where they had a marvelous time — the hurricane went somewhere else — and Gertie returned raving about the wonderful dish she had eaten one night at dinner. Bob asked her what it was called, and she said, "Pot luck!"

The time a local car dealer brought out to Medway a gleaming new SUV for her to test drive. She immediately said, "It's the wrong color," but she got in, drove all over the plantation so it was coated with mud from undercarriage to roof, then got out, remarked again, "It's the wrong color," and walked into the house.

"I miss her every day," Bob said.

Sam recalled picking up Bill Gosewisch in Columbia, where he lived, and driving him down to Medway for a party. He didn't know who his passenger was until he opened a page of *The Sands Ceased to Run* and showed Sam his picture as a young German soldier. Gosewisch confided that he had sneaked food to Gertie and looked after her in Nazi Germany.

The men talked about the challenges of maintaining an almost 7,000-acre preserve, with the complications of aging buildings, unruly coastal weather and unpredictable wildlife. I shared some of the frustrations Sidney had recorded in his plantation journal of the 1930s, and they nodded in agreement. "My biggest regret is I didn't keep a day-to-day diary," Bob said, adding a few minutes later, "It's all-consuming. This place will eat you up if you're not careful." Today, he and his staff deal with many of the same problems Sidney did, as well as new ones, such as the intrusion of nuisance animals including coyotes and wild pigs.

On the way out the door for a walk around the grounds with Sam, I met two smiling, laughing women whose names I knew well from my reading and research: Wanda McFann and Oneathea Rogers. Like Bob and Sam, they have worked at Medway for decades.

Sam took me on a walk around the immediate grounds. We couldn't go into the house, of course, but he showed me the one-room building where all the diaries and albums I had pored over at the College of Charleston's Addlestone Library were once kept — the shelves now bare of all but a few moldering old books. In the stable are three horse-drawn buggies awaiting horses and a driver with a firm hand. We opened the door of the tiny, one-room smoke house where Sidney had escaped the constant company to write, sometimes with Landine sitting quietly beside him, and strolled to the log cabin with its terrace overlooking the home reserve lake, site of so many luncheons, dinners and parties given by Gertie, Bokara and the four grandchildren. Small brass plates on the patio wall bear the names of favorite pets, including Gibbie the ape. Sam confided that one of the dogs had developed a taste for liquor. Sam and I circled around, through Grandmother's Garden, where Gertie's beloved Clippy is buried under a stone with the misspelled engraving that identifies him as "A FAITHFUL FREIND." It's also a fitting memorial to Gertie, a notoriously bad speller.

Everything is in tip-top shape, thanks to the couple Bob still calls "the new owners" even though Gregory Callimanopulos and his family bought Medway seven years ago. "I learn something new every day," Bob said, adding approvingly, "The new owners keep us extremely busy." Sam, who sees things that assure him Gertie is never far away, nodded his head and told me, "Gertie was happy when Mr. C bought this place."

After a few more words of good-bye, punctuated by the whinnying of horses in the nearby pasture, I climbed into my car and headed home. The first raindrops splattered my windshield.

It was not until I was halfway down the driveway that I realized I had not seen the cemetery, where Sidney's body and Gertie's ashes are interred, and I briefly considered going back. But I realized I didn't need to. Gertie's spirit is indeed everywhere at Medway. In the last line of *The Time of My Life*, she wrote, "Medway permeates my soul. It's home." And so it remains.

Acknowledgments

———— • ————

Writing a book is always a journey, sometimes a literal one. My journey writing *Gertie* began with my dear friend Linda Harral, whose curious mind has been intrigued by everything from Chinese foot-binding practices to South Carolina plantations. It was the latter that brought Gertrude Sanford Legendre to her attention. Linda began telling me about Gertie's adventures one day, and after she got to the part about Gertie escaping over the Swiss border during World War II, I had to stop her and ask, "Wait, wait, this all happened to *one* woman?" By now, I hope my readers are saying the same thing.

My partner on this journey is my husband, Leo, who not only encouraged me at every crossroad, but also came with me as logistics man and driver when I visited Fishers Island and, later, traced Gertie's path from the Paris Ritz Bar to the German-Swiss border during her captivity under the Germans. At the same time during this trip to Europe, we celebrated our fortieth anniversary. I couldn't ask for a better companion in travel or in life.

Writers of biography spend a great deal of time in archives, and this was certainly true with *Gertie*. My thanks go to Harlan M. Greene and his helpful staff in the Special Collections Archive at College of Charleston's Addlestone Library. I am grateful to Harlan's assistant, Mary Jo Fairchild, for answering my initial email query about the GSL Papers in such a cheerful and encouraging manner. During my hours in the Special Collections Archive, the staff extended every courtesy to me, from carting boxfuls of files for my use to loaning me sharpened pencils when I left mine at home. One of these archivists, Sam Stewart, was extraordinarily helpful in delivering high-resolution files of the many photos used in this book.

Likewise, biographers depend on family members of their subjects for information that sometimes evades archives. Gertie's elder daughter, Landine Legendre Manigault, graciously welcomed Leo and me to her home in Connecticut and we spent a pleasant summer afternoon in her backyard garden as she told us about Gertie's dark side.

Landine's four children — Sandy Wood, Wendy Wood, Gay Manigault and Pierre Manigault — shared memories of their GG through telephone conversations, face-to-face meetings and e-mails. I also enjoyed my interviews over lunch at the Barony Restaurant at Moncks Corner with Gertie's long-time secretary, Doris Walters. The visit to Medway described in the epilogue brought me into the realm of the plantation's long-time land manager, Robert Hortman, and Sam Washington, chauffeur, house man and jack-of-all-trades. Gertie's Charleston friends Pete and Connie Wyrick, Coy Johnston II and Dana and Virginia Beach were forthcoming and helpful during face-to-face interviews, and Carola Kittredge Lott shared her memories by phone.

In the publishing process, I was fortunate to have Gertie's youngest grandson, Pierre Manigault, and John Burbage of Evening Post Books in my corner. It was wonderful to have the expertise of book designer Gill Guerry and executive editor Michael Nolan. My daughter, Elizabeth Smith Dowling, provided a place for me to rest my head during numerous research trips to Charleston.

During the time it took to research and write Gertie, I was fortunate to have all these people to help me, as well as the encouragement of my family — parents Bruce and Dot Yandle, son Adam, brothers Bruce and Eric Yandle and aunt Susan Middleton — history-loving friends, and fellow writers, many of whom provided blurbs for the book.

Finally, I am grateful to Gertrude Sanford Legendre herself for having the foresight to recognize her own importance and to leave behind such a comprehensive archive of her unique experiences. How I wish I had known her!

Kathryn Smith
Anderson, South Carolina
April 2019

Notes

Foreword

The account of Gertie's capture and the look back at her life to that point is based on her autobiography *The Time of My Life* and her memoir *The Sands Ceased to Run*. An early version of this chapter appeared in the *Proceedings of the South Carolina Historical Association*, 2018.

Chapter 1:
Gilded Age Girl

Material about Aiken, including the description of Sherman's activity there during the Civil War, comes from McDonald and Miles, *Images of America: Aiken*. (It's hard to believe that Kilpatrick spent $5,000 in 1864 currency on matches, which would have been a fortune. Perhaps he bought them with Confederate dollars!) Other sources on Aiken history are Wilkins's *A Splendid Time;* "Horses of Aiken, South Carolina," https://www.travelandleisure.com, February 2, 2017; and "Town and Country," http://towncarolina.com, undated. One of the many amusing stories about Aiken's wealthy visitors in *A Splendid Time* is the account of Evalyn Walsh McClean's misplacement of her 45.52 carat Hope Diamond. She found it wrapped in a newspaper and stuffed into the horn of her gramophone – just as she had left it.

Robb's *The Sanfords of Amsterdam* provides the background on Gertie's family and the relationship between her parents, as does Gertie's autobiography. Her memories of childhood come from her autobiography, as well as her albums in the GSL Papers. Her recollection about Aiken Preparatory School may be faulty, as the school did not open until 1916. (An earlier school, the Aiken Institute, accepted both male and female students, according to *A Splendid Time*.) The amazing Mrs. Hitchcock appeared on the cover of *Time* magazine on August 18, 1930. Information about her death and internment comes from https://www.findagrave.com.

Henry Shelton Sanford information, both pro and con, comes from the fawning biography *Henry Shelton Sanford* by Molloy; the more balanced *Henry S. Sanford* by Fry; and the withering *King Leopold's Ghost* by Hochschild, as well as *Images of America: Sanford*. Christopher Dickey's lecture on Gertie at the College of Charleston, February 28, 2017, attended by the author, also provided information on grandfather Sanford's dark past.

The GSL Papers contain some of John Sanford's speeches on behalf of tariffs, one of which touted the "excellent wages" paid to a "girl weaver" at a Philadelphia carpet factory. Such a worker could earn $13 a week, Sanford said. (This compared to the $18 per month Sanford was paying his kitchen maid, also ascertained from the GSL Papers. The stark income inequality among these captains of industry and the people who worked for them in the Gilded Age was not equaled until the 21st century.)

The letters regarding Ethel Sanford's marriage are in the GSL Papers. Bokara's recollection about the later unhappiness of the union comes from her autobiography *Not What I Expected*.

Information about Stephen Sanford, the Stephen Sanford & Sons Carpet Company, Hurricana and other family interests and activities in Amsterdam, New York and environs comes from Ewing and Norton's *Broadlooms and Businessmen* and Robb's *The Sanfords of Amsterdam*. Incidentally, Amsterdam's most famous native son is the actor Kirk Douglas, born there in 1916 as Issur Danielovitch – later changed to Demsky – to impoverished Russian immigrants. His father was a ragman, the lowest rung on of the social and economic totem pole. "Izzy" Demsky changed his name to Kirk Douglas prior to enlisting in the navy during World War II. The actor wrote of his childhood in his autobiography *The Ragman's Son* (Simon & Schuster, 1988).

Miscellaneous: Sidney's letter to Gertie about their energy levels is in the GSL Papers. The recollection of Gertie dressing as an Indian princess comes from interviews with Gay Manigault and Carola Kittredge Lott. The letter to Ethel from Gertie, from the GSL Papers, is used as written, with mistakes cited. However, Gertie was a notoriously bad speller and Sidney wasn't much better. From this point on, letters quoted in the book are corrected for minor spelling and punctuation errors to avoid the distraction of constant [sic] notices.

Chapter 2:
Everyone Seemed to Be Dancing

Going forward, Gertie's autobiography and her other writings inform the book, and quotes are usually cited in the text. The amount of Stephen Sanford's estate comes from *The Sanfords of Amsterdam*, with the conversion to current dollars done by https://www.usinflationcalculator.com. (This website is used for all monetary conversions in the book.) Those curious about the Triangle Shirtwaist Fire, which killed 146 employees, can learn more from the excellent biography of Frances Perkins by Downey titled *The Woman Behind the New Deal* (Doubleday, 2009).

Background on the staggering wealth of the Sanfords and their class comes from Cable's *Top Drawer* and Kaplan's *When the Astors Owned New York*. The latter book provides the information that Caroline Astor's propensity to deck herself in jewels led to her being mocked in her later years as "a walking chandelier" and "a dozen Tiffany cases personified."

The account of the crisis of the outbreak of World War I comes from Leuchtenburg's *The Perils of Prosperity* and Whyte's biography *Hoover*. Gertie's personal memories come from her autobiography and a typescript in the GSL Papers of an interview with someone identified as "Gainfort." Information on Foxcroft School is from *Top Drawer* and the school website, https://www.foxcroft.org

The description and other details about the Sanford home at 9 East 72nd street comes from a site visit by the author and "How Sheik! Qatar is on an Upper East Side Townhouse Tear," https://observer.com, February 3, 2014. Sometime after John Sanford's death in 1939, the home and an adjoining mansion were purchased by the Lycée Francais, a private school. The emir bought the properties for $26 million. After extensive renovations, the 45,000-square-foot mansion was touted as the largest single-family residence in New York.

Miscellaneous: Rose Brind, the loyal servant who spent her life with Gertie, married a man named Sherin and took his name, but she is called Rose Brind throughout the book for simplicity's sake. According to Gertie's autobiography, Rose's husband was an alcoholic who briefly served as the Legendres' butler but was dismissed for chronic drunkenness. Rose remained married but lived apart from her husband.

Chapter 3:
Every Inch the Successful Huntress

Information on the outrage about the death of Cecil the lion comes from "Cecil the Lion Died Amid Controversy," https://www.nationalgeographic.com, October 15, 2018. Statistics on changes in hunting practices come from a review of Philip Dray's book *The Fair Chase*, by Stephen Budiansky, *Wall Street Journal*, April 28, 2018. Budiansky cites another interesting statistic regarding present-day Americans and hunting: 20 to 25 percent of the rural population still hunts. "Given the still overwhelming male cast to the sport, this suggests that nearly half of all rural males hunt," he writes.

The account of Theodore Roosevelt's experiences comes from Di Silvestro's absorbing book *Theodore Roosevelt in the Badlands*. According to one source, the western buffalo herds that had numbered in the millions had dwindled to a few thousand by the time Roosevelt reached the west. Other sources include Ward and Burns, *The Roosevelts, An Intimate History*; "All 512 animals Teddy Roosevelt and his son killed on safari," https://www.vox.com, February 3, 2016; and Roosevelt's own book *African Game Trails*. Writing before embarking on the safari, Roosevelt insisted that, besides game needed to feed his own entourage, he planned to kill no more than one male and one female of each species. His kill list portrays nothing of the kind. The Fairborn quote is from Millard's *The River of Doubt*.

Sources for the section on Paul J. Rainey include Herne's *White Hunters* and "Ripley librarian hosts Paul J. Rainey Program," *Southern Sentinel*, Ripley, Mississippi, August 21, 2010. According to Herne, Rainey sought a white hunter who would help him film a lion attack, and one hunter died in the attempt. Rainey himself died of a cerebral hemorrhage on his way to South Africa in 1923.

Gertie's contemporary album and correspondence in the GSL Papers give a good account of her overseas travels. The battlefield at Verdun must have been a sobering place; Combined French and German losses totaled 300,000 men. Laddie's *Time* cover was March 31, 1923. The *New York Times* ran its account of the jewel heist on October 4, 1924. Ethel Sanford's obituaries and Gertie's words about her mother's death and subsequent travels in Egypt are found in the GSL Papers.

The wedding announcement for Margaret Thayer and Harold Talbott ran in the *New York Times*, July 23, 1925. Gertie's account of her first safari is derived from her autobiography and the travel journal she kept that is in the GSL Papers. A document in the GSL Papers, "Hunting Big Game in East Africa," spells out the laws governing safaris at the time, many of which the Sanfords and Talbotts violated. The information about elephant slaughter comes from Rexer and Klein's *American Museum of Natural History* and "Elephant Slaughter, African Slavery and America's Pianos," https://www.npr.org, August 18, 2014.

Chapter 4:
The Roaring Riviera

In addition to Gertie's autobiography and albums, Tompkins' *Living Well is the Best Revenge* and Vaill's *Everybody Was So Young* provide background on the Murphys and the Riviera colony in the 1920s, as does, of course, Fitzgerald's *Tender Is the Night*. Calder's *Willie* gives an explanation of Gertie's view of Somerset Maugham, who maintained an elaborate home at Cap d'Antibes. While she frolicked in the bay in the summer of 1928, he was fifty-four years old and diligently writing a play, *The Sacred Flame*. Gertie claimed the film of her free boarding feat was lost while the participants could still remember what happened, yet her granddaughter Gay Manigault remembers watching it when she was a child, long after Sidney and Morris were dead. "Look Inside the Most Expensive House on Earth," about Villa les Cèdres, was published at https://www.bloomberg.com, October 12, 2017.

Background on the Legendre family comes from an interview with Landine Manigault and http://www.thepastwhispers.com/Old_New_Orleans. Information on the Legendres' Audubon Place home comes from "Audubon Place Mansion Sells for $5 Million," https://nola.curbed.com, May 19, 2014 and a site visit by the author. https://www.findagrave.com provides information on the Legendre parents. Other information comes from the GSL Papers, which include Morris Legendre's papers.

Regarding Phillip Barry's play *Holiday*, Professor Potter was portrayed in the original Broadway version by Antibes regular Donald Ogden Stewart, who would later adapt both *Holiday* and Barry's better-known play *The Philadelphia Story* into screenplays. Hepburn and Grant also starred in the film version of *The Philadelphia Story*.

Miscellaneous: Black velvets are made with Guiness beer topped with champagne. Laddie saved the life of Lady Mountbatten in 1931 when she attempted to swim to shore from a yacht anchored off Cap d'Antibes, according to an account in the *New York Times*, August 11, 1931: He "dove from the *Lizard's* deck, fully clothed, and swam rapidly to the spot where she was struggling."

Chapter 5:
The Queen of Sheba's Antelope

Background on the American Museum of Natural History comes from Rexer and Klein's *American Museum of Natural History;* Preston's *Dinosaurs in the Attic*; the museum's website, https://www.amnh.org; "Museum Has Funds for 4 New Wings," *New York Times*, May 7, 1929, and site visits by the author. Carl Akeley gave his life for his work, dying of dysentery in the Congo in 1926. His second wife, Mary, who had noteworthy credentials as an explorer, accompanied him on this last, fateful journey and led the expedition to its successful conclusion. The Akeley Memorial Hall opened in 1936, with the elephant grouping as its centerpiece.

Gertie's accounts of the Abyssinia expedition are taken from her autobiography and an article she co-authored with Sidney, "In Quest of the Queen of Sheba's Antelope, Part I" that appeared in the museum's *Natural History*, January-February 1930 issue. Newspaper reports include "Girl Got 7 Monkeys for a Bottle of Brandy," *New York Times*, August 21, 1929; and "Girl Scientist's Mistake Delights Abyssinian King," Associated Press, October 2, 1929. The GSL Papers contain various documents about the expedition, including the pay for the native staff. Salaries ranged from $10 to $20 per month, with fines for infractions as high as $5.

Frank Meier, the bartender at the Ritz, is worth a book himself. Lovers of cocktails and their history will lap up his book *The Artistry of Mixing Drinks*, which is entertaining and informative on many levels, not the least of which are the advertisements for all manner of beverages and accoutrements for the smart man and woman of the day. Meier's recipe for a "dry" martini contains equal amounts of gin and vermouth. He would no doubt be surprised by the bare hint of vermouth in most martini recipes today. A fascinating window into Meier's World War II activities is offered in "This Legendary Bartender Served Hemingway and Aided the Resistance Against the Nazis," https://munchies.vice.com, February 4, 2017; and Mazzeo's *The Hotel on Place Vendome.*

Miscellaneous: French Somaliland became the independent nation of Djibouti in 1977. Donald Carter's text accompanies the beautiful silhouettes of animals by Ugo Mochi in *Hoofed Mammals of the World*.

Chapter 6:
Jungle Trail Leads to Altar

Information on St. James' Church comes from an author site visit and the church website, https://www.stjames.org. Doris Walters described Gertie's limited churchgoing habits in an email with the author. Gertie's recollections of her wedding and honeymoon are from her autobiography. Sidney's admission that he was "not what you call a vital person" is quoted from his book *Land of the White Parasol and a Million Elephants.* His lovelorn letters come from the GSL Papers. Newspaper accounts of the wedding were pasted into some of Gertie's albums, also GSL Papers. In *Time*, Gertie recalls spending her wedding night at "the Waldorf," but the Waldorf Astoria had been closed since May 1, 1929 and later demolished to make way for the Empire State Building. The present-day Waldorf Astoria opened in 1931.

Information about the stock market crash comes from Klingaman's *1929*. The account of the effect of the Great Depression on the Stephen Sanford & Sons

Carpet Company and its merger with Bigelow-Hartford comes from Ewing and Norton's *Broadlooms and Businessmen*. John Sanford's letter to Sidney is found in the GSL Papers.

Chapter 7:
Mistress of Medway

Beach's excellent books *Medway,* about the history and natural beauty of Gertie's home*,* and *Rice and Ducks*, about the transformation of the Lowcountry from rice plantations to hunting preserves by wealthy northerners, inform this chapter. Gertie's anti-semitism is documented in letters to Sidney in the GSL Papers, including one stating, "You know how I hate Jews." Sidney also made numerous disparaging comments about Jews in his plantation diary, GSL Papers. Both made positive remarks about Bernard Baruch, in their letters and other writings, however. Baruch's picture given to Mary Sanford is in the GSL Papers.

Gertie's autobiography and Sidney's plantation diary are both crucial sources in describing the challenges and rewards of reclaiming the plantation house and land. Other documents in the GSL Papers informing this chapter are a packet of illustrated real estate papers advertising Medway; Gertie's pro-and-con list for its purchase; the wedding gift list; a list of household purchases 1929-30; the 1933 farm inventory; the couple's 1934 asset list; and numerous Medway photo albums. Landine Manigault described Sidney's smoke house retreat, and Pierre Manigault provided the information that hiring the Gourdine family was a condition of the sale of Medway to the Legendres. The last remaining member of the Gourdine family working at Medway is Sam Washington.

The descriptions of how most South Carolinians were living during the Depression comes from Golay's *America 1933* and Moorhead's *Gellhorn*. The information about income taxes in South Carolina comes from "Statistics of Income for 1933," accessed at the Internal Revenue Service website, https://www.irs.gov.

Landine Manigault shared her childhood experiences in an author interview. Bokara Legendre's recollections come from *Not What I Expected*.

Miscellaneous: During World War II, the government condemned three thousand acres of Medway land to build the Naval Weapons Station, according to Sandy Wood.

Chapter 8:
From Indochina to Iran

Information about the American Museum of Natural History comes from site visits and the museum's annual report for 2017. Franklin Delano Roosevelt dedicated the Theodore Roosevelt Rotunda at the museum in January 1936.

Gertie's autobiography and Sidney's book *Land of the White Parasol and the Million Elephants* provide the narrative for the Indochina portion of this chapter. The review of his book is found at https://www.kirkusreviews.com. Gertie's Southwest Africa journal in the GSL Papers, her autobiography and Sidney's book *Okovango Desert River* describe their grueling safari in that unforgiving land. The account of the expedition to Iran comes from Gertie's autobiography and Persian journal, GSL Papers, and Sidney's unpublished manuscript Persian Paths. There is a copy of the latter in the GSL Papers, but Landine Manigault very graciously loaned the author her personal copy for several months. Gertie's account of when the elusive wild ass was shot differs in her contemporary journal, which said it happened at the start of the

trip, and her autobiography, which said it was a last-minute coup. Perhaps she was trying to inject some suspense into her book. Gertie's travel albums, GSL Papers, provide much detail and color for this chapter.

The information about the shah of Iran comes from https://www.britannica.com/biography/Reza-Shah-Pahlavi. The shah abdicated in 1941 in favor of his son, Mohammed Reza Pahlavi, who ruled Iran until being overthrown in 1979. In *The Time of My Life*, Gertie observes that the mullahs were then reversing the reforms of the shah. "Return from an Expedition into Iran" appeared in the *New York Times*, January 13, 1939.

Miscellaneous: According to the profile of *Holiday* at the film website https://www.imdb.com, the first movie version was released in 1930 with Ann Harding as Linda, Everett Horton as Johnny and Mary Astor as Julia. The film received Academy Award nominations for best actress (Harding) and best adaptation. The Vermilye quote comes from his book *Cary Grant*.

Martha Gellhorn's wry observations in *Travels with Myself and Another* include this gem: "If you are not nuts for the English in England, you are close to vomiting over the English in the Orient." This was apparently evident to Sidney and Gertie in Africa as well.

Chapter 9:
The Gathering Storm

The account of the stable fire comes from *The Sanfords of Amsterdam* and "Stable Fire Kills 26 Sanford Racers," *New York Times*, January 10, 1939. The letters between Gertie, Sidney and her father are in the GSL Papers. The information on Medway activities comes from Sidney's plantation diary and Gertie's Medway albums, both GSL Papers, and an interview with Doris

Walters, who told the author about Gertie providing a hot meal to the plantation children.

Sources for the account of the looming war in Europe are cited in the text. Sidney's description comes from his plantation diary.

John Sanford's death was reported in the *New York Times* and the *Amsterdam* (N.Y.) *Evening Recorder*, both September 27, 1939. Additional information comes from *The Sanfords of Amsterdam.* The *New York Times* reported Gertie's delayed arrival on October 7, 1939. Sidney wrote about his father-in-law in his plantation diary. The account of the funeral and burial is from the *Amsterdam Evening Recorder*, October 4, 1939, and https://www.findagrave.com. Laddie, Mary and Janie eventually joined John and Ethel Sanford in the cemetery in Amsterdam.

Broadlooms and Businessmen and *The Sanfords of Amsterdam* describe Laddie's interests after John's death. Sidney's sour words about his brother-in-law are from his plantation diary. A letter from A.R. Conover of Stephen Sanford & Sons to Gertie is the source for the estate matters.

Bokara's birth and other family activities leading up to Pearl Harbor are documented in Gertie's Medway albums and Sidney's plantation diary, all GSL Papers. The wills of both Gertie and Sidney were accessed at the Probate Court of Berkeley County. Gertie tells the story of the last months at Medway and the move to Washington in *The Sands Ceased to Run.*

Miscellaneous: Laddie and Mary Sanford lived on at the Los Incas estate in Palm Beach, which was famous for Mary's parties for forty years. The house was razed in 1978.

Chapter 10:
Member of the OSS

The Sands Ceased to Run provides the backbone for this and the next two chapters, along with Gertie's OSS album and the letters exchanged with Sidney, all found in the GSL Papers. (The letters and album are digitized and available on line at http://lcdl.library.cofc.edu.) Two outstanding and enjoyable books about the war-time capital, Brinkley's *Washington Goes to War* and Dalton's *Washington's Golden Age,* provide background for the year Gertie spent in Washington with the OSS.

The information about Bill Donovan and the OSS comes from Waller's *Wild Bill Donovan*, McIntosh's *Sisterhood of Spies* and Lankford's *The Last American Aristocrat.* Carola Kittredge Lott, whose mother, Carola Kittredge, also worked for the OSS, said in an interview that Gertie and David Bruce knew each other socially and he suggested she come to work for him. Gertie shared her pay situation with Sidney in letters. Originally, she was paid the same thing as Bokara's nanny. By December 1942, her pay had risen to $175 per month. (Of course, she had other means of support.) Field Marshall Dill developed pernicious anemia and died in November 1944. He was the first non-American buried in Arlington National Cemetery.

In 1943 when Gertie was letting her house in Georgetown go, she heard to her displeasure that Harry and Louise Hopkins were interested in renting it, having decided to move out of the White House, where they had lived since their marriage. "It's a nice house and I would rather see nice people get it, but it is too expensive for most Washingtonians," Gertie wrote to Sidney. The Hopkinses found another house to rent.

Information on the toll of the German bombardments of London and the rest of England comes from Webb and Duncan's *Blitz Over Britain*. Tommy Hitchcock was said to be an inspiration for Tom Buchanan, the polo-playing husband of Daisy in Fitzgerald's *The Great Gatsby*. However, he seems to have had none of Buchanan's boorish qualities. Olson's books *Citizens of London* and *Last Hope Island* provide background material for this chapter. *Last Hope Island* provides, among other facts, the toll taken by the V-1 and V-2 rockets. Bruce's descriptions of his war-time activities are from his diary, edited by Lankford, *OSS Against the Reich*.

The account of Bruce's hijinks in France with Hemingway comes from *The Last Aristocrat*. The war marked the end of the marriage of Martha Gellhorn and Ernest Hemingway, described in Moorhead's *Gellhorn* and Mazzeo's *The Hotel on Place Vendome*.

Miscellaneous: Bing Crosby was the No. 1 box office draw in the country and was a passionate entertainer of the troops. This led in part to him being voted the most admired man alive in a poll taken in 1948. Gertie played golf with him in England, admiring his swing, and had him as a guest after the war at Medway. Gertie pasted Sidney's September 23, 1944 letter in her OSS album with the notation at the top "Letter written 3 days before my capture."

Chapter 11:
Bagged

Gertie's memoir, her autobiography, the OSS album and the letters exchanged with Sidney continue to inform this chapter. Information about the war-time Ritz comes from *The Hotel on Place Vendome* and an interview with Colin Peter Field, head bartender at the Bar Hemingway, at https://

www.hemingwaysociety.org/, August 9, 2017. The full name of the driver, Dick, appears in Waller's *Wild Bill Donovan*. Gertie's Walter Mitty-esque fantasy is from an early version of *The Sands Ceased to Run*, GSL Papers. Stalag 12A was primarily a transit camp where new POWs were interrogated and processed. The conditions were notoriously bad and got worse during the Battle of the Bulge. Records in the National Archives World War II Prisoners of War Data File at https://aad.archives.gov show that both Papurt and Dickson died there. The brief mention of Gertie's capture and the picture captioned "Bagged" appeared in the November 13, 1944 edition of *Newsweek*.

Chapter 12:
Gertie's War

Waller's *Wild Bill Donovan* and Christopher Dickey's article "The Socialite Spy Who Played So Dumb She Outsmarted the Nazis," https://www.thedailybeast.com, September 25, 2016, provide the account of Donovan's reaction to Gertie's capture. Sidney's correspondence with the provost marshal is in the GSL Papers. Lankford's *The Last Aristocrat* and Waller's *Wild Bill Donovan* tell of the spymaster's Normandy invasion misadventures.

In addition to Gertie's previously mentioned writings, McIntosh's *Sisterhood of Spies* contains details of her captivity. Her prison letter to Marian Hall is in the GSL Papers. Reba Z. Whittle was returned to the U.S. in January 1945, according to "Honoring WWII AF Flight Nurse," https://www.af.mil, March 31, 2016. Gertie's observations of German life behind the lines are in memos she wrote for Donovan, GSL Papers.

The SD was the intelligence component of the SS. The Gestapo operated under the

SS as well. As Lynne Olson points out in her most recent book, *Madame Fourcade's Secret War*, most people in occupied Europe drew no distinction among the various security agencies and referred to all of them as the Gestapo, which is what Gertie did in her books and letters. The building which housed the Gestapo in Berlin was destroyed in the last months of the war and is now the site of the Topography of Terror museum, according to https://topographie.de. The house where the Wannsee Conference was held is now a holocaust museum, according to https://www.ghwk.de. For sharing the location of the nearby Gestapo guest house, where Gertie was held, the author is grateful to Peter Finn, author of the forthcoming book on Gertie's war-time experiences, *A Guest of the Reich: The Story of American Heiress Gertrude Legendre's Dramatic Captivity and Daring Escape from Nazi Germany*.

The *Reader's Digest* article titled "Nazi Murder Factory" appeared in the November, 1944 edition. Information about the discovery of the camps comes from "Liberation of Nazi Camps," at the U.S. Holocaust Memorial Museum website, https://encyclopedia.ushmm.org. Gen. Ernst Kaltenbrunner was found guilty of war crimes and hanged at Nuremburg in 1946. The information about the criminalization of listening to BBC broadcasts is from the organization's website, https://www.bbc.com.

In its official history, found at http://rheinhoteldreesen.de, the Rheinhotel Dreesen says it had a cellar of 84,000 bottles of "the finest wines" at the time of the Allied capture, adding, "Once occupied by the American forces, though, only a fraction of this." Gen. Eisenhower stayed at the hotel for a week after the liberation of Bonn.

Miscellaneous: The Wannsee Conference

is the subject of a riveting film, *Conspiracy*, with Kenneth Branagh as Heydrich, and was an integral plot element in Robert Harris's alternative history novel *Fatherland*.

Chapter 13:
The Damages of War

Gertie concludes her memoir *Sands* with her debriefing in Dulles's apartment. From there, Gertie's OSS album, an early manuscript of *Sands* and correspondence with Sidney, all in the GSL Papers, and her autobiography inform the post-war story. Waller's *Wild Bill Donovan* and correspondence from Donovan in the GSL Papers cover her debriefing in Washington. The dissolution of the OSS is also from Waller's book.

Bokara's recollection of her mother's return is from her autobiography. The other descriptions are from letters written to Sidney. In one letter, Gertie wrote of her long lunch with Bob Jennings, which is different from what she wrote in *The Time of My Life*. There she simply said she ran into Jennings on the street in New York on V-E Day. Gertie's attempts to sell her story to various magazines and newspapers comes from correspondence in the GSL Papers. The May 6, 1949 receipt from William-Frederick Press in the GSL Papers gives the disappointing sales figures for *Sands*. (If it is any consolation to Gertie in the great beyond, the author paid more than $100 for her copy in 2016!)

The rumors of infidelities were shared with the author by Landine Manigault, Sandy Wood and Wendy Wood. Sidney's denial in a letter to Morris is in the GSL Papers. Bokara wrote about her hatred of riding in her autobiography, Landine stated hers in an interview with the author. Both mentioned a particularly odious riding master in Aiken. The Hawaii album is in the GSL Papers. The information about Janie's husband is from "Pansa, Ex-Diplomat, Is Drowned in Italy," *New York Times*, July 10, 1946. Doris Walters is the source for the inheritance of the estate by Bokara and Landine.

There are many letters from Bill Gosewisch, the two Ursulas and other friends Gertie made during the war in the GSL Papers, as well as receipts for the CARE packages she sent. The information about the Medway Plan comes from Robb's *The Sanfords of Amsterdam* and Beach's *Medway*. A March 1, 2017 news release from the City of Charleston and an account the same day in the Charleston (South Carolina) *Post and Courier* provide details on the installation of the commemorative plaque and the ongoing relationship of Charleston and Flers de l'Orne.

The account of the Yale-Smithsonian expedition to India is from *The Time of My Life*, with added details about Ripley's life from his obituary in the *New York Times*, March 13, 2001.

Albums in the GSL Papers provide photos of the quail shoot by Toni Frissell and snapshots of the family beach vacation in Southampton. Sidney's letters to Armant are also in the GSL Papers.

Miscellaneous: Phillips Oppenheim, who was mentioned by Sidney in his March 27, 1945 letter to Gertie, was a popular and prolific writer of thrillers.

Chapter 14:
Widow, Bride, Divorcee

Gertie and Bokara wrote of Sidney's death in their autobiographies. Landine shared her memory in an author interview. When it came to sudden deaths, the Legendre men rivaled the Kennedy family. Morris died in 1953 in a plane crash that also claimed the life of his new bride — he

had divorced Nancy after the war — and Armant died in a fall from a bridge ten years later. Hennen's son, Jimmy, died in the last weeks of combat during World War II. The letter to Armant describing Sidney's grave is in the GSL Papers. In a *New York Times* article on April 21, 1980, reflecting on her husband's untimely death, 81-year-old Ellen Barry said, "I feel like I've sort of made do ever since."

The correspondence with attorney Buist is in the GSL Papers. Piggy Weeks was a frequent visitor to Medway even before Sidney's death, and appears in numerous photos in Medway albums in the GSL Papers.

Gertie's account of her second expedition with Dillon Ripley is taken from *The Time of My Life*. Dick Mack is an interesting figure. His fellow "Bonesman," George H.W. Bush, stuck with him until the end of his life in 1979, when he died of cancer at age fifty-three, according to "Bush Opened Up to Secret Yale Society," *Washington Post*, August 7, 1988. In *Not What I Expected*, Bokara accused Gertie of having an affair with Mack years before Bokara knew him, though Gertie volunteered, "I just want you to know I never went to bed with him," when Bokara announced their engagement.

Although Gertie refers to Mahendra as the king of Nepal, he was actually the crown prince at the time of her visit. Gertie did, in fact, return to Kathmandu with Bokara in 1963, staying in a hotel that had been the maharaja's palace, according to *Not What I Expected*.

When Doris Walters came to work for Gertie in 1964, one of her first jobs was purging the office files of any mention of Weeks. The postcard and the 1950 letter are the only two pieces of correspondence the author found in the GSL Papers. The biographic details about Weeks are taken from a brief bio that accompanied an article he wrote for *U.S. Naval Medical Bulletin* in 1943, and the Legendre-Weeks wedding announcement, *New York Times*, March 30, 1951. The account of Weeks's activities in the navy are from Thomas's *Sea of Thunder*. In Herman Wouk's Pulitzer Prize-winning novel, *The Caine Mutiny*, two officers concerned about the behavior of the fictitious Captain Queeg board Halsey's flagship to report evidence of Queeg's instability to Admiral Halsey. From there, the case would have gone to the fleet medical officer – who would have been Piggy Weeks. One of the officers loses his nerve and they return to the *Caine*.

Landine Manigault shared her concerns about her mother's remarriage in an interview. Bokara's account of those childhood years is from her autobiography. The history of the log cabin comes from interviews with Robert Hortman, Gay Manigault, Pierre Manigault and Sandy Wood.

The information on Fishers Island comes from an author site visit, a brief interview with island resident John Klimczak and the article "Fishers Island is the Anti-Hampton," http://www.avenuemagazine.com, July 2, 2018. Klimczak said in 2018 that the island has 227 full-time residents and 3,300 summer residents. Landine Manigault's interview was the source of the information about Laddie and Mary Sanford's involvement in their nieces' lives. Bokara also wrote about her aunt and uncle in her autobiography. Another source on the Laddie Sanfords is Robb's *The Sanfords of Amsterdam*.

The account of Gertie's 1952 expedition to Africa and meeting with Dr. Schweitzer come from her autobiography, her French Equatorial Africa album in the GSL Papers

and a short documentary made by Kurt Wentzel called *To the Land of Lamido*, also in the GSL Papers. Upon meeting the giant lamido or sultan of Rei Bouba, Wentzel said, "We felt like the little people in *Gulliver's Travels*." Background on Schweitzer is from his biography on the Nobel Prize website, https://www.nobelprize.org.

The chapter's conclusion comes from the letter from Dr. Daniels, GSL Papers; Bokara's autobiography; the interview with Landine; and Piggy Weeks's obituary, *East Hampton* (New York) *Star*, September 28, 1968. The highly placed official Landine spoke of could have been Gertie's old friend Harold E. Talbott, who served as secretary of the air force in the Eisenhower administration. Dean Sheehan, director of operations at the McCall Center, provided background on Carnes Weeks Jr.'s work with addiction.

Chapter 15:
Second Act

Interviews with Gertie's family, friends and former employees paint the picture of her life after her second marriage ended, as well as the sources cited in the text. Carola Kittredge Lott's piece about Gertie appeared in *Town & Country* in April 1995, including her description of Gertie's voice as "gravelly." Doris Walters shared the story of Gertie's cold turkey abandonment of smoking and the subsequent lip cancer.

Albums in the GSL Papers document Gertie's extensive travels, including the round-the-world trip with Bokara in 1963. (In *Not What I Expected*, Bokara erroneously states the year was 1961.) The account of their trip to Siberut was drawn from Bokara's book and a manuscript Gertie wrote, "Mentawai," in the GSL Papers. It is uncertain if the expedition had any results. The IUCN includes all species of gibbon on its

Red List of endangered species today.

The author initially interviewed Gertie's granddaughter Wendy Wood in Charleston at, appropriately, Kudu Coffee and Craft Beer, and later by email. Email interviews were conducted with granddaughter Gay Manigault and grandson Sandy Wood. Pierre Manigault was interviewed in person and by email and also shared his answers to an email questionnaire sent by a Los Angeles screenwriter, Rebecca Robinson, who is developing a script about Gertie.

A joint interview with Connie and Pete Wyrick produced details about the mounting of the production of *Porgy and Bess*. Details about the history of *Porgy and Bess* comes from the article "Charleston's Porgy and Bess" on the website https://www.charlestonmuseum.org/. Information about Gertie's interest in visual arts comes from documents in the GSL Papers (including the results of her Famous Artists Course Talent Test) and Beach's *Medway*. The Wyricks also gave details about the publication of Gertie's autobiography by Wyrick & Company. The many letters from friends and fans about the book are in the GSL Papers.

Doris Walters was an exceptionally helpful, clear-eyed and forthcoming source for Chapters 15 and 16. Over lunches at the Barony restaurant in Moncks Corner, she reminisced about her years working for Gertie at Medway and the many personalities she encountered along the way. She was also kind enough to review the manuscript, and it was a happy day for this author when she said the book had captured the Gertie she remembered to a T. Interviews with Gertie's former employees Robert Hortman and Sam Washington also contributed to these final chapters.

Gertie's friends Coy Johnston II and Dana and Virginia Beach recalled details about socializing at Medway in an interview at the Beach home in Charleston. The sample guest list comes from documents and photo albums in the GSL Papers, Doris Walters, Bokara's autobiography and Jameson Parker's wonderful blog post, "An Adventurous Lady," http://readjamesonparker.com, May 10, 2013. Gay Manigault was especially helpful when it came to describing Gertie's signature event, the New Year's Eve costume party.

Miscellaneous: *Garden & Gun* circulation and readership profile is from its print media kit, found at https://gardenandgun.com. Charles Baskerville had a brief career as a nightclub columnist for *The New Yorker* during Prohibition, when he wrote under the nom de plume Top Hat. Doogie Bocook's husband Kenyon met his end in a fall from a Manhattan window. According to a report in the *New York Times* on September 9, 1961, he jumped from the fifteenth floor of their Park Avenue apartment while his wife was vacationing on Fishers Island. Gertie's good friend Peggy Talbott died the same way less than a year later, leaping from her Fifth Avenue apartment window. She was despondent over her husband Harold's death five years before, according to a *New York Times* report published July 16, 1962.

Chapter 16:
Saving Medway

The story of Gertie's final years and the decision to leave Medway to Bokara was pieced together from interviews with her grandchildren, daughter Landine, Bokara's autobiography, friends Coy Johnston II and Dana Beach and former secretary Doris Walters. The subject is still a painful one, and the author is grateful to all involved for being so forthcoming.

Virginia Beach's description of coming to

Medway in 1989 is from her book *Medway*. Information on Hurricane Hugo comes from the Charleston (South Carolina) *Post and Courier*, https://www.postandcourier.com; *The* (Columbia, South Carolina) *State,* https://www.thestate.com, and the National Weather Service, https://www.weather.gov/. Interviews with Bob Hortman, Coy Johnston II, Sandy Wood and Dana Beach contributed to this section, as did photographs in the GSL Papers and Beach's *Medway*.

Dana Beach, Coy Johnston II, Sandy Wood and Pierre Manigault told of Hugo's effect on Gertie's plan to leave Medway to the Audubon Society and her ultimate decision to put the house and land into separate conservation easements. The website https://www.ducks.org was helpful in understanding the work of Ducks Unlimited in this field, as was an article in *Forbes* magazine, "Asphalt is always the last crop," June 15, 1998, and Beach's *Rice and Ducks*. April Wood of Historic Charleston Foundation shared her organization's role. Information about Belle W. Baruch comes from Brockington's *Plantation Between the Waters* and a site visit to Hobcaw Barony. It was a rare treat to listen to Virginia Beach's audiotape interview with Gertie on February 2, 1996, GSL Papers. Her voice was raspy, but she had a full grasp of the here and now and was looking ahead, as always.

The account of Gertie's last months and death comes from interviews cited in the text. Bokara's role in her mother's last years and the disposition of Medway comes from her autobiography and a *New York Times* article, "Gertie's Ghost," October 16, 2011. Her humorous monologue "Mummy Was a Wild Game Hunter" was accessed at https://www.youtube.com.

Bokara's real estate transaction in California is described at https://blockshopper.com and in New York at https://therealdeal.com. Her philanthropy was tracked in an on-line search that turned up numerous listings in annual reports of charities. The largest, listed as between $50,000 and $99,000, was given to the Rainforest Action Network in 2017-18. This may have been a bequest, as she died in December 2017.

The accounts of the sale of Medway comes from *The Post and Courier*, "Historic Medway Sells for $11 Million," April 14, 2012. Bob Hortman provided details about the restoration of Medway's interior after Gregory Callimanopulos became its owner.

Miscellaneous. Valium is a familiar drug for treatment of anxiety, but readers may not be familiar with Vioxx, prescribed for arthritis and chronic pain, which was taken off the market in 2004 because high-dose, prolonged use was associated with heart attack and stroke.

Epilogue

This chapter is a straightforward account of the author's first and only visit to Medway in October 2018 and her interviews with Bob Hortman and Sam Washington there.

Sandy Wood shares a humorous anecdote about bringing a friend to Medway. When the friend saw Clippy's grave, he remarked, "How nice of your grandmother to bury the gardener in his place of work."

Bibliography

Archives

Gertrude Sanford Legendre Papers, Special Collections, Addlestone Library, College of Charleston

Books

Beach, Virginia Christian. *Medway*. Charleston: Wyrick & Company, 1999.

Beach, Virginia Christian. *Rice and Ducks*. Charleston: Evening Post Books, 2014.

Brinkley, David. *Washington Goes to War*. New York: Alfred A. Knopf, 1988.

Brockington, Lee. *Plantation Between the Waters: A Brief History of Hobcaw Barony*. Charleston: The History Press, 2006.

Byrd, Wilkins, editor. *The Splendid Time: Photographs of Old Aiken*. Aiken: The Historic Aiken Foundation, 2000.

Cable, Mary. *Top Drawer: American High Society from the Gilded Age to the Roaring Twenties*. New York: Atheneum, 1984.

Calder, Robert. *Willie: The Life of W. Somerset Maugham*. New York: St. Martin's Press, 1989.

Dalton, Joseph. *Washington's Golden Age: Hope Ridings Miller, the Society Beat, and the Rise of Women Journalists*. Lanham, Maryland: Roman & Littlefield, 2018.

Di Silvestro, Roger L. *Theodore Roosevelt in the Badlands*. New York: Walker and Company, 2011.

Dulles, Allen Welsh. *Germany's Underground*. New York: Macmillan Company, 1947.

Ewing, John S. and Nancy P. Norton.

Broadlooms and Businessmen: A History of the Bigelow-Sanford Carpet Company. Cambridge, Mass.: Harvard University Press, 1955.

Fry, Joseph A. *Henry S. Sanford: Diplomacy and Business in Nineteenth-Century America*. Reno: University of Nevada Press, 1982

Gellhorn, Martha. *Travels with Myself and Another*. New York: Eland, 1978

Golay, Michael. *America 1933: The Great Depression, Lorena Hickok, Eleanor Roosevelt, and the Shaping of the New Deal*. New York: Free Press, 2013.

Herne, Brian. *White Hunters: The Golden Age of African Safaris*. New York: Henry Holt, 1999.

Hochschild, Adam. *King Leopold's Ghost: A Story of Greed, Terror, and Heroism in Colonial Africa*. Boston: Mariner, 1998.

Kaplan, Justin. *When the Astors Owned New York: Blue Bloods and Grand Hotels in a Gilded Age*. New York: Viking, 2006.

Klingaman, William K. *1929: The Year of the Great Crash*. New York: Harper & Row, 1989.

Lankford, Nelson D. *The Last American Aristocrat: The Biography of Ambassador David K.E. Bruce*. Boston: Little, Brown and Company, 1996

Lankford, Nelson D., editor. *OSS Against the Reich: The World War II Diaries of David K.E. Bruce*. Kent, Ohio: Kent State University Press, 1991.

Legendre, Bokara. *Not What I Expected*.

Bloomington, Indiana: Balboa Press, 2017

Legendre, Gertrude Sanford. *The Sands Ceased to Run*. New York: William-Frederick Press, 1947.

Legendre, Gertrude Sanford. *The Time of My Life*. Charleston: Wyrick & Company, 1987.

Legendre, Sidney. *Land of the White Parasol and the Million Elephants: A Journey Through the Jungles of Indo-China*. New York: Dodd, Mead & Company, 1936.

Legendre, Sidney. *Okovango Desert River*. New York: Julian Messner, 1939.

Leuchtenburg, William E. *The Perils of Prosperity, 1914-32*. Chicago: University of Chicago Press, 1958.

Mazzeo, Tilar J. *The Hotel on Place Vendome*: *Life, Death, and Betrayal at the Hotel Ritz in Paris*. New York: HarperCollins, 2014

McDonald, Janice and Paul Miles. *Images of America: Aiken*. Charleston: Arcadia Publishing, 2011.

McIntosh, Elizabeth P. *Sisterhood of Spies*. Annapolis, Maryland: Naval Institute Press, 1998.

Meier, Frank. *The Artistry of Mixing Drinks*, Paris: Fryam Press, 1934.

Millard, Candice. *The River of Doubt: Theodore Roosevelt's Darkest Journey*. New York: Doubleday, 2005.

Miller, Mary E. *Baroness of Hobcaw: The Life of Belle W. Baruch*. Columbia, South Carolina: University of South Carolina Press, 2006.

Mochi, Ugo and T. Donald Carter. *Hoofed Mammals of the World*. New York: Charles Scribner's Sons, 1971.

Moorehead, Caroline. *Gellhorn: A Twentieth Century Life*. New York: Henry Holt and Company, 2003.

Olson, Lynne. *Citizens of London: The Americans Who Stood with Britain in Its Darkest, Finest Hour*. New York: Random House, 2010.

Olson, Lynne. *Last Hope Island: Britain, Occupied Europe, and the Brotherhood that Helped Turn the Tide of War.* New York: Random House, 2017.

Olson, Lynne, *Madame Fourcade's Secret War: The Daring Young Woman Who Led France's Largest Spy Network Against Hitler*. New York: Random House, 2019.

Preston, Douglas J. *Dinosaurs in the Attic: An Excursion into the American Museum of Natural History*. New York: St. Martin's Press, 1986.

Rexer, Lyle and Rachel Klein. *American Museum of Natural History: 125 Years of Expedition and Discovery*. New York: Harry N. Abrams, Inc., Publishers, 1995.

Robb, Alex M. *The Sanfords of Amsterdam: the biography of a family in America*. New York: William-Frederick Press, 1969.

Rogers, Agnes. *Women Are Here to Stay: The Durable Sex in its Infinite Variety Through Half a Century of American Life*. New York: Harper & Brothers, 1949.

Roosevelt, Theodore. *African Game Trails*. New York: Scribner, 2010.

Sanford Historical Society, Inc. *Sanford*. Charleston, South Carolina: Arcadia Press. No copyright date given.

Smith, Kathryn. "Gertrude Sanford Legendre: South Carolina Adventuress, Naturalist and World War II Spy." *The Proceedings of the South Carolina Historical Association* (2018): 135-45.

Thomas, Evan. *Sea of Thunder: Four Commanders and the Last Great Naval*

Campaign, 1941-1945. New York: Simon & Schuster, 2006.

Tompkins, Calvin. *Living Well is the Best Revenge.* New York: Viking Press, 1971.

Vaill, Amanda. *Everybody Was So Young: Gerald and Sara Murphy: A Lost Generation Love Story.* New York: Broadway Books, 1998.

Vermilye, Jerry. *Cary Grant.* New York: Galahad Books, 1973.

Waller, Douglas. *Wild Bill Donovan: The Spymaster Who Created the OSS and Modern American Espionage.* New York: The Free Press, 2011

Webb, Edwin and John Duncan. *Blitz Over Britain.* Tunbridge Wells, Kent: Spellmount Ltd., 1990.

Whyte, Kenneth. *Hoover, an Extraordinary Life in Extraordinary Times.* New York: Knopf, 2017

Interviews

Landine Legendre Manigault, June 17, 2018

Pierre Manigault, Wendy Wood, Peter Wood, Gay Manigault by email, various dates

Harlan Greene, Head of Special Collections, Addlestone Library, College of Charleston, various dates

Doris Walters, June 26, 2018, September 28, 2018, March 8, 2019 and by email

Robert Hortman and Sam Washington, October 24, 2018 and by email

Connie and Pete Wyrick, January 24, 2019 and by email

Dana Beach and Coy Johnston II, October 23, 2018

Virginia Christian Beach, September 26, 2018 and by email

Carola Kittredge Lott, November 28, 2018 and by email

April Wood, Historic Charleston Foundation, January 10, 2019

Site Visits

Florida
Henry Sanford Museum, Sanford

New York
Fishers Island
Sanford Home, New York City
St. James' Church, New York City
American Museum of Natural History, Africa Hall, New York City

South Carolina
Aiken
Cypress Gardens, Berkeley County
Hobcaw Barony, Georgetown County
Medway, Berkeley County

Europe
Bar Hemingway, Hotel Ritz, Paris
Arlon, Belgium
Luxembourg City
Wallendorf, Germany
Diez Castle, Diez, Germany
Rheinhotel Dressen, Bonn, Germany
Petersberg Hotel, Konigswinter, Germany
Oberpleis, Germany
Konstanz, Germany
Kreuzlingen, Switzerland

Miscellaneous

Christopher Dickey lecture, College of Charleston, February 28, 2017

Publication and internet sources are cited in full in Notes

Photo Credits

All photos in this book are from the Gertrude Sanford Legendre Papers used courtesy Special Collections, College of Charleston Library, with the following exceptions:

Page 8 - Henry S. Sanford by Matthew Brady, Library of Congress

Page 18 - Charlotte Noland, Foxcroft School Archives, Middleburg, Virginia

Page 20 - John Sanford home, author photo

Page 73 - Nyala exhibit, American Museum of Natural History, author photo

Page 89 - Ripley painting of Medway House, by kind permission of P.H.S. Wood

Page 99 - William Donovan, Library of Congress

Page 204 - Medway, Brandon Coffey Photography

Reading Group Guide

———— • ————

Questions for Discussion

1. Gertie was able to live such an adventurous life in part because her family was quite wealthy. How did her father John Sanford support her dreams? How did he fall short?

2. What were some of the factors that influenced Gertie as a girl so that she wanted more than the life of leisure accepted by many of her wealthy peers? How was she similar to her peers?

3. Gertie's big-game hunting experiences began when she graduated from high school. What was your reaction to the game, including five lions, that she shot on her first African safari? What were some indications that she thought the hunting was excessive?

4. Sidney and Morris Legendre entered Gertie's life in the summer of 1928. What qualities do you think each brother had that appealed to Gertie? What about her appealed to them?

5. Gertie's summer on the storied French Riviera brought her in contact with some of the most famous personalities of that time and place. What did you think of her estimations of writers Somerset Maugham, F. Scott Fitzgerald and Ernest Hemingway?

6. Gertie's 1928-29 expedition for the American Museum of Natural History was quite different from her first safari, but she found it much more rewarding. Compare the two experiences. How did the expedition help her mature?

7. Medway grabbed hold of Gertie and Sidney's hearts and never let it go. Do you have a similar connection to a home or property?

8. If Gertie had been asked to rank her priorities in life, she might have said, "Adventure first, husband second, children third." She might even have ranked her dogs before her children. Why do you suppose she and Sidney had children? Were you disturbed by her cavalier approach to motherhood? Do you think Sidney would have been a more attentive father with a different wife?

9. Gertie found her OSS experience both exciting and stultifying, and she sometimes railed against her treatment by the men in the organization. Do you think she might have found more challenging assignments if she had been a man? Would she have handled them well?

10. The trip to see the front that landed Gertie in Nazi hands can be seen as foolhardy or simply unlucky. What is your take on her misadventure? How did she make the best of her situation and manage not to jeopardize OSS agents in the field?

11. After the end of the war, Gertie resumed some of her pre-war activities, but her eyes had been opened by the misery she saw in war-torn Europe. What did you think of the assistance she gave friends such as Bill Gosewisch and the unknown Europeans she helped through the Medway Plan?

12. Sidney's sudden death in 1948 was a dreadful blow to Gertie. What do you think attracted her to her second husband, Carnes Weeks? Besides his addiction problems, why else was their marriage doomed?

13. Dr. Albert Schweitzer was one of the greatest personalities Gertie met, in her opinion. Do you think what she saw at Schweitzer's compound and his famous reverence for all life had any influence on her laying down her hunting guns? What else led to her awakening as a conservationist?

14. Gertie was glad she had gotten to see the far corners of the world B.T. – Before Tourists. As you read about all the places she visited, which appealed to you the most? Which one place would you like to go?

15. If you could have attended one of Gertie's New Year's Eve parties, what would your costume have been?

16. Gertie's decision to leave Medway in the hands of her daughter Bokara had long and sad consequences for her family. How might she have handled this differently? Did her actions indicate her love of Medway was stronger than her love of family?

17. Gertie died on the 52nd anniversary of Sidney's death. Do you think this was anything beyond coincidence? How would you imagine their reunion in the afterlife?

18. Under the conservation easements, Medway's buildings and land are protected from development. Do you think this is a permanent situation, or do you think future court challenges may overturn easements such as these?

19. What is Gertie's greatest legacy?

Enhance Your Reading Group Meeting

Author Kathryn Smith would love to call in or Skype with your reading group. You can contact her through her website, www.kathrynsmithwords.com. Here are some other ideas for making your book club discussion of Gertie more fun, just as the real Gertie might have done.

Invite all your members to come in costume, perhaps choosing one of the themes Gertie used at her famous New Year's Eve party, like "Come as Your Favorite Fairytale Character" or "Come as Your Favorite Cocktail."

Show the Katharine Hepburn-Cary Grant film *Holiday*, based on Gertie and her siblings.

For a special dessert, serve Gertie's famous Medway Snow. The recipe was provided by her long-time secretary, Doris Walters.

2 envelopes gelatin
6 egg whites
½ c. cold water
1/3 c. boiling water
¼ tsp. salt
¾ c. sugar
2 c. heavy cream
1 tsp. vanilla
1 c. flaked coconut

1. Soften gelatin in the cold water.
2. Pour boiling water into gelatin. Stir to dissolve.
3. Beat egg whites until stiff, add salt and gradually beat in sugar.
4. Fold gelatin into whites.
5. Beat cream until stiff, add vanilla and fold into egg whites.
6. Rub bottom and sides of 8" springform pan with butter. Sprinkle bottom with half of the coconut. Pour in cream mixture. Chill to set, then sprinkle with remaining coconut before serving.

Serve with raspberry sauce, using your own recipe or one of the many available in cookbooks or on-line.

Index

birth of, 6-7

bombing raid behavior of, 2, 108, 137, 140

character traits of, 2,4, 56, 84, 183, 190, 195-96, 202, 205-6

childhood of, *5, 13*, 6-21

children of. *See* Manigault, Landine Legendre *and* Legendre, Bokara Hennen

conservation activities of, 33, 172, 181, 182, 186-87, 189-93

correspondence with Sidney Legendre of, 10-11, 98-111, 113, 147, 148, 149-50

courtship and marriage of Carnes Weeks and, 150, 161, 164-65

courtship and marriage of Sidney Legendre and, 45-58

death and funeral of, 196-98

education of, 17-19, 24

employees of, 65-66, 70, 92, 94, 102, 103, 105-6, 184-85, 187-88, 196, 206. *See also* Brind, Rose; Evans, Violet; Hortman, Robert; Johanssen, Alva; Walters, Doris; *and* Washington, Sam

energy of, 10-11, 84, 184, 194

entertaining by, 20-21, 43, 93, 102, 105, 106, 109-10, 133, 136-37, 152, 175, 168, 178-79, 184-88

escape from Germans by, 141-48

expeditions of: Abyssinia, (1928-29), 3, 46-53, 72; French Indochina (1931), 3-4, 73-77, *75*; French Equatorial Africa

(1952), 169-71; India (1946-47), 153-54; Indonesia (1972), 177; Iran (1938), 81-86, *82*; Nepal (1949), 160-64, *163;* Southwest Africa (1936), 4, 78-80

fashion sense of, 41, 56, 113, 184-85

feelings for Sidney Legendre of, 53, 55-56, 58, 100-101, 121, 149, 150, 159, 161, 174

final years of, 188-96

Fishers Island home of, 169, 177, 180, 182, 183, 196, 206, 221n

German capture of, 1-4, 113-23, *122*

German imprisonment of, 4, 124-41

grandchildren of. *See* Wood, Peter Harrison Sanford; Wood, Wendeney Legendre; Manigault, Gabrielle Hamilton; *and* Manigault, Pierre

great-grandchildren of, 180, 183

health of, 92, 162-63, 164, 193-94, *197*

horse activities of, 2, 11-12, 14, 18, 30, 93, 179

hunting of, 2-4, 21-26, 30-36, 48, 51-52, 58, 76-77, 80, 84-86, 154-55, 164, 171, 172, 184, 191

hygiene, importance to, 49, 80, 119-20, 122, 128, 131, 133, 137,138, 139

Internés d'Honneur and, 134-39, 145-46, *146*

marriages of, 86, 220n

military service of 94, *95*, 100-101, 165

relationship with Sidney Legendre of, 38, 56, 58, 65, 86

Legendre, Nancy Newbold, 86, 151, 155, 220n

Legendre, Olive, 103, 159, 185

Legendre, Sidney Jennings

affection for dogs of, 69, 70, 98

anti-Semitism of, 61, 215n

appearance of, 3, 39, *39*, 41, *42, 51*, 55, *55, 67, 75, 82,* 86

business interests of, 68, 148, 150, 155-57

character traits of, 11, 53, 55-56, 71, 84, 93

childhood of, 39-40, 54

correspondence with Gertie of, 10-11, 98-111, 113, 143, 147, 148, 149-50

courtship and marriage of Gertie and, 45-58

death and funeral of, 158-59

education of, 40

expeditions of: Abyssinia (1928-29), 3, 46-53, 72; French Indochina (1931), 3- 4, 73-77, *75*; India (1946-47), 153-54; Iran (1938), 81-86; Southwest Africa (1936), 4, 78-80

family of, 39-40, 92

feelings for Gertie of, 56, 71, 81, 92, 100-101, 111, 147, 150, 160

hunting of, 51-52, 58, 76, 80, 84-86, 154-55

last will and testament of, 94-95

Medway Plantation and. *See* Medway Plantation

meeting with Carnes Weeks of, 149-50, 165

military service of, 2, 94-95, *95,* 97-98, 100-101, 149

relationship of his children with, 69-70, 71-72, 83, 89, 92, 102

relationship with Morris Legendre of, 38, 56, 58, 65, 86

Riviera experience of, 41-43, 45, 53

rumors of infidelity by, 149-50

sense of humor of, 53, 66, 68, 71, 74, 76, 79, 80, 84, 150-51

sports activities of, 40, 69, 77, 90, 155

wealth of, 39, 67

writing and books of, 64, 65, 66, 68-70, 71, 73-74, 76, 77, 78, 80, 81, 84-85, 90, 91-92, 94, 160, 207

Leopold II, 7-8, 41, 114

Leuchtenburg, William E., 16

lions, 3, 21, 22, 23-24, 31, 32, 33-34, 46, 50, 54, 68, 200, 205, 213n

Lott, Carola Kittredge, 175-76, 183, 185, 217n

M

Mack, Dick, 161-62, *163*, 164, 177, 185, 220n

Mahendra, 164, 220n

Manigault, Gabrielle Hamilton "Gay," 176, 178-80, 182, 184, 187, 198, 200, 214n

Manigault, Landine Legendre, 2, 39, 81, 88, 90, 93, 95, 103, 119, 151, *156*, 169, 179, 182

    appearance of, *69*, 70, 90, 155, *156, 168*

    birth of, 69, 77

    children of, 173, 176

    education of, 17, 70, 95, 102, 151, 159, 167

    Gertie's death and, 196

    inheritances of, 94-95, 152, 194

    marriages of, 159, 173, 176, 177-78

    relationship of Gertie with, 69-71, 83, 102, 175, 180, 194, 196

    relationship of Laddie and Mary Sanford with, 169

    relationship of Sidney Legendre with, 69-70, 71, 83, 102, 207

    Sidney Legendre's death and, 158-59, 196

Manigault, Peter, 176, 178, 181, 189

Manigault, Pierre, 176, 178-81, 187, 194, 196, 198, 200

Marshall, George C., 102, 125, 172

Maugham, Somerset, 43, 213-14n

Marx, Harpo, 41, 58

Maxwell, Elsa, 43, 44

Medway Charitable Trust, 202

Medway Environmental Trust, 193-94, 195

Medway Institute, 196

Medway Plan, 152-53

Medway Plantation

    appearance of, 62, *62*, 64, *89*, 103, 203-4, *204*, 206-7

    Bokara Legendre's ownership of, 198-201. *See also* Medway Institute

    challenges of, 62, 63-64, 66, 71, 77, 92, 93, 150-51, 194, 206

    conservation easements for, 191-92

    damage caused by missile storage at, 151, 216n

    Ducks Unlimited and, 191-92

    farming at, 65-66, 93, 155-56, 160

    furnishings at, 64-65, 92

    Gertie's disposition of, 191-94

    grandchildren's love of, 178

    Gregory Callimanopulos's ownership of, 201, 207

    guests at, 11, 68, 93, 155, 184-88

    Historic Charleston Foundation and, 192

    history of, 62-63

    Hurricane Hugo and, 189-91

    Legendres' emotional attachment to, 62, 63, 68-69, 88-89, 93, 103, 188

    Legendres' first visit to, 3, 62

    Legendres' purchase of, 3, 63-64

    log cabin at, 168, 188

    National Audubon Society and, 190-91

    renovation of, 64

    sale of, 201

About the Author

———— • ————

Kathryn Smith is a journalist, writer and American history speaker who is fascinated by women who were ahead of their time. Her first biography, *The Gatekeeper*, told the unknown story of Marguerite LeHand, private secretary and de facto chief of staff to Franklin Delano Roosevelt – the first woman to be secretary to a president, the only woman to serve as chief of staff. Kathryn is also the author of a collection of interviews with World War II veterans, *A Necessary War*, and a series of mystery novels co-authored with Kelly Durham. She lives in Anderson, South Carolina with her husband, Leo.

Visit her at www.kathrynsmithwords.com